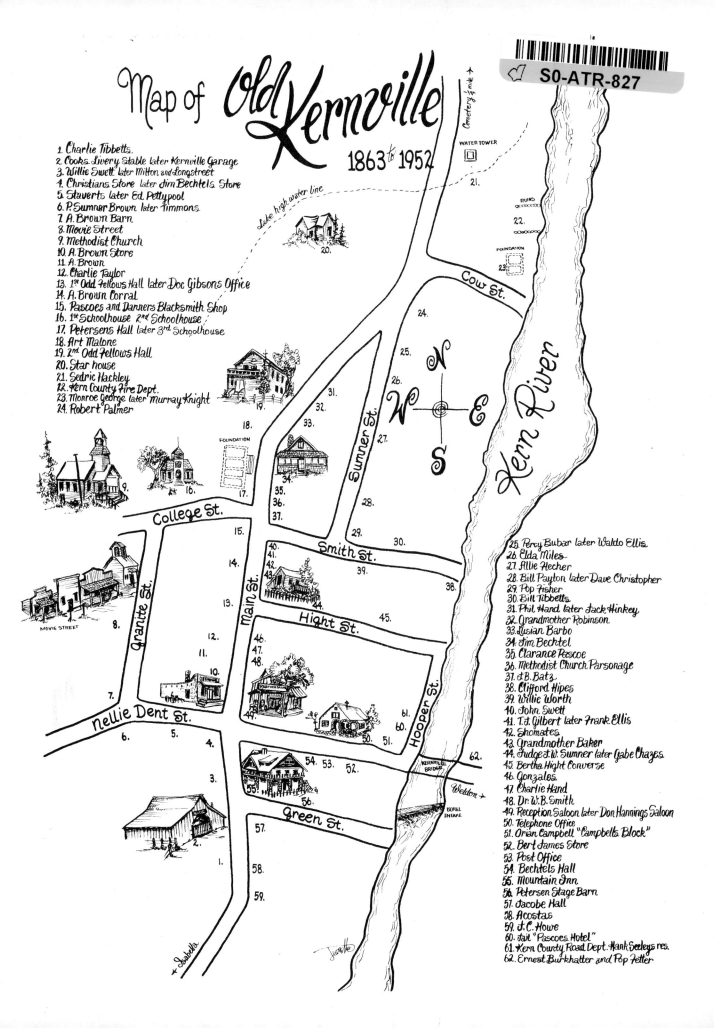

Map of Old Kernville
1863 to 1952

1. Charlie Tibbetts.
2. Cooks Livery Stable later Kernville Garage
3. Willie Swett later Milton and Longstreet
4. Christians Store later Jim Bechtels Store
5. Staverts later Ed. Pettypool
6. P. Sumner Brown later Timmons
7. A. Brown Barn
8. Movie Street
9. Methodist Church
10. A. Brown Store
11. A. Brown
12. Charlie Taylor
13. 1st Odd Fellows Hall later Doc Gibsons Office
14. A. Brown Corral.
15. Pascoes and Danners Blacksmith Shop
16. 1st Schoolhouse 2nd Schoolhouse
17. Petersens Hall later 3rd Schoolhouse
18. Art Malone
19. 2nd Odd Fellows Hall
20. Star house
21. Sedric Hackley
22. Kern County Fire Dept.
23. Monroe George later Murray Knight
24. Robert Palmer

25. Percy Bubar later Waldo Ellis.
26. Elda Miles.
27. Allie Hecher
28. Bill Payton later Dave Christopher
29. Pop Fisher
30. Bill Tibbetts.
31. Phil Hand later Jack Hinkey.
32. Grandmother Robinson
33. Lusian Barbo
34. Jim Bechtel
35. Clarance Pescoe
36. Methodist Church Parsonage
37. J. B. Batz
38. Clifford Hipes
39. Willie Worth
40. John Swett
41. T. J. Gilbert later Frank Ellis
42. Shomates.
43. Grandmother Baker
44. Judge J. W. Sumner later Gabe Chazes.
45. Bertha Hight Converse
46. Gonzales.
47. Charlie Hand
48. Dr. W. B. Smith
49. Reception Saloon later Don Hannings Saloon
50. Telephone Office
51. Orian Campbell "Campbells Block"
52. Bert James Store
53. Post Office
54. Bechtels Hall
55. Mountain Inn
56. Petersen Stage Barn
57. Jacobe Hall
58. Acostas
59. J. C. Howe
60. Jail "Pascoes Hotel"
61. Kern County Road Dept. Hank Seeleys res.
62. Ernest Burkhalter and Pop Felter

Cemetery ¼ mile →

WATER TOWER

Lake high water line

Cow St.

Kern River

N E W S

College St.

Smith St.

Hight St.

Green St.

Movie Street

Granite St.

Main St.

Nellie Dent St.

Hooper St.

Kernville Bridge

Weldon →

Borel Intake

← Isabella

Sumner St.

RUINS

FOUNDATION

FOUNDATION

North Fork Country

North Fork Country

by Bob Powers

Illustrated by JEANETTE ROGERS

WESTERNLORE PRESS . . . 1974 . . . LOS ANGELES 90041

Library of Congress Catalog Card No. 74-84608

ISBN No. 0-87026-034-0

PRINTED IN THE UNITED STATES OF AMERICA BY WESTERNLORE PRESS

Dedicated to My Mother and My Dad . . .
in loving appreciation for the many happy
memories I have of our little home by the Kern

Acknowledgments

THANKS are due many people for the help given on *North Fork Country*. To my good friend, Bob Ettner, who spent many hours editing the manuscript. Also to Jeanette Rogers for the excellent job she did on the maps, and to Don Meadows for writing the foreword. Grateful acknowledgment is given to Joan Dowd for her help with portions of the manuscript, and to Beverly Newman and Donna Bundy for typing same. Invaluable help was given by the Southern California Edison Company by supplying me with pictures for this section, and to the Louis Schuetze family and William B. Myers for their help in research on the Edison story.

Those old-timers living on the Kern River who spent so much time helping me on this project are too numerous to mention here, but some of those who were of the most help were Ida B. Pascoe and John and Gail Wofford. W. Harland Boyd of the Bakersfield College and Inez Pettijohn of the Kern County Library were two who were a great help by sharing with me their knowledge as to where information might be found on early happenings on the Kern.

Foreword

For thousands of years the Kern River scoured channels through mountain granite and boulders to form magnificent canyons and valleys. During thousands of years the river created water falls, rough crags and mountain meadows in a land of silent splendor unrelieved by human occupation. Then people came to the river to grab riches, escape the flurry of civilization or to fuse with the natural environment. Their impact on the country was as great as that of the river.

In a previous book Bob Powers has told the story of the river and how people came to the South Fork to raise cattle and find contentment. Now he takes the story across a mountain spur into the North Fork where the river is more active and where miners, cattle men, engineers, adventurers, homesteaders and creative people have found satisfaction in expressing themselves. They adapted the land to their need and became a part of it. Some of their efforts have been lost under water, but many old-timers can remember and talk about when Whiskey Flat, Old Kernville and Isabella were places of importance. Neon lights, paved streets and motels have replaced candles, trails and shanties but the spirit of the river still guides the lives and happiness of the mountain people who live along the Kern. They are isolated but not provincial. Bob Powers has collected the ingredients of his homeland and alloyed them into a rare amalgam of mountains and men.

—Don Meadows.

Quinta de los Prados,
July 1974

Table of Contents

Looking north up Main Street in Old Kernville, 1916. A. Brown Store, at left, was the oldest store in Kern County up until the town had to be moved in the early 1950s.

Old Kernville

THERE will never be another town like Old Kernville—at least in the opinion of the old-timers who were once its residents. This is understandable because there was something unique and very special about this quaint old community that is difficult to express. Aside from its picturesque setting, homey atmosphere, shaded streets, rustic taverns and historic backgrounds, Old Kernville was as temperamental as it was interesting and charming. On Saturday night it could be as wild and unruly as "Old Man River" on the rampage; yet, on a bright Sunday morning it could be as serene and peaceful as the murmuring Kern in its most pensive mood.

Not only will Old Kernville continue to hold an enviable place in the hearts of those who once lived there, but will also be long remembered by the visitors who came there to enjoy its seclusion, attend church, take in a dance, or become involved in an old-fashioned, no-holds-barred brawl.

Unfortunately, Old Kernville, originally called Whiskey Flat, is only a memory—the site itself buried part of each year beneath the waters of Lake Isabella. But only a few miles upstream a new town has risen to take its place. First called

New Kernville, it soon became known simply as Kernville; and its fame spread as being one of California's most picturesque mountain villages.

The story of the settlement of Old Kernville has been told many times and with as many variations, but an account of the actual happenings can best be obtained through writings. Probably the most authentic story was written in 1910 by Alice Maude Brown, whose father, Joseph Warren Sumner, was one of the first to live in the area. Mr. Sumner married Mary E. Dakin in 1843, and in 1853 he left his wife and family in Maine to come to California in an attempt to make enough to be able to establish a home for them. By 1870 he had accomplished this goal, and they came to live with him in Kernville. Mary Josephine, his oldest daughter, was 26, and Alice Maude was 22. The son, Elisha Payson, who did not come with the family to California, died a year later in Saco, Maine. Mr. Sumner, a Master Mason, became Justice of the Peace in 1870 and, as he served in that capacity for 30 years, became known to all as "Judge" Sumner. The following is Alice Brown's account as given to her by her father in 1870:

1

Old Kernville, 1916. Street on left is Nellie Dent, which went east out of town to cross the bridge over the Kern River. Building is the famous Mountain Inn, owned at this time by the A. Brown Company and operated by Bill and Lou Calkins.

Judge Sumner, one of the first to settle on the North Fork of the Kern River.

Mrs. Mary E. Sumner, wife of Judge Sumner.

In 1860 a man by the name of Lovely Rogers had a mule which got away from camp in Keysville. Mr. Rogers trailed him a way and, as is the custom with miners, he took his pick along with him. He came across some rock which at once attracted his attention. He broke it up, took it back to camp and showed it to Father, who told him he thought it was fine paying rock. Lovely Rogers worked this mine for some time; later Father bought it and called it the Sumner Mine. He sold a third to Mr. Caldwell and a third to Mr. Oders. They put up a little stamp mill, setting it at right angles to the big 80 stamp mill that stands on the site now. The mine paid well, other parties came in and opened up other mines.

Mr. Caldwell built a house about half way between Kernville and the mill, the chimney of which is still standing. Shortly after that, my father built the adobe building that Mr. Gilbert sold a short time ago to Longs. Those were the first buildings put up. As soon as Father commenced working the mine and crushing rock, a man by the name of Hamilton set up a saloon across the road from Mr. Caldwell's house. Father and Mr. Caldwell told him he couldn't have a saloon there but if he wanted, they would move his things, consist-

Lovely Rogers on his mule in front of original discovery later called the Sumner Mine. This mine eventually became part of a group of mines on the same vein known collectively as the Big Blue Mine.

ing of a tent and a couple of barrels with a board across them for a bar, down to a little flat, something over a mile away. And if he didn't want them to, they would anyway. So he pitched his tent in the flat and called it Whiskey Flat, which was the beginning of Kernville. In 1864, Capt. Peck, who owned some of the mines, had the name changed to Kernville.

There were a dozen small quartz mills located in and around Kernville at one time, but the Big Blue Mine—originally known as Sumner Mine—continued as the leading producer over the years. A report from the Kern River mines to the *Courier* by C. Schofield on June 3, 1871, said that the Big Blue was in steady operation and keeping a 16 stamp mill going. The men had been working with an open cut to the depth of thirty or forty feet and about seventy feet across the vein. The growth of Kernville during this period is best described by the Saturday issue of the *Havilah Miner*, June 7, 1873:

KERNVILLE: This little town is making rapid strides toward city proportions. During the last five months it has doubled in population. Some buildings are now in the course of erection, but are put back in consequence of an insufficiency of lumber. Jos. Frietach has thoroughly refurnished the Olympic Hotel. Fitzgerald and Best have established one near the Big Blue Mine, and Peterson and Nelson have opened a first class hotel at the northern end of town. Mr. Green, an accomplished gentleman, lately arrived from San Francisco, is waiting for lumber to erect a building for general merchandise purposes. The Brown Brothers and J. J. Murphy are doing a good business.

Again on November 22, 1873, the *Havilah Miner* gives us the following news of the founding of Quartzburg, on the long flat that lies to the north

Alice Sumner Brown, age 10 years. Mrs. Sumner sent this picture to her husband when he was living in Keysville in 1858.

Left to right, 80 stamp mill for the Big Blue Mine and the White House. Taken in 1889.

of Old Kernville cemetery and west of the river. Formerly called Cove Flat, it was the spot where the first house in the area was built by Joseph Caldwell.

A wonderful state of progress is going on in Kernville and "Two Villas" adjacent. The construction of buildings continues steadily . . . The busy hum of men seems to pervade that entire section of country from there to the Big Blue Mine mill. But about the new town; it is a mile from Kernville and about a quarter from the Sumner or Big Blue Mine. Sixteen houses have appeared there during the last few months and more are in the course of construction. We propose to call it Quartzburg on account of its proximity to the largest mine in the state and perhaps on the Pacific Coast. Maurice Fitzgerald has purchased a billiard table and will open a saloon in the enlarged portion of Fitzgerald's Hotel. Lumber for the construction of a general merchandise store is on the ground.

Then again, the *Havilah Miner,* dated February 21, 1874, recorded the following:

We made a short trip to Kernville last Monday, and found the town steadily progressing. The large mercantile establishment of A. D. Green and Company is doing a tremendous business, all the hotels are doing well. At Quartzburg, several new houses have lately been put up, and this place shows the same magical growth as Kernville does. The Big Blue is producing its regular amount of quartz, and the vein is enlarging.

Another article followed about a town just up the river that lay about a half-mile south of the Kern River Golf Course. First called Burkeville, after E. R. Burke, manager of the Big Blue Mine and Mill at that time, it was later called both Milltown and Millville.

The handsome little town of Burkeville holds her own and keeps pace with the improvements of other successful mining towns. The mill has been improved in many ways, the old overshot water wheel has been removed for a turbine, which does the work admirably with much less water. Col. C. Strong has his house

nearly completed and handsomely furnished; the parlor is ornamented with a splendid piece of furniture in the shape of a Knabe piano, on which the Colonel's accomplished wife and daughter executed entertainingly.

The home of Col. C. Strong mentioned in the preceding news item was the most impressive building in Millville and became known as the White House. Most of the shopping was done in Kernville. A boarding house was set up close to the mill for single men. Below the White House and back against the bank was the old adobe building that was the second house built on the Kern River. This home, built by Joseph Sumner in 1860, was sold to Mark Wyatt when Judge Sumner moved his family into Kernville. The Gilbert family next owned this home. All that remained of his old home in 1973 was part of the root cellar built of native stone which set against the bank of the mill ditch.

The same issue of the *Havilah Miner* ran the following article about Kernville:

KERNVILLE: Peterson and Nelson Ball—These gentlemen will give a splendid ball at their new hotel in Kernville next Monday. Havilah ought to turn out in full, and give the "Kernville Hotel" boys a regular old fashioned benefit. They deserve good treatment from Havilah, and will sure treat you well in return—let's go to the ball, and not come home till morning.

In 1874, Senator John P. Jones of Nevada acquired the controlling interest in the Big Blue Mine and placed Edwin R. Burke in charge as manager. It was decided that the 16 stamp mill was insufficient for the mammoth operation they had in mind; so in that same year Burke employed Joseph Cyrus, who had a ranch across from Kern-

Mrs. Mark Wyatt and Irene (Gilbert) Dalley stand in front of the old Judge Sumner home at Millville.

4

ville, to build an 80 stamp mill in place of the old one. Cyrus was an expert millwright and after coming across the plains in 1850 was engaged to build several of the best quartz and sawmills in the central counties of the state. From 1868 to 1874 he was employed in railway bridge work in California and Oregon.

As lumber was very hard to get in any volume, Burke hired Robert H. Evans to build a sawmill on the west slope of Greenhorn Mountain. Evans worked only oxen in his mill operation. Dave Stockton told about helping his father, Robert Stockton, bring back oxen that had wandered over Greenhorn in the winter after being turned out to fend for themselves. They were so wild that Dave claimed Evans left them yoked together in teams all summer with their tails tied together. Evans also constructed a road between the sawmill and Kernville that later was known as the Wagy Flat Road and, still later, Sawmill Road.

Water was taken out one and one-fourth mile above the mill and close to where Kernville now stands. A ditch was constructed to carry enough water to run a fifty-six inch turbine.

The Sumner shaft ran along the largest vein, which was from six to eight feet thick and had well-defined walls. Working this shaft were steam hoists and two large Cornish plunger pumping engines. One of these engines had a sixteen-inch column, and the other a twelve inch. When these pumps were installed in 1876, some 100 miners were laid off while the job was being completed. A surface tramway was built, and parts of the roadbed for the track can still be seen from the highway south of Kernville. A miner rode a string of three five-ton cars down the canyon to the terminus of the track on the hill behind the mill. There the cars were dumped into a 60-ton bin. The empty cars were pulled back up by mules. In later years, the ore was hauled to the mill by large trucks, but a mule was still being used to pull the loaded cars out to where the ore was hoisted for loading into the trucks. Burke was quoted in 1876 as saying that the average run paid $15 per ton and cost $5 to handle, with an average of one hundred tons a day being taken out and crushed. This company also operated a reverberatory furnace (to roast concentrates), made by Henry Concentrators.

During the latter part of the 1870s, two hundred miners were employed at the mine, most of whom were Cornish miners called "Cousin Jacks." In Kernville at this time, there were six or seven

Looking south down the main street of Kernville in 1888. The Kernville Hotel on the right was built by N. P. Petersen in 1873.

stores, four saloons, a brewery, three hotels, a livery stable, and other businesses and homes balancing out the community.

In 1879, Senator Jones withdrew his support from the Kernville project and E. B. Clushman, who had been bookkeeper at the mine, leased and operated the mine for about a year. Then in 1881 the mines were leased and operated by a group of San Francisco importers doing business under the firm name of Michels, Freidlander, and Company. They ran a drainage tunnel under the mine at about river level and intersected the main shaft at 240 feet. In addition, work was carried on 120 feet below this level. They took out a large amount of very profitable ore.

In 1883, failure of the eastern companies with which they were doing business forced the San Francisco Company to dispose of its holdings in the mine. The Kernville employees had not been paid for two months when the plight of the financiers reached them. In spite of the assurance of Morris Jacoby, manager of the company store, that they would receive their back pay, uneasiness developed which finally turned into sabotage of the mine. An incendiary fire in 1883 completely burned and destroyed the Sumner shaft, surface buildings and equipment. The total loss amounted to $250,000. The fire swept through the entire mine and was said to have smoldered for many years. This caused the ground to cave in, rendering the mine unworkable. The remaining buildings were allowed to fall into decay. Creditors who took over the mine soon faced continuing problems of holding the property. And, in 1884, the Big Blue Mine was sold at Sheriff's auction held in Bakersfield.

Foundations on the floor of the glory hole of the Sumner Mine as they appeared in 1974. These foundations were constructed in 1876 to support the steam hoists and Cornish pumping engines used in the Sumner shaft. An incendiary fire in 1883 completely destroyed the surface buildings and equipment, spreading underground, and causing a huge cave-in that rendered the mine unworkable.

From 1883 until 1907 there was virtually no work done at the Big Blue Mine. Then in 1907 the Kern Development Company leased the property. The water power ditch was reconstructed, a new water turbine and penstock installed, the 2,000 foot tunnel reopened, and the Donkey shaft rebuilt and named the Cove shaft. Although never developing much commercial ore, they continued to lease the property until 1926.

It was during the period that the Kern Development Company had the property leased that the

Big Blue gold mill of Kern Mines, Inc. (1939).

following took place. It was a peaceful Sunday afternoon in Kernville. The year was 1913 and, as usual, a small group of people were sitting on the front porch of the Kern River Hotel when the stillness was broken by the cry of "fire" that rang down the tree-lined street.

The fire was in a drainage tunnel that came out close to the river above town, and was called the Graveyard Tunnel, as it was located just above the cemetery.

A woman, fishing upriver, discovered the fire and hurried back to report it to Constable Clarence Pascoe. Pascoe went straight to the Kern River Hotel to round up some of the miners who boarded there. Willie Long, his nephew, Creighton Long, and Bill Wharton were the first to grab their miners' lamps, some tools and buckets, and take off for the tunnel. The three men filled their buckets with water and disappeared into the mine.

In a few minutes, other men arrived and tried to follow them in, but the gas forced them back. They were able to go in far enough to see the three men lying on the tunnel floor.

6

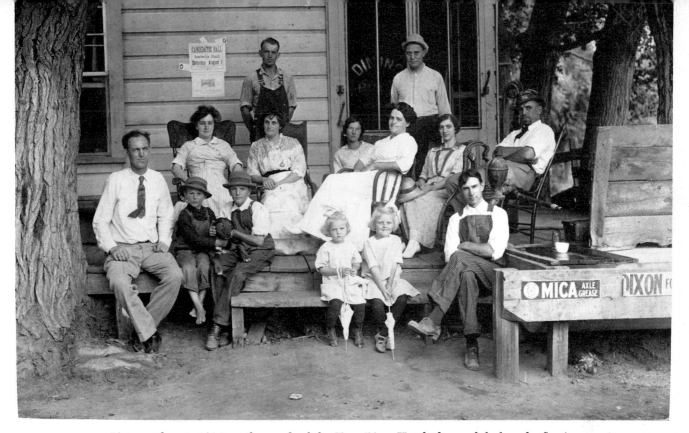

Picture taken in 1913 on the porch of the Kern River Hotel, the week before the fire in the Graveyard Tunnel of the Big Blue. *Front row, left to right*—Will Wharton, unidentified, Merle Hight, Sjrostrom sisters, Willy Long. *Seated, left to right*—Mrs. McCloud, Mrs. Sjrostrom, Eunice Stavert, Grandma Stavert, Flossie Stavert Hand, unidentified prizefighter from Taft. *Back row, left to right*—Creighton Long, E. Lovett.

A request was telehoned to Bakersfield for fire equipment, which arrived about midnight, along with several firemen. The first fireman who entered was overcome by gas as his mask was equipped only for smoke. He was taken to the Kern River Hotel, where Flossie and Eunice Staffert were able to revive him. The bodies of the three miners were not retrieved until the next day. They were taken to the I.O.O.F. Hall to wait the arrival of the coroner from Bakersfield.

In 1927, Mr. Jubien of New York leased the Big Blue, Sumner, and Nellie Dent mines. Diamond drilling and drifting were carried on from the 260-foot level. This lease was abandoned, and no ore extracted. Then the American Smelting and Refining Company leased these same mines in October of 1931 and carried on an extensive exploration program, but relinquished their lease in 1932. In 1934, A. V. Udell organized a group which later became the Big Blue Mining Company. More modern milling practices were used and extensive development work was carried on until April 1935, when the company was forced to seek reorganization under Section 77B of the Federal Bankruptcy Act.

Kern Mines, Inc. in 1936 bought out the Big Blue Company under supervision of the Federal Court. Owner Charlie Long started the last work to be done on the Big Blue Group of mines. All the machinery was reconditioned, and the Big Blue was again producing gold. Dr. W. L. Rogers was president of Kern Mines, Inc. and Dr. John W. Prout was the geologist. A miner by the name of Irvin Knutsen was brought in from Colorado as superintendent. Knutsen brought with him miners from Colorado, but there were also quite a few locals included. Bobby and Archie Luthy, remembered as first-rate miners, were two of these; as were Waldo Ellis, Jerry Sanders, Joe Loveall, Sam Moyer, and Dutch Ellis. Probably the one person who more people associate with the Big Blue Mine in its last years of activity was Jim Jorgensen. Jim, his wife, and two daughters moved into Old Kernville in 1936. Jim went to work at the Big Blue as maintenance man and just a general, all-around handymen. His jobs included hauling steel and occasionally ore to the mill. In 1940 Jim and his family moved into the old Tibbetts' house on the Big Blue property. The old house sat on the flat along the river just west of Judge Sumner's original home.

Jim Jorgensen, maintenance man and later watchman for the Big Blue Mine, sits by a chunk of the ore from the famous Big Blue Mine.

In 1942, after World War II had started, the mine was caught in a breakdown. There was still gold there, but it was classed as non-strategic. It was just too much of a hassle to get powder, steel, and men, so it was closed for good. The only man to remain on the payroll was Jim Jorgensen. He moved up the hill to the old white house that was built by Col. C. Strong the year Senator Jones had taken over the Big Blue. Jim was maintenance man and watchman until the Corps of Engineers acquired the mill site in 1956. When the Jorgensens moved from the white house, it was left vacant. Vandals so completely destroyed this old landmark, which was then 83 years old, that it had to be demolished. The last building left of the group at the Big Blue was the guest house, built in 1936 to house visiting dignitaries. Vandals also razed this building and, in 1972, set it afire. Being set ablaze at night, the building was totally involved before the county fire department was able

to respond. Only a chimney was left standing as a landmark of some 110 years since the discovery of the Big Blue. The owner of the Big Blue property in the 1960s, fearing injury to sightseers, had the headframe over Big Blue burned—destroying forever another link to the historic past of the Kern River Valley. Cement foundations remain that supported the old mill, but for the most part only the abandoned mine dumps up canyon bear mute reminder of the mine that started the town of Kernville.

By 1869, Judge Sumner had purchased a ranch across the river from his mill. And in 1876 he filed on more adjoining land. Here the Judge developed the first commercial orchard in the Valley with many acres of the finest apples, pears, and peaches. He also cultivated quite a few acres of plums, and dried many tons of prunes on the ranch.

Another phase of the Judge's diversified farming operation was a large dairy. For many years he furnished the surrounding area with their dairy needs.

Most of the buildings, except for the ranch house, were built of adobe brick. After he sold his house by the Big Blue Mill, Judge Sumner always lived in town with his family and had a foreman run the ranch, one of which was Add Cross.

Robert Palmer, Jr. was another local rancher who made the Sumner ranch the headquarters for his meat business. Robert, who was living in Old Kernville at the time, had a small bunch of cattle and periodically would slaughter beef and deliver meat to various towns and mining camps in the vicinity.

Big Blue headframe, blacksmith shop, hoist house and primary crusher (designed by Sam Moyer).

Open air milking parlor on the old Sumner Ranch, 1890s. Bill Calkins doing the honors.

Creamery and Ice and Cold Storage Plant on the Sumner Ranch taken in 1903. The last of these buildings disappeared below the waters of Lake Isabella in 1969.

The Old Milk Wagon crosses the Kern River during high water. from the town of Old Kernville to the Sumner Ranch. Ernest Andress and Mr. Hand on board, 1890s.

Andy Brown, Kern River pioneer.

Alice Brown.

There were always quite a few hired men living on the ranch. When questioned about what was on the bill of fare at mealtimes, they were most likely to answer "prunes and sowbelly." Besides all the fruit raised there, they also had quite a bunch of hogs. And, of course, there was always plenty of milk, cream, and cheese on the table.

In 1904, the Kern River Company purchased the water rights on the Sumner ranch for the Borel power plant, and the once flourishing ranch soon faded to only empty fields. The last physical evidence of the old Sumner ranch to remain was the adobe walls of the dairy building that could be seen standing northwest of the Kernville Airport. Some one hundred years after they were constructed, the rising waters of Lake Isabella took their toll, and the brick walls returned to the ground from which they came.

Judge Sumner, one of the best known pioneers of this mountain region, lived out his days in Kernville. He died in 1911 at 92 years of age. His wife, Mary, died two months later at 85.

A. BROWN COMPANY

A name closely associated with that of Judge Sumner in Kernville was that of Andy Brown. Andy had been born in Ireland. After coming to Philadelphia as a youth in 1852, he sailed around Cape Horn and landed in San Francisco. In the mid-1860s, Andy arrived in Kernville. After working in the Big Blue Mine for a short time, he showed such promise that he was picked by Judge Sumner to be one of his foremen in the mine. In 1873 he married the Judge's daughter, Alice. Two children born to this family were P. Sumner,

The A. Brown Store taken in the 1870s. Stagecoach is from the Telegraph Stage Line.

named after his grandfather and called "Summy," and M. Elizabeth, who became the wife of Dr. Edward M. Pallette of Los Angeles. In 1869, Andy Brown purchased a brick store building from Kitteridge and Company, and with it two and one-half acres on Main Street in the middle of Kernville. North of the store and set back from the street, Andy built his young bride a fine home. The *Havilah Miner* reported in its February 21, 1874 issue that, "Mr. Andy Brown's new house is finished and is the handsomest private residence in town." On this same parcel of ground was built the Odd Fellows Hall. On the north end was a blacksmith shop, which for a time was operated by Clarence Pascoe and Lee Danner. Later a planing mill for Brown's lumber operation was con-

structed there. Just north of the A. Brown house, Andy built a home for Charlie Taylor, the head man in his company. At the back of this property, the company owned several old buildings and sheds which included the first Kernville School. Moved back against the hill in 1898, when a new school was built, this collection of sheds and old buildings was used in the forming of Movie Street in the 1930s. Andy Brown kept acquiring property in Kernville until the early 1900s, resulting in the community often being referred to as the A. Brown Company town. The standing of Andy Brown in the town of Kernville is pointed out in an anecdote related by Anna Tibbets, who was teaching there in the early 1900s. Anna was discussing the Creator with one of her students and

Andy Brown's home, built in 1874.

Inside the A. Brown Sawmill, 1894. The only men identified in this picture are Newt Walker, upper left corner; Jim Walker, lower left corner; and Bert Hight, second from right on middle row.

12

asked, "Who has dominion over all the trees, mountains, and waters?" Without a moment's hesitation, the boy answered, "Andy Brown."

Brown purchased, in 1871, a ranch at Weldon from Alexander Forsyth on which he constructed a flour mill in 1877. His holdings on the South Fork eventually amounted to more than two thousand acres and extended as far down the Valley as the Murphy Ranch, which lay just southeast of Rocky Point. Although most of this acreage was watered from ditches diverted from the South Fork, part of the Murphy Ranch was supplied by water coming from the "North Fork." A tunnel was driven through Rocky Point to bring the water out on grade with the land to be irrigated. With a general store in Weldon, Kernville, and eventually one in Havilah, the flour mill at Weldon, a sawmill on the Greenhorn Mountains, as well as a fleet of freight wagons that kept the roads busy to the railhead in Caliente, Andy Brown built up what was virtually a business empire in the Kern River Valley.

Brown's Sawmill, which it was called after Andy reopened it in the 1890s, was originally the old Evans' Mill, which had been closed down for several years following the Big Blue fire. Andy kept a crew of local men working there most of the year. In the 1890s the Walker brothers worked there along with Bert Hight. The lumber was hauled down the mountain on freight wagons pulled by eight-horse teams. Most of the best teamsters in the Valley made this run at one time or another. Bill Alexander, known as Bill Alec while still a lad in his teens, was among those who

P. Sumner Brown and Elizabeth Brown Pallette, 1880.

drove teams down the steep, crooked grade to the Valley floor.

Bill had many a wild tale to spin about those trips down the mountain. The lumber wagons were pulled by what was known as a jerk-line team. Eight to ten horses or mules were used for each wagon. The teamster rode the wheel horse on the left side, on a saddle built like an English saddle. He controlled the team by a single rein hooked to the left leader called a jerk line. The brake on the wagon was operated by a length of leather or rope, known as a brake strap. On one trip down this mountain grade the brake strap on Bill Alec's wagon broke, and the weight of the loaded wagon quickly forced the team into an uncontrolled run down the crooked road. To make Bill's position even more precarious, the narrow dirt track dropped off sharply on the right; and on the left was a steep cut bank. Bill knew he would not be able to make the next turn. He did not relish the thought of getting tangled up with eight horses fighting for their lives, to say nothing of

Logging scene—A. Brown's Mill on Greenhorn. In those days it was strictly horsepower to get the logs to the mill.

An A. Brown teamster pauses in front of the Mountain Inn with a load of lumber from A. Brown Mill.

the load of lumber that would become airborne; so he decided to jump. Just in the nick of time, he spotted a small bush growing on the road bank. Working up in his teamster's saddle to a crouch, he sprang for the bush as he passed by. As luck would have it, the bush was rooted deeply enough to hold him, but none too long. As the wagon thundered by, the roots pulled free, and he dropped onto the road behind the wagon. Luckily none of the horses were killed. And with the help of fellow teamsters driving the same road, he was able to get his wagon patched up and reloaded. Then with the team none too worse for wear, except for a few of the horses limping somewhat, he started on down the mountain before darkness set in.

The early teamsters and lumbermen were known for being a hard-working, hard-playing bunch of boys. One best remembered for his good sense of humor was Percy Bubar. Percy had teamed on most of the big construction jobs in Kern County as he was exceptionally good at handling hookups where thirty or more horses and mules were involved. In the early 1900s, Percy worked a short time for the Los Angeles Water and Power Company during the construction of their aqueduct through the Mojave Desert. The company had construction camps scattered every few miles. Percy was enjoying an evening meal in the Sand Canyon Camp when the following incident occurred that was most typical of him. As was the custom, food was set out on long tables, family style, and passed back and forth as needed. Some of the big shots from the Los Angeles office had come up, and the local bosses were entertaining them at one end of a long table. From about

ten feet, Percy asked for someone to please send the butter down. One of the local foremen, wanting to impress the visiting dignitaries, stated, "Just eat your dinner, Mr. Bubar, and don't worry about the butter." Not uttering a word in reply, Percy stepped up on the bench, then the table, and walked ten feet, scattering food and dishes along the way. He calmly picked up the butter and walked back down the table to his seat. His fellow workers thought it was great. And, needless to say, when he asked to have anything else passed, haste was made to send it on its way.

Another teamster with a good nature was Charlie Hand. Charlie had been herding goats on the Mojave Desert in 1900 when he decided to seek employment in the Kern River Valley. His first job was driving team for A. Brown at his sawmill. Charlie loved to play poker and would often stay up all night, then be on the job the next day. He had the knack of being able to go to sleep any time or place, and if he stopped his team going up hill to let them rest, he would catch a few winks of sleep to supplement the time he had lost. Charlie, like Jimmy Durante, had a prominent nose and took a lot of good natured kidding about it. One time Charlie was playing cards at the Mountain Inn. Suspense was high, and Charlie had his cards up under his nose taking a peek to see if he would call or drop out. Hoping to distract him, one of his buddies across the table quipped, "Charlie, wipe your nose; it's running." Quick as a flash, Charlie come back, "You wipe it; you're closer to the darn thing than I am."

Soon after Andy's son, Sumner, married he took his bride, the former Jessie Lee Cartwright, on a visit to the A. Brown sawmill. As Sumner took care of the problems that had arisen since his last visit, young Mrs. Brown, fresh from the big city

Boarding house at Millville, 1890s. Seated on left, Mrs. Charlie Tibbetts and her two boys, Harry and Rosewell. Man seated on porch to left is Percy Bubar, and the girl on the step is Stella Gilbert Barbeau. All others, unidentified.

Dick Fuggitt, taken in 1917 when he was in the freight business with Charlie Hand; wife, Addie; and, *left to right*, daughters, Mildred Fuggitt Stubblefield and Elizabeth Fuggitt Crowder.

Main Street of Kernville, 1914, looking south. First house on left, Mrs. Baker; second, Judge Sumner, later Gabe Chavez. On right is old A. Brown Barn, first Odd Fellows Hall, A. Brown Store and, at the far end, the Robert Christian Store. Note cows taking their leisure in the street.

of Los Angeles, wandered off a short distance in the surrounding timber. She was a little startled to hear the cry, "timber," ring out; but not knowing what it meant, she soon forgot about it. A few minutes later, a huge cedar tree came crashing down, the uppermost limbs missing her by only a few feet. As she screamed in terror, the young husband came rushing to her side, white and shaking. Needless to say, the fallers also were somewhat shaken too, as falling a tree on the boss's wife was not the best way to get a raise. To sum it all up, young Mrs. Brown did not wander out of camp on any subsequent visits, nor did she forget what the cry "timber" meant.

In 1887, Charles C. Taylor arrived in the Valley and, after working two weeks on the Sumner Ranch across the river, went to work for Andy Brown in the store. For many years Charlie Taylor was Andy's top man. He not only ran the store; but in 1901, when the A. Brown Company operations were incorporated, he was designated as secretary and general manager. By 1904, Andy Brown had extensive real estate holdings. When he retired and moved to Los Angeles with his family, he left Taylor to assume executive leadership of his corporation.

Among others to work for A. Brown in his store at Kernville was Ed Pettypool, who had run the A. Brown store in Havilah for a period of time. Ed was a first-rate carpenter and did a lot of building and repair work for the A. Brown Company.

Charlie Hand pulls up in front of the Reception Saloon with his load of beer. He named all his trucks, and this one he called the Blue Bird. Note hard rubber tires on the truck, and tops of beer kegs padded with straw.

Pettypool family in Old Kernville, 1914. *Left to right,* Ed Pettypool, Nellie Pettypool Milligan, Lottie Pettypool, and Gertrude Pettypool Suhre.

The Charlie Hand Stage dubbed the Morning Glory in front of the A. Brown Store. Driver, Phil Hand, *right front*, year about 1916 or 1917.

Phil and Myrta Glezen both waited on customers in the old brick building before they moved to the South Fork to take over the Onyx Store.

View of Old Kernville, 1914, looking south from Brewery Hill.

Yes, during the early 1900s it could rightfully be said that Kernville was an A. Brown town. The Company owned the town's only hotel, The Mountain Inn, as well as many houses which were rented—such as the house Dr. Smith lived in. The Company also employed a large number of men in the lumber mill at Wagy Flat as well as on their ranches, such as the Murphy Ranch close to Kernville. The key to the whole conglomerate was the A. Brown Store. Although small stores had operated off and on at various times during the early days of Kernville, they did not last long. They lacked the capital needed for wholesale purchases at the right prices. The A. Brown Company, with stores at Weldon, Havilah, and Kernville, on the other hand, could buy in volume and sell for less. Also, A. Brown wagons, on return trips from hauling flour and other items to Caliente, were able to bring supplies into the Valley at a fraction of the cost of their competitors. Besides, many of the people in the Valley who worked for the A. Brown Company ran up such a bill, that they did not have much to collect after their A. Brown bills were paid.

BECHTEL

Then, in 1918, James R. Bechtel moved to Kernville, leased the old Robert Christian building that had been used in years past as a store, and opened a grocery store. He bought one of the first solid-tired Moreland trucks and hauled his entire grocery stock to his store from Bakersfield. Some of the things featured in his store that were not common at that time were fish, fruits and vegetables, bakery bread, and ice cream. He was the first to

install a gasoline pump where the customers could see how much gas he was getting. The sign on this new type gas dispenser read, "See what you buy, buy what you see." Jim's business grew so fast that he bought a parcel of property on Nellie Dent Street. This property, which once contained a Chinese gambling house, was the last remaining piece of land in Kernville which had belonged to the Chinese settlers that came into the Valley during the Gold Rush. Just east of the Mountain Inn in Old Kernville Jim built first his dance hall, with a pool hall and barber shop in the front area.

It became well known throughout the Valley as Bechtel's Hall. Second, he built the Cedar Bark Building that opened as a restaurant, with Mrs. Carpenter as the first leasee. When she gave up her lease, Mr. and Mrs. Matlock took over the restaurant for the remaining years before it was finally remodeled to become the Kernville Post Office. This building was moved to what was then called New Kernville and became Johnson's

Bechtel family in front of Mountain Inn. *Left to right*, Pearl Bechtel, Edith Bechtel Long, and Jim Bechtel.

Jim Bechtel's Store, Old Kernville, formerly the Robert Christian Store, on far right is the A. Brown Store.

Tackle Shop. In back of this building was the well and tank house that supplied the southern end of the town with water. This was the town's first water system. Still having vacant property facing the street just south of the main street, he bought three of the Edison Company's surplus houses and moved them onto this property, which was back of the tank house and dance hall, and used them as rentals. Jim built a combination store and service station. Some of the names appearing in the old record book from Bechtel's Store in 1920 are: Josie Acosta, Frank Apalatea, George Bandy, Matt Burlando, Mrs. Baker, Dad Buzzard, Bill Calkins, Art Carlson, Floyd DeWolf, Dick Fuggitt, Wayne French, Cora Ellis, Don Hanning, Merle Hight, W. D. Joughin, Martinez, John Noyer, Howard Petersen, Dr. Smith, Clint Steadman, C. B. Tibbetts, and I. S. Wofford. Matt Burlando and Irvin Wofford paid their bills by bringing in a butchered beef. It would hang in quarters in Jim's walk-in refrigerator. When a customer came in to buy meat, a quarter was taken down off the hook and cut to their individual order.

In 1920, Bechtel bought the property in Old Kernville north of what was originally Cook's Livery Stable, converting what had been the home of Mr. and Mrs. Martinez into a service station and cafe. He leased this to Rae Longstreet and her sisters. Rae later bought the property and took Bill Melton in as a partner after her sisters returned to Ohio to live.

In the ensuing years, Jim built a garage on his property east of the store building on Nellie Dent Street, which was first leased by Aubrey Strain, son-in-law of the Matlocks. He later purchased the block of property across the street from his store building from Jerry and Bertha Converse. This property had one old miner's shack on it with a retired miner living in it. He soon began building new rentals on this property, but the old shack remained for the miner to live in as long as he cared to do so. This property later became known as Bechtel's Court. When the town was moved upriver, many of these houses were moved and placed on Sirretta Street.

Through the years Jim also bought property throughout the town, remodeled the houses and then resold them. He also had another water well and tank house behind his home, which served the northern part of Kernville with water.

Left to right, **Bert's Store, Post Office (later Johnson's Tackle Shop in New Kernville), and Bechtel's Hall. In the right foreground is part of what was called the Liar's Bench, where a bunch of old-timers could always be found swapping tall tales. This was where the troubles of the world were settled in those days.**

Up until this time most of the people in Kernville each had his own water well. These wells were usually located on the back porch and fitted with a hand operated pitcher pump. When Jim Bechtel's neighbors, such as Clarence and Ida B. Pascoe, saw how convenient it was to have water piped into the house, they got Jim to let them hook into his water system. Big business put a crimp in Jim Bechtel's love of the outdoors; he wanted more time to hunt and enjoy the country, so he sold his grocery store to a young fella named Bert James.

JAMES

Bert's father, Billie James, came to work in the Big Blue Mine in 1880. When Bert was born, the James family was living in Keysville. An interesting event took place on that occasion and was related as follows: When Ava James felt that her time had come, Billie rushed to Kernville for Doc Gibson. Of course, in those days of horse and buggy, it took some time to drive the eight miles to Kernville and return. When they realized the doctor would not make it in time, Mrs. William Walker was called in to assist. When the doctor arrived some six hours later, he was just in time to check the healthy baby and return to town. The job of naming the young son came next. The James's had already more-or-less settled on the name Burton; but because memories of the Burton-Walker feud was still alive, Mrs. Walker threw a fit. The name Bert was finally settled upon.

Bert ranched until 1929, when he bought the grocery business from Jim Bechtel. It was known from that time on as "Bert's Store," and he continued to run the store just as Jim had, giving credit to many of the locals. Some bills were left unpaid for years, and still others were never paid. It might be that Bert did not make much money, but he made a lot of friends.

When World War II broke out, Bert was not only faced with the big job of running a grocery store during war time but he also had the responsibility of raising his thirteen year old son, Clint. Clint's mother had died some years before.

Within the year, Helen Ramsey, a Kansas schoolteacher came to Kernville and very soon became a very important part of Bert's life. Helen had been raised on a cattle ranch, and from the beginning she fit easily into this rural life.

Helen was hired to teach in the Kern Valley High School, which was then a two-year high school located east of Old Kernville close to a place called the Old Mile sign. Clint was in Helen's classes for the first two years of high school. In 1944, Bert James and Helen Ramsey were married. Clint later jokingly said that his dad married Helen to get a built-in tutor.

As has been the case with so many schoolteachers who married local men and remained in the Valley, Helen became a welcome addition to the social and cultural life of Old Kernville. She even found time from her duties as a storekeeper's wife to be active in a variety of local clubs and organizations, and was the first to form a bridge club in the Valley.

In December of 1949, Bert and Helen moved their home to property on the east side of the Kern River in what was soon to become the town of New Kernville. In 1953 they moved the grocery business to their newly finished store in what was then called New Kernville.

It was not long before they turned the grocery business into Clint's able hands, and then the James's learned the secret of happy retirement—to stay busy. They did not sit back with their hands folded. They continued to operate the James Trailer Park while remaining active in community life. Although slowed down some by the years, at 75 Bert still had that outdoorsman's love for hard physical work and could still put in a good day's work cutting firewood or at a variety of other jobs he found to do.

THE SCHOOLS

The history of any pioneer town is not complete without the story of its early school. The Kernville Union School District, which included the original Kernville School, is most unique in that when it was formed on April 6, 1932, it had included within its boundary five former districts. These districts were: (1) the original Kernville School District, established May 5, 1868; (2) the North Fork School District, formed February 9, 1921, which lasted only eleven years before consolidating with the Kernville District on April 6, 1932; (3) the Palmer School District, formed May

Bert and Helen James when they were married, 1944.

11, 1883, changed in name to the Isabella District in 1905, and finally annexed to the Kernville Union School District in 1948, and (4) the Vaughn District which came in January 23, 1950. The Vaughn School District, established April 3, 1905, had its schoolhouse at Bodfish. The Havilah School District, (5), founded November 9, 1866, had the distinction of being the first public school in Kern County. It was annexed to the Vaughn District in 1920.

When the Kernville School was established in 1868, with an enrollment of 26 children, the first teacher was Mrs. Carrie Tilly. Adam Hamilton, founder of the town of Whiskey Flat, was clerk. Hamilton had established an earlier school in 1868 with an enrollment of 26 children, the first 1863, but this was not a public, tax-supported school. Another longtime district clerk was Judge Sumner, who served two terms, with a total of 21 years.

By 1880 the average daily attendance had reached 59, and two teachers, Hattie Gould and Lizzie Yates, were hired to teach the children.

A group of pioneers pose for a picture in front of the first school in Kernville, 1897, the first community center. *In back, left to right,* Lottie Swett, John Swett, Bill Curtis, Jim Craig, Sumner Brown, Jack Shomate, Charles Sherman, Ed Churchman, Bill Swett, Bert Hight, Bertha Hight, May Hight, Mr. Smith, Mrs. Smith, Edith Swett, at that time the Kernville schoolteacher. *Front row,* Milta Ross Wirth, Lina Finley, George Barber, Lena Fuggitt, Kate Shomate, Annie Shomate.

Teaching conditions in the Kernville School in the early years were poor. In 1907, the teacher, Ethel Carter, wrote, "The porch of the schoolhouse needs new flooring, and the pump should be repaired, otherwise the property is in good condition. The school grounds should be fenced. Heavy wagons continually cross the grounds very near the building and have made it very rough and dusty."

The following year Esther L. Rothwell, Kernville teacher, wrote, "The Kernville School has been slow and backward for years. It is in a very bad condition now on account of the unexpectedly short term this year. Very little interest is shown in the school work by the trustees or the community in general. The boys and girls cannot be trusted to play together, so there should be a fence around the yard and one separating the boys from the girls' playground. The children are happy but restless and unambitious. It is impossible to secure results from this school that you would naturally expect."

In 1914, Freda Hand, sister of Charlie Hand, wrote of the Kernville School, "One criticism might be made as to the furnishing of the school rooms, and that is that we have had to use the old desks which have served for another generation of children, and are not only very much carved and mutilated, but most of them are unfitted in

Second school in Kernville, built in 1898. Note the Methodist Church just past the left corner of the school, and the stile in the front fence.

20

Kernville School, 1932. *Back row, left to right*, Louis Tibbetts, Arthur Allen, Kern Trumbull, Elsie Price, Anna Petersen, Elinor Potter, Carol Diltz, Florence O'Brien, Beverly Mergenthaler, Delmar Price. The three girls at top, Phyllis Hight, Helene Fisher, Carolyn Pascoe. *Middle row*, Margaret Hand, Doris Frazier, June Potter, Grace Petersen, Bernice Robinson, Gayle Mendleson Walker, Mrs. Bessie Robinson (principal), Betty Robinson, Clara Malone, Florence Price, Betty Ann Tichenor, Betty Radcliff. *Second row*, Jackie Levy, Johnny Osenbaugh, Billy Longstreet, Henry Petersen, Charles Tibbetts, Ellis Byrom, William Petersen, Allan Tuttle, Bobby Robinson. *First row*, Dick Pascoe, Raymond Pascoe, Harvey Malone, Howard Potter, Lyman Petersen, Delynn Bales, Donald Mergenthaler, Richard Acosta, Bobby Stains.

Carrie Tilly, first schoolteacher in Kernville, 1868.

size and position for the children who occupy them."

The teacher in 1916-17, Emmett Berry, had the following advice for teachers coming to Kernville: "Any new teacher coming in will have to learn to understand the people here, look past many irritating incidents, and be firm in their decisions."

Teachers did not stay long in Kernville in the early days. The period from 1906 to 1918 was probably typical, the average stay being only one and one-half years.

There are always many interesting stories that can be told about any of these country schools, and the Kernville School was no exception. One such story had to do with the day the teacher thought the flu bug or some other such medical disaster had come down on the town's population. What had her scratching her head was that it seemed to be showing up on the boys and then only on three or four in the same grade. On this particular day there was an especially heavy run on the boys' outhouse. The truth finally came to light some 60 years later; it seemed that some of

Kernville School, 1947—Jo Anne Mills, Donna Keillor, Mary Anne McNally, Ruth Wren, Arlene Apalatea, Mary Lou Denison, Jimmy Maxwell, Lee Gouldin. *Second row*, Jo Anne Thompson, Colene Worrell, Linda O'Connell, Marilyn Apalatea, John Gibson, "Butch" Jackson, Franklin Petersen, Donald Dodson, Kenneth Kane. *Front row*, Bud Malone, Ted Martin, Bobby Crowder, Larry Wagner, Melvin Butterbredt, J. L. Hall.

the boys felt they were going to need some help on their test the next day. So they went over to the schoolyard after dark and suspended the appropriate textbook on a heavy cord down one of the holes of the outhouse that was not used too much. The next day when they came to a question that stumped them they would ask to go to the outhouse. The teacher went through the normal precautions of checking the pockets of the boys' bib overalls and shirts and even checked the outhouse later to see if she could find the reason for so many boys to do so well on one certain test. I guess it could be said that she did not look far enough. You can bet that if she had discovered the ruse that day there would have been a stink raised that would have made the West Point incident seem insignificant.

When the last school in old Kernville was opened, the *Bakersfield Californian* reported on Monday, August 22, 1938, the following news item:

New Structure Replaces Historic Kern County Structure. Using Charles Dana's famous expression "When a man bites a dog, it is news" as a maxim, completion

Kernville School, 1940, grades five through eight. *Back row, left to right,* Roy Frakes, Howard Potter, Richard Acosta, Harvey Malone, Bobby Robinson, Agnes Barney, Jane Christopher, Roberta Fulton, Iown Scott, June Walker. *Second row,* Margaret Burton, Beverly Welch, unidentified, Doris Jorgenson, Joyce Jorgenson, Mrs. Keenholtz, Jo Leen Hall, Maxine Hall, Jo Ann Mergenthaler, Evelyn Hackley. *Third row, left to right,* Ronnie Campbell, Jack Ellis, Willard Malone, Donald Mergenthaler, Red Harris, Clinton James, George Barney. *Bottom row,* Jack Finin, Stanley Malone, Bobby Pinkley, Jim Ellis, Don Pascoe.

of the new $26,946 school structure at Kernville ranks as big news in Kern County. The trustees have built the school out of regular tax funds without floating a bond issue or obtaining P.W.A. help. Architect Stanton Willard of Symmes and Willard reports the new building shown above (article included photograph) contains two classrooms which by means of a sliding partition, may be made into an auditorium, complete with stage and stage equipment. Designed to serve as a community structure, the building contains a modern kitchen and a room which is being offered to the County to be used as a branch library. Blinds, linoleum and stage equipment are being installed now. Shown at right is the old school building, now used as part of a movie set. Many pioneers of Kern attended classes in this structure.

On the same page was the following:

Kernville Kiddies to Find New Building for Classes.

KERNVILLE—August 22 (Special). The opening of the school term in September will find the children of Kernville and vicinity housed in a modern schoolhouse which was built to meet the needs which have developed with a rapid increase in growth in the community. The construction of this building, with most of the conveniences to be found in the newest of city school buildings, has been a step out of the "little red schoolhouse" era for Kernville.

The new structure was built beside the old building, which was only recently torn down and moved away. During this process old papers were found under the floors which caused many old time residents to reflect on their own school days. Among old timers whose names appeared on old spelling, geography and history papers are May Booth, Etta Bole, Mamie Ross, John Hooper, Charley Beaty, William Walker; with the date November 6, 1882 after his name, Hal Walker, Klosa; on a grammar paper, Carrie Tilly, Edna Beaty and Bertha Hooper.

Under a picture of the old school was noted:

The only school building to remain is one which antedates that recently torn down. With its quaint belfry, it forms a picturesque part of atmospheric Movie Street. Last minute preparations are now being made by a group of men under the direction of the Kernville Union School Board so that the new building will be in readiness for school opening.

The first year of the Kernville Union School District, 1932-33, recorded an average daily attendance of 41 pupils. The first teaching principal was Bessie S. Robinson, who had served the previous two years in the same capacity at the Kernville School. Mrs. Florence Pascoe was district clerk during this term.

The Kernville Union School District covers 295 square miles of territory with a 1970-71 assessed valuation of $26 million. It encompasses most of Lake Isabella's perimeter and the North Fork of

Last grammar school—Old Kernville.

the Kern River, which lies above Kernville. Much of the area is mountainous and includes the summits of three of Kern County's highest peaks — Greenhorn Mountain, Breckenridge Mountain, and Piute Peak.

One of the best things that ever happened to the Kernville Union School District occurred when they hired Woodrow W. Wallace as their teaching principal in 1946. "Woody," as he came to be known, started his teaching career in 1941 in Strathmore, California. After a year at Strathmore, he was drafted into the Army and served in the 81st Infantry Division. Before long he was sent to Officers Training School at Fort Benning, Georgia. After becoming an instructor, Woody went to England with the 8th Corps Headquarters and, working his way up to the rank of captain, spent time in France, Germany and Holland.

Upon discharge from the service, Woody attended the Paramount graduate school. Not wanting to return to Strathmore, Woody was prepared to apply for a teaching position in the Southland when he was informed of a possible vacancy in Kernville.

He came to Kernville and met Bill Stewart, one of the school trustees, who showed him around town. Bill introduced him to other members of the school board which included Sedric Hackley, Ida Ray, Orian Campbell and Edith Gouldin. The school board liked Woody immediately and he accepted their offer of the teaching principal position. This started Woody Wallace on the job as superintendent in a school with an enrollment of only 103 students in 1946-47, and by 1970-71 had grown to a high of 711 students. During this same period the school employees also increased from 8 to 50.

Selma Cooper

Cleone Shaw

Aida Martin DaMant

Woodrow W. Wallace

Naomi Horton

Frances Douglas

Mary Grant

Because of the newly formed Lake Isabella, Kernville School was forced to relocate below the dam on Erskine Creek Road in 1953. Accelerated growth and enrollment of the school in the early 1950s was caused by the heavy influx of construction workers and their families for the Isabella Reservoir project. The first 20 years Woody spent at the Old Kernville School were most memorable. His job included teaching the 7th and 8th grade combination with as many as 39 students, along with supervising the teachers. He coached three sports and, due to the lack of secretarial help, he kept all the books. Being under two federal laws created even more of a secretarial burden, and it was some years before the County even furnished him a typewriter.

The flood of 1950 placed additional pressure on Woody. When the Kernville bridge washed out, children living on the east side of the river had to make a 52 mile round trip to attend school. The one bus driver, Guy Shultz, was also the janitor, and if he would have had to make this trip he could not have swept the floors. So for two months Woody made this trip with a busload of children each morning and night.

In 1948, when the Isabella School joined the Kernville Union School District, their building was moved to Kernville to serve as a classroom for the fourth grade. Two additional temporary classrooms had been built in the schoolyard to house the sixth grade in which Mrs. Francis Douglas refereed 54 children, and the fifth grade, with Mrs. Felix riding herd on an additional 54 students. The main school building, built in 1938, housed Principal Wallace and the seventh and eighth grade combination.

Also in this building was a small kitchen in which Thyra Apalatea, Callie Dodson and Lucille Seeley put out meals for over 200 students. Eating arrangements required that the students fill their trays and return to their individual classrooms, where the teachers could supervise the eating.

In 1949, when the South Fork school building was condemned because of an earthquake, some of the children were sent to Kernville. Along with the extra children, part of the agreement was that a teacher be furnished, who was Cleone Shaw; also Boss Petersen, bus driver-custodian until his retirement in 1971; and Lutie Petersen, who worked in the kitchen. All three of these people stayed on at Kernville. With their help the Kern-

ville School was able to handle the additional load.

When Ada Martin first moved to the Kernville School from the Vaughn School with the upper grades, she was given a room for her third and fourth graders in the Methodist Church, which stood in back of the schoolyard. According to Ada, this made a perfect classroom. The following year the Vaughn School building was moved into the schoolyard. Mrs. Martin was given a room for her 30 students, while Mary Grant and Selma Cooper each had their rooms for first and second grades, with more than 30 students in each—a total of over 100 students in this small building.

Many of Woody's former students had children who went through the full eight years under Mr. Wallace. One of these was Marjorie (Martin) Powers, who graduated out of Woody's class in 1947. By 1972 five of her children had also graduated from the Kernville School.

Although Woody was relieved of teaching duties after the school moved below the dam, he still had a big job as superintendent because of the continued growth. He relates that the only reason he was able to do such a fine job for so long was because of the excellent help he had in the way of school employees and school board members. He had nothing but praise for the board members over the years. These dedicated citizens who put in so many years of unpaid service have listed among their members Bill Stewart, Sedric Hackley, Benny Burton, Herman Wagner, Orian Campbell, Ida Ray, Foster Webb, Barney Campbell, Edith Gouldin, Frank Phillips, Bill Stephens, Ken Thompson, and Thyra Apalatea. By 1972, Thyra had served 20 years as secretary of the school board.

School custodians who took an interest in their work and excellent bus drivers also made Woody's job much easier. Some of those remembered by teaching staff and students alike include Guy Shultz, Boss Petersen, Junior Robinson and Bobbie Robinson. Those working in the kitchen over the years included Mrs. Grace Theobald, Beulah Hall, Lutie Petersen, and Lorena Bell.

Of course, any school is only as good as its teachers; and although Kernville had its outstanding teachers in the first 80 years of its existence, Woody had the knack of acquiring good teachers and keeping them. The following is a list of teachers who came to teach in the Kernville School, transferred to the new school at Isabella, and

Kernville Methodist Church, built in 1898.

many of whom stayed on to retirement: Ada (Martin) DaMant, Mary Grant, Selma Cooper, Warren Axe, Cleone Shaw, Naomi Horton, and Frances Douglas.

In the fall of 1968 a new Kernville elementary school including kindergarten through sixth grades was constructed. Kernville again had a school building.

In 1974, Woody Wallace submitted his resignation as district school superintendent, thus ending a truly outstanding career that spanned 28 years.

Besides its unique formation from five former districts and its phenomenal growth, the Kernville Union School District has also become a model of scholastic excellence for the community. Students who have had the opportunity to attend this school are indeed fortunate.

THE COMMUNITY CHURCH

Almost as surely as each pioneer town would have a school, there also would be a church. In many small communities for years there was usually only one church, for that was all it could support. During the horse and buggy period, not many would travel 15 or 20 miles to attend a church of like faith, but would attend the one in their home town. In some towns the first church was Catholic, in others, Presbyterian. And, in Kernville it was the Methodist Church that for many years fulfilled the town's spiritual needs. People who had belonged to churches of other denominations before moving to this country town often faithfully attended and supported the Community Methodist Church.

The Kern River Circuit of the Methodist Church had been organized in 1870, but it was not until July of 1874 that the first quarterly conference was held in the town of Kernville. At this time a Sunday School was organized, with Richard Williams as the superintendent. The name was changed to the Kernville Charge. The area covered not only included Weldon and Glennville, but also Walker's Basin and Tehachapi. It was a 200-mile trip around the charge and most of the ministers made the rounds three times between each quarterly conference, or about every two and one-half months. Then in 1884 the town of Kernville suffered financial disaster with the $250,000 Big Blue Mine fire. On February 9 of that year, the fire's effect on the church, as well as the town, is reflected in the Quarterly Report for the Second Conference held at Kernville:

Dear Brethren:

Since making my last report the business interests of the town of Kernville have suffered from financial depression from which they have not recovered. This of course affects the interests of the church. There has been a falling off at the Sabbath Eve congregation owing we think in measure at least to removal of families to other localities of late, however the congregation has been very good. Have endeavored to be faithful in the duty of visiting from house to house the number of Pastoral visits made during the quarter 69. Have taken no benevolent collection because of depression in business interests making money scarce. On the whole we are not disheartened but still hopeful of good results from efforts put forth. The work is God's. He will care for it and his workers.

Respectfully submitted,
CHARLES W. HOWELL,
Preacher in Charge.

In 1898, some 28 years after the Kern River Charge was first organized, Kernville still did not have a church buliding in the community. Services were held in the school. They had bought property at the west end of College Street, but could not gather enough money to start building. Then a group of the Kernville men, who were not church members, decided to help the Lord's work along and started giving plays in the Reception Saloon, the proceeds going for lumber to build the church. One of the actors in those early productions was Harold Calkins. Because his acting ability and mannerisms reminded some of his co-workers of Bill Neigh, a famous actor of that time, Calkins was given the nickname, Bill—a name that remained with him the rest of his life.

Reverend J. C. Livingston was the pastor during this period. Being an expert carpenter himself and possessing a great deal of determination, he pushed ahead with the construction of the church. This was in 1898. The following year after they had finished this building, Livingston helped the congregation at Weldon build a church. Only one minister served the two communities until 1948. At that time, the Weldon Church and the Highland Chapel of Bodfish became one circuit, and Kernville and Johnsondale became another.

Although there were many men who were faithful to duties of the church in those early days, it was then, as it has been down through the years, the women who carried the biggest share of the load. The first women to be mentioned in church records for the Kernville Charge were Harriet Johnston, wife of Dr. F. A. Johnston; Sister Plummer; Sister Robinson; Jennie Alberts; Josie Belknap; and Hettie Gould, an early Kernville schoolteacher. Another of the Valley women who attended and worked in the Methodist Church all

Dave and Nettie Hight Yarbrough.

her life was Lottie Pettypool. Lottie started Sunday School at Onyx in 1886 with Ella Smith as her teacher. In 1949, when they had the 50th anniversary celebration of the building of the Methodist Churches, she sent the following item reminiscing about the early church:

With the building of the Kernville Church, Mr. Livingston was blessed with the faithful, untiring aid of Mrs. Edith Taylor, whose memory is dear to all of us. Through Mrs. Taylor's efforts, often came the answers to prayers mentioned. How well some of us remember the fine ice cream socials given under her direction ably assisted by Mrs. Josephine Belknap. Mrs. Taylor, being a minister's daughter (daughter of Jesse L. Bennett), and Mrs. Belknap, a minister's wife, the truth of faith by works was in their blood. It would take volumes to give an account of the valuable assistance those two Christian women gave our pastor. Mr. Livingston spoke of Mrs. Taylor as the backbone of the church—the main spoke in the wheel.

Another person who was active in the Methodist Church was Nettie Hight Yarbrough. For the celebration she sent this letter:

Kernville, California
February 26, 1949

Dear Friends:

Not being able to attend the table talk, at the 50th anniversary celebration of the building of the churches, I shall have a quiet little chat with you in reply to Rev. Banghart's request.

I was born in '68. At that time there were no churches and no ministers here, other than some miner who happened to be well versed on the Bible. Many of the meetings led by the Bible teacher were held in my home. Every home had a Bible. When a young couple started out in life they were made a gift of a Bible. Many evenings were spent reading and discussing it. People seemed to lean on God and his great strength. They needed his love, too, to help them through the many great problems of life. Children

Lottie Pettypool leaves Havilah for Kernville on Petersen Stage. Tom Gonzales is the driver.

Mrs. Josie Belknap, taken in 1905. Mrs. Belknap was very active in the early church and would many times preach the service for funerals.

were faithfully taught the love of God and his great wisdom. Every night we kneeled by our sweet loving mother saying our prayers. Then we God blessed, and kissed each good-night and cuddled down in our beds of new mown hay. The morning was greeted with our little prayers of song. This song told of the bright sun coming up, the dew floats away, good morning bright sunshine, the little birds say all the lovely flowers and sweet song birds. The song ended thus: Our Heavenly Father, how kind and how good.

After each little hand and face was washed we had a good breakfast. We were taught table manners and kindness to old people. We each had some little duty to perform. They told us how the ants worked and all that the bees did so we were their "ants" and "bees" to get in wood, drive the cattle home and to help mama and papa. We loved it.

Then we moved to Kernville from the old Greenhorn Mountain to attend school. The school house for many years was used for Sunday School and Church. In public school the day was always begun with the Lord's Prayer. After the town grew larger and several religious groups were represented some objected to teaching religion in schools so the prayer was discontinued. The church worship services were all held in the one room school house. Mrs. Josie Belknap (then Miss Josie Sumner) was our minister and Sunday School teacher. Sunday School was held at the hour of ten. It seemed that every child attended and loved it. At 11 A.M. church was held for mothers and fathers who could not attend the 7 P.M. service that night. Many mothers had to stay home to put the little ones to bed. That way everyone was able to go to church each Sunday. There were no fretful, sleepy, crying children to upset the evening meeting. We all loved the beautiful old songs. "Dare to be a Daniel" was a favorite song. "Shall we meet beyond the River?" "When Jesus was here Among Men, He took the little children as lambs to His fold, I'd like to have been with Him then" and many others just as beautiful.

28

After Sunday School we remembered that we were to "keep the day Holy." We would walk over the hills in the springtime and gather wild flowers. Many times we would use them to decorate the graves of those who had gone on. The day was mostly spent in different homes, singing and visiting. No romping, no dancing, a day of quiet and rest, not for a few, but for all, they wanted it that way.

We were taught never to take the life we could not give. Miss Josie Sumner preached many funeral sermons. Funerals were held in the homes, there being no other building large enough. Mrs. Belknap kept up this good work until Reverend Bennet came to us. He was with us many years and most beloved by all. You may all know the story from here on. May God bless and keep each and every one of you.

Your friend,
Nettie Hight Yarbrough,
Kernville, California.

Another faithful worker in the Kernville Methodist Church was Ida B. Pascoe. When Ida B. and her husband, Clarence, moved to the Kern River Valley in 1902, she was no stranger to the area as she had made frequent visits over a span of twenty years previous to that time. The following article, written by Mrs. Pascoe, gives some of her unusual church background during this period:

My father Reverend O. D. Dooley, more often called Parson Dooley, was a Cumberland Presbyterian Preacher of the pioneer days. Father preached for many years in the South Fork Valley, Hot Springs Valley, Havilah, and Kernville. In his early ministry, father traveled the hard way—on horseback over the mountain trails to get to his appointments. Then later with a span of horses and wagon. As a small child, I remember Mother, my brother, and I coming over to the South Fork Valley with Father when he came to preach, which was once a month. We would travel all day long and in the late afternoon would come to

Methodist Aid Society held on the Tilly Ranch. *Front row, left to right,* Ida B. Pascoe, Mrs. Tibbetts, Anna Andress and daughter, Grace, Mrs. Hight (Converse), Grandmother Stavert. *Back row,* Gladys Coit and son, Marvin, Fannie Converse, Mrs. Gabe Chavez.

Mr. and Mrs. Henry True's ranch or the Johnson or Smith ranch where we stayed all night.

Father preached in the Weldon schoolhouse, the Scodie schoolhouse, and many times in the homes of different families. Several times father brought with him Reverend Baldwin and they would hold protracted meetings for a week at a time. Father built many churches throughout the state. He was active in his work all through his ministerial life. His last mission was when he was called to Merced to dedicate a new Cumberland Presbyterian Church that had just been completed; Father being the oldest minister, this honor was bestowed on him. Father became ill while at Merced, and two weeks after arriving home he passed away at the age of 86 years. He organized and built the Cumberland Presbyterian Church at Glenville in 1866. [This was the first church built in Kern County and was still being used in 1973.]

In 1973, Ida B. had attended the Kernville Methodist Church for over seventy years. She helped form the first choir and was president of this group for many years. It was this choir that virtually held the church together for many years. The members met faithfully for practice every Wednesday night and were in church every Sunday, come rain or shine. They bought their own robes, chairs, and music. These members also gave $25 annually toward the minister's salary, although most of them gave their tithe to the church. This group put on Spring and Fall Fashion Shows and Home Talent Shows to raise money for the church. Waldo Ellis and Gladys Campbell were another two who served many years with the church choir.

As stated before, to the greatest degree it was the women who kept the church going. While there will undoubtedly be many missed who were equally important in their contribution to the church activities, others not previously mentioned were: Ethel Crotser, Lorena Hipes, Oleta Barnes, and Lola Maud Ellis.

The Methodist Conference moved their ministers every two years, but each minister who came to the Kernville Church had something special to contribute. Although there were certain ministers who especially endeared themselves to those of their charge, it would be rather boring for those not acquainted with the church to list all those that served here. One of those mentioned most often, though, begins with Jesse Lee Bennett. In an outline of the life and activities of Reverend Jesse Lee Bennett recounted by Mrs. Gwenevere Hooper, she reminisced, "That Father Bennett laid a solid foundation in establishing the Methodist

John and Gwenevere Wyatt Hooper, 1894.

Church in the Kernville Circuit is attested by the fact that many were drawn to take great interest in the work of the church. Among those perhaps best remembered by me were the daughters of Judge Sumner, Mrs. Andrew Brown and Josie Belknap. Judge Sumner was for many years the superintendent of the Kernville Sunday School, and his daughters took an active part in the work —Mrs. Belknap playing the organ and Mrs. Brown leading the singing. Also, they each taught a Sunday School Class, and it was from Mrs. Brown that I learned the Lord's Prayer. Now whenever I attend Lodge and hear the Lord's Prayer, my thoughts go back to Mrs. Brown. In later years Mrs. Jessie Brown, wife of Sumner Brown, the son of Andrew, also taught in the Kernville Sunday School."

Others best remembered were the Reverends J. C. Livingston, Clark A. Newton, W. E. Banghart, and Donald Nelson.

When the Valley celebrated the 50th anniversary of the dedication of the original church buildings of Weldon and Kernville Community Methodist Churches in November of 1948, some of the former pastors who were not able to attend sent letters. The following is one sent by Reverend Arthur D. Willett, who had served the Valley churches for a period of one year around 1920. Although Reverend Willett lived in the Valley only a little over a year, one can tell from reading his letter to the churches that his stay here made a lasting impression on him as it has on so many who have lived here. It was partly the near perfect climate there along the Kern where the desert meets the mountains, but for the main part it was the people. The spirit of unity that prevailed and their concern for each other that made the Kern River so unequal.

Madison, Wisconsin.

When the announcement of the 50th anniversary came, the first thing Mrs. Willett said was "Let's take a plane out and surprise them." How we should like to have done just that! But circumstances just wouldn't permit such a jaunt. But every year we say to each other "Is this the year that we go to Kernville and Weldon?" When we left we never dreamed that we would not be back to visit real soon. But here these many years have passed.

Our coming and the little time we spent among you may have seemed very drab to you—just another minister and his family. But to us who were born in, the middle-west and went to school in Boston, the life of Kernville was very exciting. There were only seventeen houses and the school, church, and the store—but there was the river, and the mountains and Bull Run and Box Canyon and Dr. Smith with his nose for quartz veins and trout. And there were the Yucca blossoms on the side of the mountain with an odor so sweet that it nearly made one faint, and the hummingbird that had its nest in the old barn on the bend of the river, and the carpet of pink foliage in the canyons —the California quail with its topknot and brood of little ones that scattered when I came near. And there was Jerry Converse, the dreamer who periodically went to search for the pot of gold on the South Fork, and his good wife who helped bring Donald into the world—at least she and Dr. Smith were present on the occasion. Donald lives just back of us and is a chemist for the state and works in the University Bio-Chemistry building. I always tell him, when we get the notion to go fishing on a trip, that the best trip I ever planned, he spoiled. I had arranged with Mr. Pascoe next door to the parsonage, to go up the river 75 miles with packs, to fish for the golden trout up there that he told me about. And we were to start the morning that Donald came. Of course the trip was off—off I fear forever. Being a native son, Donald looks forward to visiting also. What I fear for me is that the romance of those early days will have vanished—even many of the people. Who was that very intelligent brother at Isabella, with the long hair, who said to me once "Padre, don't bury me in the Kernville Cemetery. I don't want someone rolling over and asking 'Well, who shot you?'" And who was the old lady who used to make a pound cake for the parents when the new baby arrived? And who was it that used to make coffins out of pine boards—the kind that were broad at the shoulders and narrowed down to the feet and to the head? And what fun the boys had at the egg-hunt on the lawn of Mrs. Pettypool—a lovely lady in a large place next to Brown's store?

Hold on! I'll be reminiscing and living over every day of the glorious time I had there. And if I should start on Weldon (and Arthur who is now a minister) climbing the pulpit pedestal while I was trying to preach, and the experiences with all of the lovely people who lived there and at Onyx and up to Walker's Pass and down river to the dam and Havilah "where there is gold" and the good lady who asked me if I didn't want to come to her place and take a bath—I didn't know she had hot sulphur water—I was under the impression that she thought I really needed a cleaning-up—well if I should start in on all of those good folks, this letter would never get sent. It would make a book. (Every Sunday School and church where I have been, and when I was superintendent of the Eau Claire District, has heard about Ella Smith— Mrs. Tom Smith—as I knew her and the work she has done so faithfully for these many years. And how her daughter has at last taken her mantle to carry on in the same prophetic and faithful way.) Please stop me before it is too late! Maybe it is almost too late now, so I'll throw myself back on the horse's haunches and pull in on the bit. In other words, I'm going to get this to the post office. I didn't realize that the time was so short. Say, did Doc Smith ever join the church? He told me that he didn't feel good enough. Well that kind of stumped me because I had just come out of the U. S. Cavalry where men weren't good either— but they weren't his kind either. As Captain Huff said to me one time when I talked to him about his drinking, "Padre, these new silk stockings and carnation cologne are ruining me." Doc seemed to me to be just about the best kind of a man that I had ever met— and yet he wasn't good enough to join the church!

Here I stop! Love to you all.

Say you know I always had a tender feeling for the Cannell Meadows because my mother's maiden name was Cannell and she never left the Isle of Man until my father brought her to America. And so to that bunch of Manxmen who turned cowboys on the South Fork—all hail!

This letter was neither dictated nor read. Bishop Mitchell always used to have written "dictated but not read," so he wouldn't be blamed for mistakes in spelling etc. How he used to shove things off onto his secretary. I'm virtuous. I don't have a secretary so I'll assume all the blame.

Should I tell the pastor, Mr. Banghart, how we used to get the week's meat? Monday, shoot a jack. Wed. get some trout. Friday some eggs from Bob Neill. Sat. a chunk of beef from the butchering at Onyx. And wood! Why just pick up bull cones or dig up the roots of a Juniper tree. Yes, I saw Old Belle in the mountains twice. She was supposed to pull me around the circuit but I gave her her liberty.

Mrs. Willett tells me to send her love, too.

A. D. WILLETT.

Dr. William B. Smith, 1915.

DOCTOR SMITH

Old Kernville had its share of doctors down through the years. None, though, will live longer in the hearts of the mountain residents than Dr. William B. Smith.

Dr. Smith was born in Pomona in 1883. In the process of growing up and acquiring an education, he became acquainted with a variety of vocations, of which one was mining. The mining bug hit Bill Smith early in life, as it had his father and other members of his family.

In 1915, Dr. Smith, who had just finished his internship in Chicago, established residency in the town of Randsburg with his family which included his wife, Madge, a son and a daughter. They were doing fine when, as Dr. Smith put it, "one morning I woke up and looked out the window and the air was filled with dust; people were leaving town on every road out." With most of the people departing, Dr. Smith decided that he had better seek a more prosperous town in which to practice medicine. Later that year he loaded his worldly possession and little family in their Model T. As they drove over Walker Pass and down through the South Fork, they decided to make a

side trip to Kernville before going out through Havilah and up the San Joaquin Valley.

Dr. Smith and his family stayed in Kernville two weeks with a Mrs. Converse. A doctor was needed in Kernville, so he returned to Randsburg to move the rest of his belongings. He took Merle Hight, who was then a lad of 12, with him. It was snowing and after an unsuccessful try to get over Walker's Pass, they tried the Tehachapi route— only to become hopelessly sunk in a drift several miles outside the town of Tehachapi. They spent a cold night burning fence posts under a tree to keep warm. The next day they found a ranch house. The obliging farmer hooked up his team of horses and helped them over the pass.

Besides the local populace and those working in the Big Blue Mine, the Southern California Edison Company was starting a major project to bring water through 16 miles of tunnels and flumes to power hydro-electric generators. This was to become the Kern River 3 Powerhouse. At one time there were 3,000 men working on this project. Although they had a company doctor, he did need help. When the company doctor left and went to Big Creek, another Southern California Edison community, Dr. Smith handled all the cases by himself.

In those days there were practical nurses in every community who served as midwives when doctors were not available, and worked alongside the doctor when there was one in town. One of these midwives was Mrs. Converse and many babies in the Kernville area were helped into the world by this gracious pioneer. Another practical nurse who worked with Dr. Smith at the Edison Company hospital at Hospital Flat was Mrs. Anderson. She not only worked with Dr. Smith there, but also stayed in his home between her assignments of nursing in private homes.

Dr. Smith delivered babies, not only all over the Kern River Valley, but also in the town of Havilah and in Walker's Basin. Some of the children he delivered who are still living in the Valley are from the families of Weaver Hand, Marvin Powers Sr., Art Malone, Earl Pascoe, and Matt Burlando. There were no hospitals in the Valley, so in most cases—after receiving a phone call or having a message delivered personally—he would make an emergency house call. Starting up his Model A Ford, many times in the middle of the night, to drive to some isolated ranch to deliver a baby was commonplace for him.

After the Edison Company finished their plant at K. R. 3, the medical business dropped off sharply and Dr. Smith was heard making the statement to Mrs. Anderson that the people of Kernville were disgustingly healthy.

About this time Judge Vrooman, judge for the Kern River Judicial District, died and Dr. Smith was appointed to the job. This was in 1922 and he held the position for nine years. Court was held in the old Oddfellows Hall, and one winter, when business was slow all around, the townspeople hired the Doctor to paint the outside of the building. In reminiscing about the job which he did by hand and with no help, he said that it took him most of the winter. It was painted green with no trim whatsoever.

The cases Dr. Smith presided over covered everything from deer poaching to bootlegging whiskey. Remembering his years as judge, Dr. Smith recalled a case that concerned poaching deer. One day Mrs. Polkinhorn, wife of Havilah rancher Jim Polkinhorn, heard a shot. She looked out to see a local citizen crawling through the fence into their alfalfa field to where a doe lay dying from a rifle shot. Off to the west the rest of the deer herd was scattering into the hills. As the season was closed, deer came down into the Polkinhorn fields every day. They had become fairly used to cars coming by on the road, so the kill had been as easy as shooting sitting ducks. Mrs. Polkinhorn silently let the poacher drag his game from the field and, as soon as he departed, called the constable, Clarence Pascoe. Mr. Pascoe talked it over with the Judge, Dr. Smith, then decided to talk to the guilty party. This they did, but also in on the discussion was a wealthy rancher friend of the accused poacher. The Doctor and the constable convinced the man to plead guilty and let the local court handle it, so the date for the handling of the case was set.

The rancher showed up in court in Kernville at the Oddfellows Hall, bringing in his friend to appear before the Judge. After the preliminaries of recording the plea and recording the acceptance of the guilty plea, Judge Smith asked if the accused was ready to have the penalty imposed. Upon receiving an answer to the affirmative, Judge Smith gave the sentence. He said he could hardly send the poacher to jail in Bakersfield as it was so far away and that, since it was a first offense and just one deer, he would let the man off with a

fine. He fined him $200 for possession of an illegal deer. Dr. Smith later said he almost had to patch a hole in the roof of the Oddfellows Hall as the defendant shot to his feet in protest. He and the rancher were both talking at once, claiming the trial was outrageous and the deer was not worth more than $20. Doc Smith said, "Wait just a minute, I'm not finished." On top of the first $200, he also found the man guilty of trespassing on the property where the deer was feeding. After another violent storm the rancher friend advised the defendant to pay the fine, but told the Judge that he would remember the incident. The case report was sent to Bakersfield and was shortly followed by a letter of congratulations from the District Attorney's office. Doc Smith was fast becoming known as a man who could not be swayed by friends or politics.

Another case concerning Dr. Smith occurred when Constable Pascoe received a phone call notifying him that several deer were staggering around in a canyon off the South Fork. Rumor had it that there was an illegal whiskey still in that same canyon and, having no deputies, Mr. Pascoe took Judge Smith with him to investigate.

About halfway up the canyon near Walker's Pass they passed a speeding car. Although they recognized the occupants, they made no attempt to stop them as they had no proof of illegal involvement.

A few miles further up the canyon, near the end of the road, they found the bootleg operation. Tucked back under a big rock was as nice a still as you would ever want to see. Although no one was in attendance, it was evident that the operators had just left as the heat under the coils of the still was still causing a pencil size stream of the clearest 100-proof mountain dew to flow into a five-gallon jug. Nearby was the pile of sour corn mash from which the deer had eaten the day before, unwittingly blowing the whistle on the bootleggers. Constable Pascoe and Dr. Smith completely destroyed the whole operation, even though Dr. Smith admitted he felt badly about tearing up anything that had been set up with as much skill and was working as perfectly as the little still. Even though neither of the investigators were drinking men, they decided to take the four gallons of 100-proof whiskey and a new 25-30 rifle acquired as evidence. Although they had strong suspicions as to the owner of the still, they were never brought to trial because of lack of sub-

Kernville, California, *looking north*, home and office of Dr. William B. Smith on right, next door Charlie Hand, two A, Brown rentals, and last Gabe Chavez.

stantial evidence. Doc Smith fell heir to the mountain dew when it was left in custody of the court, and used it in his practice. When he moved to Delano some years later he still had more than a gallon left.

Dr. Smith had many other part time activities which included choir member, preacher, and gen-

Old Doc Smith "sounds off for a dollar." Taken at his desk in April of 1968.

eral trouble shooter for the whole area. One hobby that he admitted cost him a great deal of his hard earned cash was the mining bug. Some 55 years after coming to the Kern River Valley he was still as enthusiastic about trying to get that 'beautiful free gold out that God had put there." However, he freely admitted that "a little gold corrupts, more gold corrupts a little more, and millions of dollars corrupts completely."

One of his business ventures in the Valley was meat butchering. He figured if he could take the meat from the producer to customer in one step he could make money. Doc went to Charlie Taylor, who handled the finances for the A. Brown Company, and borrowed money—quite a lot. Things were set up and going fine when he found the meat had to have government inspection, and he would have to pay for the inspector to come up from Bakersfield each time. So the slaughter house business was terminated almost before it started, but not soon enough to keep Doc Smith from losing $5,000.

As his four small children were growing up, he was busy night and day. One case comes to mind where a man was injured some 16 miles above Kernville on the Edison job. It was evening before

Tibbetts Brothers, 1900 era, *standing left to right*, Fred and William; *seated*, *left to right*, Frank and Charlie.

Doc Smith received word of the accident. Nevertheless, he departed immediately in his Model A. Realizing the man needed more medical attention than he could be given in Kernville, he gave him first aid, bundled the patient in his car, and started for Bakersfield. The patient survived the trip over roads that were not much more than cow paths, and which took them through Havilah and Caliente. The next day the Doctor stayed with the man until he was out of danger and then started the long trip home. This is only one of the many instances where he gave untold hours to his profession, many times receiving only a verbal thanks from his patients for payment. This was typical of pioneer doctors, though.

Doctor Smith said he kept busy running the lives of everything and everybody in the Valley, including the jackrabbits and rattlesnakes. He fished and prospected, and generally just enjoyed life to its fullest.

In 1931, Dr. and Mrs. Smith decided that their family of teenagers, which included a son, DeWitt, and three daughters, Nancy, Harriet, and Betty, would have to be moved to where they could be closer to high school. So the town of Delano was chosen. Doc Smith soon built up his medical practice in this farming community of 3,000 residents, as the people found that he treated everyone with compassion rather than concern of payment. He also played an important role in the town's activities. When Doctor Smith was 62, he was the mayor of the city of Delano, trustee of the Methodist Church, secretary of the high school board of trustees, member of County Council of Boy Scouts, and was also teaching an adult Sunday school class in the Methodist Church. He was called on to lecture from time to time. In his more than 60 years of active practice, he delivered over 3,000 babies.

He was a homespun philosopher of fame, and his many friends knew him as "Limerick Bill." He kept in touch with his many friends in the Kern Valley and elsewhere with a constant flow of letters.

After some 40 years in Delano, he was still practicing medicine. A knock would come at his door, and old Doc Smith would call out with a booming voice that could be heard to city hall, "COME IN!" He received pay for only a small portion of the services he rendered, but was dedicated to his work and loved those he treated. These characteristics, coupled with his deep faith in God, made him an outstanding example of our country doctors of bygone years.

In later years he wrote his autobiography and ended it with the following paragraph:

This seems to be a good place to end this tale of a country doctor, his life, and his beliefs. It has been on the whole a privilege and a joy to have lived on this marvelous earth for more than 75 years and I have little material goods to leave my dependents but the beauty and the wonder of the good earth I leave to all.

Truly a good place to end.

TIBBETTS

The Roswell Tibbetts family was another who came in the early days of the settlement of the Kern River Valley and stayed on.

Roswell Goodspeed Tibbetts was born in Liberty, Maine, in 1930 and while quite young, chose to follow the sea. It was as second mate on a vessel that rounded Cape Horn that he arrived in San Francisco in 1850; the voyage had taken six months.

The lure of the gold fields caused young Tibbetts to give up the life of a sailor. He placer mined on the Feather River for a time, and later worked in the celebrated Comstock Mine of

Nevada, and at Truckee and the Sierra Valley in California. During this period he transported mail between Sierraville and Truckee, wearing snowshoes during winter months.

Also during this time he married Mrs. Helen Branch Norcross, and her son, Charles, from a former marriage, was adopted by Roswell when he was four years old. Three more sons were born to Roswell and Helen—Fred in 1863, William in 1866, and Frank in 1869.

In 1874, Roswell Tibbetts brought his family to Kernville, where he built and operated the American Eagle Hotel. He made many acquaintances in the Valley and counted Judge Sumner as one of his closest friends.

In 1881 the Tibbetts sold the hotel and moved to Calico, where they built another hotel. Mrs. Sarah Hight, a widow, and Mrs. Orr arrived from Kernville and assisted Mrs. Tibbetts in setting up a dressmaking business, a bakery and a skating rink within the hotel.

While they were living in Calico there was an unusual mail carrier that delivered mail from that town to Bismarck, some miles away. This was Dorsey, a collie dog who daily made the round trip across the desert alone, delivering his charge with clocklike precision.

Following a fire in 1887, the family moved to Huron, in Fresno County, where Mr. Tibbetts opened a livery stable. He also homesteaded 160 acres, part of which was still in Fred's family in 1973.

But Huron was not for the elder Tibbetts and he returned to Kernville in the early 1980s to open a store and meat market, which he operated with the help of his two younger sons, Will and Frank.

Fred had a stamp mill in Keysville for a time and was a mining developer in Rhyolite, Bullfrog, and other Nevada towns. In 1882, Fred married Emma Bell Gould and this union was blessed with one boy and three girls.

William remained in Kernville where he first raised cattle under the name of Cross Brothers and Tibbetts, the brothers being John and Addison. William later operated the Caliente-Kernville stage line and made other investments. He married Anna C. Munch in 1895, and their two daughters were named Florence and Hazel.

Upon the family's return from Calico, Frank worked in his father's store and was later employed at the Big Blue Mine. In 1894 he married Elizabeth Cross, sister of John and Add Cross.

Dorsey, U.S. Mail Carrier, 1883.

Two daughters who died in infancy were interred in the old pioneer cemetery in Kernville. A son, Marion, was born while Frank was working the Keysville mines and a daughter, Maybelle, was born later. In 1900, Frank moved his family to Bakersfield where he opened a grocery store with his father.

Charles Branch Tibbetts was the oldest child. He worked in the Big Blue Mine for several years after he arrived in Kernville. He hauled gold bearing quartz on contract; hauling 24 tons daily with a four horse team and averaging $10.00 a day over expenses.

He invested his savings in cattle and land near Kernville, establishing his headquarters for the cattle business opposite the old mill with the TT brand. He continued in the cattle business until 1897, when he went to Alaska. After packing 1,500 pounds of supplies over the Chilcoot Trail, he built a boat and floated the supplies down the Yukon to Dawson.

Charlie packed supplies into the mountains for the Kern River Company (later the Edison Com-

Left to right, Cecil and Earl Pascoe; *seated,* Clarence Pascoe.

pany) and at one time contracted to furnish meat for the company. On June 7, 1893, Charlie married Emma L. Klosa. Born to Emma and Charlie were Roswell, a daughter, Carla, and Harry, who drowned in the Kern River in 1913. In 1973, the fifth generation of Tibbetts to live in the Valley were the children of Norman, Roswell's son.

PASCOE

Another family who played a big part in the development of the Kern River Valley were the Pascoes'. Jeptha and Henry Pascoe came west with the original Donner Party in 1858. It was only by chance that they happened to be with the group that split off and took another route for the last leg of the journey into California, thereby missing the tragic circumstances that the remainder of their wagon train were exposed to on Donner Pass. Jeptha Pascoe settled in Glenville area in the early 1860s, while it was still part of Tulare County. When the election of 1867 took place after Kern County was formed, he was the first constable elected for District No. 2, the Linns Valley District. Jeptha Pascoe married Allie Whisman, and they raised a family of eight children, most of which were born in the Glen-

ville area. The first of Jeptha and Allie's boys to live and work in the Kern River Valley was Clarence.

In 1902, Clarence moved his wife, the former Ida B. Dooley, and year-old son, Earl, into Old Kernville. When Clarence Pascoe came to the Kern River, his first job was hauling ore with teams from the Big Blue Mine to the mill. He was a first-rate blacksmith, so he soon gave up hauling. With Lee Danner, as his partner, he opened a shop located on the corner of Main and College Streets.

Clarence Pascoe was best remembered as the local constable. He was appointed to fill the unexpired term of Hal Walker, who had died in office. Clarence served a total of twenty-five years in this office and built up an enviable reputation.

In those early days, there were at least five saloons in the old town. When the cowboys and miners converged on Old Kernville every weekend, they would create quite a law enforcement problem. The Kern River Company was still building their canal to the powerhouse, later known as Borel; and many of their men came into town to celebrate as well as quite a number who worked upriver on the Edison K. R. No. 3 power plant between 1914 and 1921.

Clarence made a success of his constable job because he possessed those certain qualities of character and manner which are so necessary to every good lawman. During his entire career, in spite of many tense and delicate situations, he seldom had to use his gun. At an early rodeo at the Wofford Ranch, Lucien Barbeau asked Constable Pascoe if his deputies were there. Clarence allowed as how the deputies were around there somewhere and wondered what the problem was. Well, Barbeau exclaimed that Newt Walker was pretty drunk and was going to end up shooting someone if he was not hauled in. Newt Walker was a gunman of considerable ability, and under certain circumstances, would shoot to kill with only the slightest provocation. He wore two guns and had killed two men in prior years. Pascoe walked over to where Newt was stirring up all the commotion and said, "Hello, Newt, how are you?" After visiting a few minutes, he said, "Newt, you're pretty drunk—you'd better give me your guns. When you get ready to go back to Keysville, get somebody to drive you home and you can look me up and I'll give your guns back." Newt handed the guns over just as meekly as could be. Newt later said that Pascoe was the only man to whom he would ever give his guns. On many other occasions a near tragedy was averted simply because Clarence Pascoe was the arresting officer, instead of some more excitable person or one not so wise to the ways of mountain people.

It was no easy road for the pioneer wife of the town constable of Kernville in the early 1900s, but Ida B. Pascoe was more than equal to the task. Ida was born ten miles below Glenville in the little town of Woody. Here she grew up, went to school, and married Clarence, her childhood sweetheart. She was no stranger to the Kern River, for as early as 1880 she had ridden over Green-horn Mountain with her father, Parson Dooley, to hold camp meetings in Kernville, Havilah, and along the South Fork. She also visited back and forth with the Tilly girls, spending a week or so with Carrie and Cassie Tilly on the old Tilly Ranch. May Booth, one of the Tilly stepdaughters, had married her brother, Tom. As a young woman, Ida always rode sidesaddle and could ride some highly spirited horses.

Kernville was still pretty wild around 1900. Many a night a shot rang out and someone would say, "There's another man for breakfast"—meaning that if you walked downtown the next morning before breakfast you could see another corpse or two. Bertha Converse had succeeded her mother, Mrs. Baker, as undertaker, and many times she called on Ida B. to help her wash and dress the bodies and lay them out.

In 1904, a second son, Cecil, was born into the Pascoe family. Ida worried about her two young sons when they were out of sight due to the close proximity of the Kern River. Also, too many people had the habit of shooting first and talking later. So when five-year-old Cecil could not be found one afternoon, she became quite concerned. After an hour or more of frantic searching up and down the river bank and in all the alleys, she found him curled up and fast asleep behind the big cottonwood tree in front of the Reception Saloon. When Cecil came of age, he was deputized and served under his father a number of years. Later he became constable in Old Kernville, a job which he held for twenty years. Equal to the reputation that he built up as a peace officer was the one he gained over the years for his ability to handle stock. Cecil leaned toward rodeo competition and breaking colts. The latter art became a specialty which he developed to a high degree of perfection.

Nugget, pictured with his trainer, Cecil Pascoe aboard, was raised on the Joughin Ranch on the South Fork and was truly a horse of distinction. Year is 1935.

Cecil also had great patience, which is a necessity for expert horsemen. At his ranch in Caldwell Canyon, he spent many hours working with his young horses and attributed much of his success to what he called "lots of double S." This meant many hours of saddle and scenery for the colts, or many hours of riding and hard work which could not be done overnight.

Cecil Pascoe married Florence Parr, and they had two sons, Richard and Donald. Dick Pascoe needs no introduction to rodeo fans; for by 1973 he had competed in rodeos for twenty-five years, winning top honors, including fourth place in World Cowboy Championship Ratings in bull riding. He took home about $16,000 a year in prize money, and also took his share of the large purses in team roping in rodeo. In 1972 he was still going strong, for he and his partner finished second in the Team Roping Contest at the Cow Palace Rodeo in San Francisco. With sixty-three of the best teams in the nation entered, they were beat out of first place by only one-tenth of a second on the total accumulated time for the roping of three steers.

Don Pascoe, although a top hand with horses, became a jet pilot in the United States Air Force and was flight commander while stationed in Japan. Don remained in the Air Force until 1971, although he still kept his hand in working with stock by returning to the Kern River Valley as often as his schedule as flight instructor would allow.

Mountain Inn in Old Kernville where Earl Pascoe met and courted Lucille Calkins, whose folks ran the Inn.

Earl Pascoe also grew up with stock and, at the age of fourteen, had his own packing business. The pack animals for his first pack string were burros, many of which roamed the Valley in herds in those days. When he finished school, Earl went into packing full-time, adding mules and horses to his pack string. At that time, he was packing out of Old Kernville into the high mountains by way of Cannell Meadow Trail.

In 1921, Earl married Lucille Calkins. Lucille's father, Bill Calkins, was originally from Minne-

Aubrey Pascoe when he was working for the U. S. Forest Service out of Old Isabella in the early 1900s.

Carolyn Pascoe—a top hand with livestock.

sota. When first on the Kern River in the 1890s, Bill worked on Judge Sumner's Ranch across the river from Old Kernville. The Judge had a large herd of dairy cattle, and being from a dairy state, Bill understood the dairy business — especially cheese making. He was instrumental in setting up the cheese making process that was to furnish the area for many years. He also helped develop the water wheel that powered the cream separator in the dairy. He left the Valley and went back east to work as a refrigeration engineer, and married the former Louisa Haycock. However, California was in his blood, and in 1909 he brought his family west and settled in the Los Angeles area. In 1915 he moved his wife and daughter, Lucille, to the town of Old Kernville. At that time, the newly built Mountain Inn Hotel was up for lease, so Bill went into the hotel business.

In those early days of Old Kernville, for entertainment the young people rode horseback, had picnics, or gathered at the Mountain Inn for dancing to the latest tunes on the rolls of the player piano in the lobby. This was where Earl met and courted Lucille in the evenings on the porch of the Mountain Inn, and in 1921 they were married.

The following pack season they went up the river and began building their own pack station, which was later to be known as Road's End.

Two children were born to Earl and Lucille, Carolyn and Raymond. Carolyn could ride and handle a pack outfit with the best. She once appeared on television with two mules from her string to demonstrate how to pack a mule, and to advertise "Whiskey Flat Days." Carolyn married Oscar Greene, a prominent businessman in the Valley, and their two daughters, Kassie and Kriste, also showed the inherent ability to handle livestock.

Raymond left the Valley after he returned from the service and located in the town of Bakersfield, wherh he married Pauline O'Hare, who also loved the out-of-doors. All seven of their children learned to love the mountains and were all well versed in handling stock. For many years this family spent quite a bit of time each summer at the Knapp's cabin in Horse Meadow, which created some memories they would never forget.

Another of Jeptha Pascoe's sons to live and work on the Kern River was Aubrey. He first worked for the U. S. Forest Service in the early days when all the work had to be done on horseback. Aubrey Pascoe worked out of the Valley for a few years, but later moved back with his wife, Esther, and their three children. Aubrey worked for many years for Alexander and Rudnick on the Onyx Ranch, and his youngest son, Dwight, who grew up on a cattle ranch, also became a top cowhand. Possibly the saying that stockmen and stockwomen "are born, not made" is true.

ACROSS THE RIVER

Thomas Jack Gilbert, one of the best remembered of the pioneers to settle Kern River, came to the Valley in 1872. He and his father had been working the Sierra Gordo Mine in Owens Valley that year when the earthquake struck and virtually leveled the town of Lone Pine. Thomas Jack, as he was known to the Valley residents, was born in Cornwall, England in 1853 and came to California in the late 1860s.

Gilbert learned the blacksmith trade, a vocation he followed until the early 1900s. Among the mines he smithed were the Harley Mine, Big Blue, the Bahten Mine at Havilah, and the Bright Star. At one time he had his own blacksmith shop on the main street of Kernville, just north of the Reception Saloon.

Frank Knapp cabin at Horse Meadow, taken in 1930.

On December 11, 1880, in a ceremony performed at Havilah, the Justice of the Peace F. W. Goodall married Marie A. Rene and Thomas Jack Gilbert. The new Mrs. Gilbert was born in 1860 in Germany. In 1906, Thomas Jack leased a ranch across the river and just north of Old Kernville that had been homesteaded in 1886 by Frank Thurston. In 1910 he bought the place adjoining it on the north that became known as the Gilbert Ranch, and was later named the Dalley Ranch.

Marie Gilbert went into the honey business on this old ranch and became known as the Bee Queen of the Kern River Valley. The highest point in her career as beekeeper came in 1916 when she brought in a crop of twenty-one *tons* of honey. Marie had to buy a Moreland truck to transport her sweet cargo to the railhead at Caliente. Marie and Thomas Jack Gilbert had two daughters, Stella and Irene. Stella became the wife of Lucien Barbeau, a Valley pioneer, and they had two boys, Roland and Clyde. Irene married Art Dalley, and both were still living on the old ranch in 1973.

As you travel south along Sierra Way, the old Dalley ranch house sat back from the highway and was almost hidden by trees and shrubs. Some of the outbuildings date back to the turn of the century, as did the ditch that brought water from the river to irrigate the meadows on the ranch for over 80 years. This ditch started just below what was later Camp Owen, and, until 1970, ran through a tunnel in the steep river bank just below Ewings-on-the-Kern.

Irene's daughter, Carol Luthey, and her husband, Bob, made their home across Sierra Way from the old ranch while a son, Robert, chose to make his home out of the Valley.

39

Art and Marie Malone and their family, *left to right*, Clare, Bud, Joyce, Willard, Patsy, Stanley, Dorothy, Lornie, Edith, and Harvey.

Closer to the highway are the buildings left over when the ranch was the headquarters for the Rivernook Dairy. The name of the dairy was later changed to the Mountain Meadow Dairy, and during that time it was operated by John and Billie Gobler. Next to the old dairy was a log cabin the Goblers had moved down from the Piute Mountains in 1968, rebuilding it and making it a charming home.

In 1973 the remains of the Art Malone place lay south of all the ranch buildings, marked only by a tiny weathered shed and a grove of trees. Art and his wife, the former Marie Apalatea, lived here for over 25 years. Most of these years Art worked on the ranch. It was here that they raised a family of five boys and five girls that were a definite credit to the Kern River Valley. Four of the sons and one of the daughters, Edith, served in the Armed Forces. One son, Lornie, was one of the Kern River's most decorated war heroes.

Among the honors he received while serving in the Army were the Purple Heart, the Bronze Star with three Oak Leaf Clusters for meritorious achievements, the Air Medal, and the Army Commendation Medal. After serving two years in Korea, Lornie also served as part of the renowned Swamp Rat platoon. At the end of his four-year tour of duty in Vietnam, he was presented with an engraved sword by the people of Vietnam. In 1973, after serving for 21 years, he extended his enlistment for another three years.

AL COE

Remembered as one of the Kern River's most colorful characters was Alvin Bryan Coe. Al was born in Bakersfield, California, in 1897, but by 1903 had moved with his parents to Los Angeles where he started his schooling. That year his father took up a homestead in the Imperial Valley, starved out there, then went to Lancaster, which is on the Mojave Desert. He borrowed money, but went broke in farming ventures. Having had his fill of California opportunities in 1904, Mr. Coe took his family to Cuba and Al, as a lad of seven, remembered the trip vividly. He recalled sailing around the sunken battleship, *Maine,* in the Cuban harbor, and seeing Morro Castle and the Pine Island Penal Colony.

The Coes bought 500 acres of land in Cuba and went into the honey business. Mr. Coe bought bees in hives made of hollow palm stumps and, as the bees were of the fierce little black Cuban variety, he killed the queens and replaced them with the gentler Italian queen bees purchased from the States. Before long he was shipping honey by the barrel and beeswax by the hundred pounds. As a sideline, the Coes trapped giant turtles for their shells—the shells being in great demand for ladies' combs, buttons, and various other decorative uses.

Al went to the second grade in Cuba, and received foreign language training as the teacher could speak no English. Al taught the teacher English and he, in turn, was taught Spanish, a tongue he remembered the rest of his life. Al's mother did not care for the rugged Cuban life, and his parents separated after they had lived there a year. She left, bringing Al back to the States.

They arrived in Oakland in time to see the burning of San Francisco following the aftermath of the 1906 earthquake. Al's uncle drove them through San Francisco while it was still smoldering.

In 1915, Al's mother remarried, this time to a miner. He influenced Al to take up mining, a hobby—if not an occupation—that Al kept the rest of his life. From that day forward he was never far from a mining operation and could discuss any phase of mining, milling, or geology with the competence of a mining engineer.

After finishing school he worked at a variety of jobs, including working on a grain harvester in the Imperial Valley and being a trusted employee of the Wells Fargo Company in San Francisco. Al tells of the tricks used by Wells Fargo to safely ship valuable cargo through what was then very wild country. They sometimes sent the company strong boxes full of pennies, while the real payload of gold was shipped in coffins. He also handled 70-lb. bars of silver from the Nevada mines. But this was inside work and too confining for a person of Al Coe's energies. So, in 1919, he

returned to his birthplace of Bakersfield. Here again he worked at different jobs, including that of oil field driller where he picked up his useful mechanical knowledge.

In 1920, Al Coe made his first visit to the Kern River Valley. This was a deer hunting trip with two friends, Tom Marsh and Ray Walters. He was a frequent visitor to the Valley from that time on, including trips to the Woman's Club hall on the South Fork to play the accordion for dances.

Then in 1933 he was offered a job setting up the mining equipment at the Sunrise Mine in Keysville, where he worked with such pioneer miners as George Copeland, Clyde Zook, and Roswell Tibbetts. After a year in Keysville he moved into Kernville, where he lived and worked for many years. One of his first jobs there was as a blacksmith for Johnny Potter who, with his wife, Ruth, was living and working at the Mountain Inn.

He next went to work at the Kernville Garage, which then belonged to the A. Brown Company. He was to receive 50 percent of that charged for labor and storage, and the profit off the sale of parts would be his alone. The first month he made $40.00, which was sufficient for his needs at the time.

When Ed Pettypool quit the A. Brown Company as maintenance man, Al took on that job also, getting his meals at the Mountain Inn. Mr. and Mrs. Hawkins were the cooks there, and Al remembers the pleasure they received from watching him put away great volumes of food. On Monday and Tuesday they would set out the food left over from the large week-end crowds, and Al would proceed to finish it off.

Al next went back to Keysville to work at the Keys Mine. Roswell Tibbetts was foreman, and Al Martinez and Barney Gordon were working there too. He acquired five mining claims in Keysville, registering five of twenty acres each on his claims, and bought the quitclaim deeds to two five-acre mill sites. He began prospecting in Keysville between his jobs in the mines.

A miner by choice and a mechanic by instinct, he was hired by the Mammoth Mines to repair machinery. But his natural mining instinct, together with what he had learned about hard rock mining from his stepfather, made him a valuable man underground. He could timber a shaft and read earth signs that directed the miners' picks along a vein, as well as run all the machinery used in the operation. When the Mammoth closed

Al Coe loved children and here he talks to Kevin Dowd as Kevin checks out his unusual beard. 1970.

down in 1942 by government order at the start of World War II, Al stayed on as caretaker. He walked the shaft regularly, knowing that when the mine resumed operation they would need pipe and timbers for the shafts, and shovels, and fillings for the trams and hoists—so all these things were kept.

While in Kernville, he met Hazel Edwards and they were married. They moved into a two-bedroom house on the Billy Goat claim and together they started collecting household goods. Hazel learned to paint, and an old cast-off house trailer became her studio. In the 1950s when Old Kernville had to be moved to make way for Lake Isabella, Al Coe waited sadly in the background as the old buildings were torn down or moved away. He loaded in his pick-up truck the discarded remnants of the old life and took them to his home in Keysville. Nobody else wanted such things as the sign that had swung in front of the picturesque Mountain Inn, but to Al they brought back memories, and so he kept them.

Many people have passed through Al Coe's country without being aware that he existed. A sign on Highway 155, just before the Main Dam Bridge, reads "Keysville—3 miles—a historical landmark." The road to Keysville winds along the Kern River to the southwest through blue oaks, buck brush and digger pine. As it dips down into Hog Eye Creek, you are entering what was once "Al's Kingdom," carefully mounded rock formations marking the sites of early Chinese placer mining claims. There are new additions, too, in the form of nearly 400 young blue spruce trees, which Al has planted along the creek bed. Further

on, beside the creek, is a fireplace built by the Chinese miners between 1863 and 1865. At the top of a rise was a faded, red arrow set in a mound of rocks. Nailed to a tree was a weathered, hand-lettered sign reading "A.B. Coe—Rock Haven."

Many who keep their home and belongings spotless and always in order were appalled at the sight of Al's kingdom, and would describe it as a junk yard. The place was a maze of mining equipment, giant piles of pipe and steel, stacks of lumber, a full set of blacksmith forges, bellows, electric hot water heaters, mattresses, refrigerators, chassies for more than 100 old cars, 17 rusted antique cars, tangles of wire, mountains of bolts and nuts, generators, hydraulic lifts, and on and on. He had pets such as four white ring-necked doves, a collection of dogs of all colors and ages, and maybe a hog or two and some chickens. As far as the eye could see were the results of nearly forty years of collecting things. There was a 1906 movie projector which Al used to run every Friday night at the Oddfellows' Hall in old Kernville. There were original pictures and glass negatives of the Saline Valley Tramway, which Al has since placed in a museum in Independence, a stamp mill and a gold scale that were used in local mines, a set of woodworking tools used to build the Batz house on the South Fork, vintage ore cars, and miles of track. Yes, there were old tires, rain soaked paper boxes, and ancient clothing, but "junk?" Al would snap, "There's no such thing; there's wood, scrap metal and debris—but everything has a use."

Al never made it big in business and he never hit a glory hole, but he was important in another way—he always seemed to have what his friends needed. When they could not find it anywhere else, they came to Al and his collection. In 1969 realty specialists of the Bureau of Land Management labeled Al's collection "junk" and, armed with that judgment, they set out to make him clean it up. In the summer of that year, as part of the statewide beautification campaign, Al was ordered to get rid of his collection and clear the land. They stated that he had originally registered the land for the purpose of mining—and collecting junk had nothing to do with mining. The B.L.M. later issued a second order giving Al 90 days to move his belongings. Al stood there with the paper in his hand and looked around. He jerked his red cap down over his eyes and snapped, "Hell, it took forty years to put it here; how can I move it in 90 days?" Then softly and to no one in particular, he added, "Anyway, even if I could, where would I take it?"

The third order came on January 13. The B.L.M. lodged a judgment and order signed by Judge M. D. Crocker of the U. S. District Court in Fresno. It stated, in part, "The plaintiff, United States of America, its employees, agents and contractors, are entitled to enter that 'Public Domain' hereinafter described, and remove all that personal property, hereinafter defined as 'junk', and to remove and dispose of same in such manner as plaintiff deems proper." With this order, Al was not permitted to sell anything nor to move anything out. Everything was "frozen" and technically owned by the government.

Al made several attempts to secure legal help, but the lawyers he contacted claimed full schedules and hesitated to belabor the federal government. In recounting his brief contacts with lawyers, he grumbled, "I don't see why I have to get a law man to use a lot of fancy words to protect the rights already guaranteed to me by the Constitution." On March 13, the B.L.M. conducted a tour of Coe's place for eighteen contractors' representatives. Five of these entered a bid, the highest being $29,538.00 and the lowest $500.00. The $500.00 bid came from Bud Mallory of Onyx. He and Al were friends, and he had found things he needed many times at Al's. He confirmed that there was plenty of salvage material in the four or five hundred tons of scrap metal in Keysville. The Mallorys, being antique collectors, also helped influence Bud's low bid.

The people of the community were brought face to face with the fact that the B.L.M. meant business and that Al's world, as well as part of their world, was in real danger. They all agreed that Al's collection had gotten out of hand, but to remove everything would mean to endanger the relics, the landmarks, and the antiques.

On March 30 the people contacted John Ortega, crusading lawyer with California Rural Legal Assistance, in McFarland, nearly 100 miles from the Valley. The day before the clean-up was to begin, Al met John Ortega for the first time. And, at 5:30 p.m., Ortega decided to take the case. However, he needed time—even 12 hours would help—with which Bud Mallory agreed. The attorney obtained a temporary restraining order but was not able to get proof of this order into the hands of the B.L.M. until Monday morning. This was Friday, and Mallory had been ordered to haul on Saturday and Sunday. The big trucks moved in Saturday morning, and Al stood by armed with a Revere movie camera, methodically recording every item that went into the trucks. Sunday was even worse because the looters came in the guise of tourists, all people from out of the Valley. They rummaged through boxes, poked into barrels, and took whatever struck their fancy. Al watched for a while. "Vultures," he growled, then he went into the house and closed the door. At dusk, the last of ten truckloads rumbled down the Keysville Road.

The temporary restraining order was issued for fourteen days and stayed any further removal of Coe's "unique personal chattel." It allowed Coe to remove mining equipment and restrained the government authorities from coming onto the land. The victory was short lived, as two days later, on April 8, Al was served with an order to appear before Judge M. D. Crocker. At that time, the B.L.M. would seek to dissolve the restraining order, naming fire hazard and failure to post a supercedeas bond for the protection of the government as reasons for dissolution. In addition, the California Rural Legal Assistance had requested that John Ortega withdraw from the case prior to court appearance on the 13th. They felt his caseload was too great and the time involved in Coe's defense to be excessive.

Ortega contacted George W. Granger, a private attorney in Delano, California, who agreed to represent Al in court. Judge Crocker granted a 30-day stay of judgment to allow Granger to perfect the appeal, during which time Coe would be free to move anything he wished from his collection. Granger said later that the stay would give Al about six months as it would take the B.L.M. that long to formally respond to the appeal and for a new trial date to be set in higher court.

By mid-May, most of the old car bodies had been hauled away; wreckers from most of the local garages were seen coming from Keysville with many a chassis they had left at Al's. The rest were taken by Leroy Edwards. Al donated some things to the local Ghost Town displays, and they asked him to take over the gold panning exhibition for the tourists. But there was so much to do in six months, and he just could not give away or sell things he might need—some day. "Someone might want a generator repaired, so I can't get rid of these parts . . ." and Al's voice records the items, one by one, trailing off into practical rationaliza-

China Charlie, the last of the Chinamen in Old Kernville.

to wit, and there is about the man an indescribable sense of dignity. Of himself, he says, "I'm a pack rat, a natural born scrounge, a gold rush hipster, but I'm an honorable man. My ways are strange, maybe, but I've never imposed them on anyone else. I know they laugh at me. I know the flatlanders drive in to see me like I was part of the sideshow. Thank God I've got better manners."

For whatever reason they came, he was polite, and once in awhile he would treat them to a show. He conducted a tour of the Mammoth Mine that was an unforgettable geological experience from start to finish. He recreated the grueling days of the miners so colorfully that, when you emerged through the narrow shaft into the first cavernous "glory hole" reaching 250 feet into the top of the mountain, you wanted to laugh and shout.

Al Coe was a proud man. He did not receive Social Security benefits until he was 72. He faithfully paid the possessory interest mining taxes on his claim each year. He hired a neighbor to put a 12-foot firebreak around his property each spring, and he provided what few material things that he and Hazel needed by his own industry and ingenuity. He kept an itemized ledger of each day— what he spent, what he sold, how many hours he put in at the Mammoth Mine or at one of his claims. If he used dynamite or nails, it was written down. He recorded debts, debtors and donations to the church of $100.00 a year. One of the last entries in his correspondence file was a letter from Congressman Bob Mathias, thanking A. B. Coe for a $5.00 donation to assist with Congressional printing and expenses.

The "Kernville Merchants" was one of the best teams to ever play in the Kern River Valley, taken in 1951, *Left to right;* Corky Huston, left field; Harvey Malone, pitcher; Jack Reed, catcher; Woody Wallace, right field; Dave Childes, center field; Willard Malone, second base; Tim Witt, third base; unidentified player; and last, Hy Witt, first base. Also a regular team member but not pictured here was Harold Carol.

tion. He wants to keep it all because it is all he has—his Glory Hole.

Working with Al in his battle to keep the things tied in so closely with his way of life was Joan Dowd. Joan, a local writer and the correspondent for the *Bakersfield Californian*, personally threw everything she had into the ring for Al. She used her car, equipped with bald tires, to take him to Fresno as he had no transportation that would take him so far from home. In the days Joan worked with Al she came to know and admire him as so many had before. She wrote the following about him, which seems to sum up this crusty old miner:

Today, at 73, Al is thin, tough, his beard hangs in matted curls down his chest, and his breathing is labored, but his hands are still deft and his mind is facile. He lost his front teeth to the back feet of a mule some years ago, but when he speaks, you don't look, you listen. What you hear is an intelligent man who quotes Shakespeare and mining laws with knowledgability and insight. The years have added wisdom

He was not an ordinary "junkman." I'm sure it is safe to say that Alvin Bryan Coe contributed no small part to the history and color of Kern River Valley, and will be remembered fondly by many.

There were so many other things that made Old Kernville so unique that they are too numerous to mention. Some stemmed from the fact that there were so many colorful old-timers who called this town their home. One was China Charlie, who worked for the A. Brown Company in Kernville. As was the custom with Orientals in many of the frontier towns, Charlie was the butt of many a joke, but most of the time he took the kidding good naturedly. One time some of the men put his buggy up on the barn; another time they changed the back wheels for the front; but the prank best remembered was the time they talked him into trading his gentle old mule for one who from all appearances was a young, gentle mule, but that insisted on running away every time he was hitched to a vehicle. China Charlie had no more than gotten to his seat and slapped the mule with the reins when off they went! As they charged down Nellie Dent Street in a cloud of dust and started across the bridge, the onlookers could hear Charlie yell, "Run you devil, Charlie ride as fast as you run." As it turned out, the Chinaman let the mule run as far as he wanted to; and it was related that he finally turned into a dependable mule.

There were also those who lived in and around Old Kernville, such as George and Hy James, Jimmie Johnson, William McDonald, and Clarence Allen, as well as a raft of others who were something special. There were the town barbers. Among these were Ellis Byrom, Frank Venable, and Jack Hinkey. A complete book could be written on the exploits of these fabulous characters, and of the tall tales they spun from behind the barber chair.

There was the telephone office that before the dial system was the most complete public information system any town ever had. The telephone operator, as she looked out on the street from her switchboard, could not only see who came and went into Bert James' Store and the post office, but most always would also know who was in town, and if not, where they had gone. It was almost unbelievable. One time that comes to mind that points out how this worked was the occasion when Lynn Felick's mother called from Idaho.

The beach across the river from the town of Old Kernville was always a popular spot in summertime.

Whoever was the operator at this time, I believe Lola Maud Ellis, said, "Lynn has gone to Bakersfield today, but I know where Bob (her husband) is working. Do you want me to call him?" Or another time the operator might volunteer, "She isn't home, I just saw her go into Bert's Store. Do you want me to call her again when she comes out and has had time to get home?" Or it might be, "He just went into the post office. I'll give him a call when he gets back to the Mountain Inn." An old-timer by the name of George Bandy first owned the telephone office. Then for a time it was operated by Orian Campbell, and then Don and Edith Gouldin, who owned the telephone office until the town of Old Kernville was moved to make way for the lake.

Besides the people, there were those ageless cottonwood trees that shaded the town thoroughfares for almost a century, the river so close at hand, and the long stretches of sandy beach that became so much a part of the charm of this old town. There was the championship softball team, the Kernville Merchants, and the dance bands with people such as Olive French, Sally Hooper, Slim Winslow, and many others.

THE LIBRARY

A great part of the intellectual advancement and development of any community can be traced directly to the establishment of a properly operated library, and Old Kernville was no exception to the rule.

The Kernville branch of the Kern County Free Library had been established in 1914, but it was 31 years later that the library began to function properly. This was because the few books that

Erina Hackley, Kernville librarian.

were available were kept in the A. Brown Store, and one of the clerks would have to take time from their other duties to check out books. Charlie Taylor, bookkeeper, postmaster, manager for the A. Brown Company, was the first to take on these duties, and it was handed down to other company employees until the store was sold to the Weldons. The store continued to house the library until 1945, when it was decided that the town needed a full-time librarian as well as a more convenient place in which to operate.

Six or seven people took the county test, and Erina Hackley was chosen for the job. The fact Mrs. Hackley was a wise choice was borne out in the years to come by the big part the library finally came to play in the community.

When Mrs. Hackley first got the job, the room in George Stengardt's hall that was to be used for the library wasn't yet ready. As the books had to be moved from the store, they were all carted up to the Hackley home, and placed on shelves set up in the living room.

As soon as Mrs. Hackley took the job, she did something that was typical of the special interest she took in her job over the years. In the front of each book was a slip of paper which gave the name of each person in the order in which each one had checked out that certain book. She went through each of the 300 books, listing the names of the people who had checked them out so she could get some idea of the kind of books the people of Kernville liked to read, so that she could order accordingly. Then after several months wait, the room in Stengardt's hall received a face lifting, complete with new linoleum, paint, and book shelves in readiness for occupancy. The room was

right next door to Jack Hinkey's barber shop, another cultural center of sorts.

It wasn't long before there were 3,000 books to choose from instead of 300. In the last few months that the library had been kept in the A. Brown Store, only two children had checked out books. But Mrs. Hackley was determined to change this. Not only did she get books that they would enjoy, but Woody Wallace, then principal of the Kernville School, further enhanced the program by bussing alternate grades from the school to the library each Monday morning. The library was given huge stacks of *National Geographics,* which the children devoured, along with books on almost every subject.

About this time an additional 3,000 residents entered the Valley to build the Isabella Dam. Many of these families, known lovingly as the "Dam People," lived in Kernville. A few of the local residents were a little apprehensive about that many construction people being dumped into the area all at once, and it was a pleasant surprise when it was realized that the group as a whole was a real addition to the Valley.

When the library had to be moved to what was then called New Kernville, it was initially set up in part of Kenneth and Vy Blomberg's building that later housed the Sportsman Bar. And again, Jack Hinkey was cutting hair next door. The thing best remembered about the library's stay in this building was how bad the flat roof leaked. More than once Mrs. Hackley used all the pots and pans she could scare up to catch the drips, and one time she startled the town folk by sweeping gallons of water out of the front door into the street.

For some time, Woody continued to bus the children to the library in its new location; and for a while after that, Erina took boxes of books down to the school for the children to check out.

After four years in this location, the owners wanted to remodel, so another move had to be made. The town was scoured, and no suitable location could be found, so the Odd Fellows offered to build a permanent library next to their hall. That kind of dedication to the personal literary needs of the townsfolk inspired other people to also take a special interest in the library. Helen James and Pearl Bechtel were two that faithfully brought flower arrangements to brighten the room. Things like this helped to make a visit to the library even more enjoyable. Erina retired in 1969 after 24 years of service. In 1973, Carol

Old Apalatea house, later owned by Matt Burlando. This historic landmark, known locally as the old Burlando house, was moved by Dave Mills to the Silver City Ghost Town in 1969.

South approach to New Kernville, early 1950s.

Owens was still continuing the traditional type of personalized service that has made the Kernville Library such a vital part of the community.

NEW KERNVILLE

Finally in the early 1950s, the move that had been dreaded for so long had to be made. As the time to evacuate the old town approached, the residents started looking for a spot to relocate. Some chose Mr. Irwin Wofford's town to the south, and still others wanted to move upriver. The spot chosen for the new town was then called the Burlando Ranch. This old ranch was homesteaded in 1896 by Albia Curliss and was later acquired by Andy Brown, who in turn sold it to Francisco Apalatea in 1905. Matt Burlando, son-

The merchants in Old Kernville also went to great lengths to drum up business. Above we see Willy Wirth, owner of the Reception Saloon, serving a customer out on Main Street. The year is 1903.

in-law of Apalatea, bought the ranch in 1916 for the headquarters of his cattle raising operation. Matt had passed away in 1939, and it was his wife, Lupie, that Murray Knight, a resident of Old Kernville, approached about buying her ranch for a townsite. Lupie thought a lot of Murray, and was finally persuaded to sell the property. Included in this sale was the old house that Albia Curliss had built in 1896. Earlier called the Apalatea house and later the Burlando house, it soon became a landmark. It was finally moved to the *Silver City* Ghost Town, located at Bodfish, where it was still on display in 1973.

The Kernville Development Company was formed. Others besides Murray and Zora Knight who owned shares in this company were Pearl Bechtel, Jim Meredith, Roy Orrick, and Harriet Sanders. It was not easy to get permission to build a town in this location because of all the irrigation that had been done on the ranch for years and it appeared that the water table was too high for septic systems. Not easily discouraged, the Kernville Development Company bought the land. Then, after cutting out the ditches, they dug enough holes all over the proposed site to assure the planning commission that it was not a swamp. After the lots had been laid out, the Kernville Development Company gave the land for the Circle Park and the Riverside Park, the County Fire Station, and the Odd Fellows Hall. The site that the Kernville Methodist Church was moved onto was also donated.

The moving of the town brought about several interesting happenings. In many cases, those moving were fighting a time schedule. One instance that took all the ingenuity of those involved was the day they realized the road along the river be-

Part of the first Whiskey Flat Committee, *left to right*, Ardis Walker, Lloree Knowles, Barbara Hed. James Meredith, LaVida Yeargan, and Sim Barnes.

Ardis and Gayle Walker, Whiskey Flat Days.

low the present Riverside Park was not wide enough to accommodate the buildings being moved up river. Compressors and jackhammers were brought in, and, using car lights, the men drilled most of the night. A good friend in one of the county offices happened to know where there was some dynamite that was not being used. It was rushed in so the bank could be blown off to let the houses be moved on into town.

Soon the green meadows were crisscrossed with streets. As lawns and trees were planted, it was not long before this new town had built up a reputation as a mountain resort that was hard to surpass.

WHISKEY FLAT DAYS

The town of Old Kernville, formerly called Whiskey Flat, is not forgotten though. Each year it is relived in the Whiskey Flat Celebration in February. As in most mountain resort towns, there is a time each spring before the start of tourist season when the economy needs a boost. Lloree Knowles, a local real estate broker, was the first to recommend that the community use a frontier-type celebration to try to bring more people into the Valley during this slack period. Use of the name, "Whiskey Flat Days," for the celebration was suggested by Ardis Walker, local author and

historian, in order to tie it with the town's historic past. This pioneer-type celebration was started in 1957 by the Kernville Business Association, which later became the Kernville Chamber of Commerce. Lloree Knowles was chairman of this first Whiskey Flat Days Committee, and those who served with her were Ardis Walker, president of the Kernville Business Association, Murray and Zora Knight, Jack Gray, George Stengardt, Erina Hackley, Carl Weber, James Meredith, George Artman, Sim Barnes, Barbara Hed, and LaVida Yeargan.

The first celebration ran from a Wednesday through Sunday in late March. And with a lot of hard work on the part of many of the local citizens, it was termed a success. Each year brought forth more events to make the annual celebration a little bigger and better.

Murray and Zora Knight.

Fred Kirste, best remembered Whiskey Flat Mayor.

In 1958 the Whiskey Flat Committee decided to hold an election for an Honorary Mayor of Whiskey Flat. The outcome of the election was to depend on how many votes the candidate sold at ten cents per vote. The price per vote was raised in later years to fifty cents per vote. In addition to bringing in many extra dollars to promote the event, it did a great deal to get not only the locals, but visitors also into the mood of the celebration. Murray Knight was the first acting mayor, and he and his wife, Zora, became a very colorful part of the earliest of these celebrations. This was also the year the can-can girls in their authentic costumes became part of the publicity team. In 1959, Barbara Hed became the first and only lady mayor. Campaigning as the "Pink Lady," she had the support of a bevy of can-can girls.

In 1973, after fifteen years of mayor campaigns, there was one who stood out head and shoulders above all those who held the office before or after him. This was Fred Kirste. Known as "Forthright Fred," he served as honorary mayor for the years of 1967, 1968, and again in 1972. Fred tirelessly spent countless hours of his own time, as well as many dollars from his own pocket, promoting Whiskey Flat Days. The mayor campaign added much to the color and excitement of Whiskey Flat Days.

Part of the prospective mayor's campaign included articles that appeared in the local newspapers. The following "Bull-a-Ton" sent in by Bull

Run Bob during his campaign for mayor is typical of the nature of this event:

KERN VALLEY SUN
Thursday, January 30, 1969

'Bull Run' Bob's Platform Assessed — Slightly Windy

"I, 'Bull Run Bob' Powers, after lengthy deliberation have bowed to the will of the people to debark on a winnin' campaine for mayore of Whiskey Flat. It is

Photo that appeared in the *Kern Valley Sun* during Bull Run Bob's successful campaign for Mayor shows Bull Run on his mule Sadie surveying Harley Mountain in preparation for reopening the Harley Mine and Tramway.

Sponsored by the South Fork Fish and Game Association in 1969 and backed to the hilt by his Forest Service co-workers, the boys all whoop it up when it was announced that Bull Run had won the contest with a record amount of $1,485 in ticket sales. *Left to right*, Bull Run's campaign manager, Asbury Sharpinton (Bob Ettner); John Wells; Larry Benik; Fred Kirste (Incumbent Mayor); Bill Sanborg; Ed Masonheimer; Noel Mancbach; and Dennis Murphy. Above pictured are all employed by the U. S. Forest Service with exception of Mayor Kirste.

"Cold Cash Clint" James, Whiskey Flat Mayor 1970.

my feelen that this society, or any grate society can long indure without drastic changes. But, indeed, we are in a period of unrest that cries for solutions.

"As your next Mayore, I promise to provide these simpel, yet unquestionably good ansers to problems that have plaged us.

"Be it known that my platform will be one of simplicity, good horsesence, and fare play. Not only will teritorial problems be solved, but I will bring to Whiskey Flat a new aira of properity.

"To provide these betterments, the following will be inacted:

"1. After the county seat was swiped by the flatlanders of Bakersfield in 1874 from one of hour most outstanding mountain communities, it is only fitten and proper to return it again to the mountain folk. Unbiased surveys have showed the most desirable

The Epitaph Contest has always been an interesting part of Whiskey Flat Days.

location, consideren its growth to be the beatiful and prosperious town of Bull Run.

"2. Revise the gold standard upward to $95 per ounce, so the most famous and marginal mines of Bull Run, Harley, and Big Blue may reopen. This would take the local miners off the welfare rolls and gettum eaten regular.

"3. Rebuild the tramway to the top of Harley Mountain in an atempt to spur mountain fun in the sun. This would not only provide a georgeous view of Whiskey Flat below but give the visitor a chance to see Bull Run and walk on the head of the Sleeping Giant.

"And that ain't no bull!!"

The annual Whiskey Flat Days Parade with Johnnie McNally as Master of Ceremonies was added in 1961. Lloree Knowles, who organized the first parade, was chairman for the majority of the twelve parades held up through 1973. Many outstanding entries were brought to these parades.

The Epitaph Contest began in 1959, with entries arriving from as far away as Pennsylvania that year. Other events added included the Whiskerino Contest, Authentic Costumes, Anglers Casting Contest, Horseshoe Pitchers, Trap Shoot Contest, Greased Pig Contest, Children's Animal Parade and Pet Contest, and Oldtime Fiddlers Contest. Trophies were given for the winning entries.

There were always plenty of activities planned to keep things interesting. Of note were conducted

"Dog Eared Dave" Rossback, Whiskey Flat Mayor 1971.

Harvey Malone, third generation native, was a popular mayor who held the office two successive years. He had the support of "The Pink Lady" (Barbara Hed) *at left* and her bevy of can-can girls. Barbara was the first and only lady mayor of Whiskey Flat.

tours to points of historical interest including the mining sites of Keysville and Havilah. There were barbecued beef dinners served at the Odd Fellows Hall by the Kern Valley Future Farmers of America, as well as a Flap-Jack Breakfast served Sunday morning, and the Artists' Breakfast served at Ewings-on-the-Kern. Down through the years, other things included at various times were Old Fashioned Box Socials, Old Timers Picnics and Reunions, a Candidates' Ball for those running for the office of mayor, and Talent Shows.

All of the various civic groups in Kernville did their part to add excitement and flavor of the rough and tumble life style that typified Kernville's pioneer past. The Vigilantes manned by the Kernville Lions Club staged mock holdups and shooting scrapes, and the Kernville Kapers were put on by the Kernville Business and Professional Womens Club.

While there is not space to list all those who contributed a lot of time and effort to the Whiskey Flat Celebration, some of those best remembered for doing more than their share were Leland Scott,

Lloyd Spradlin, and Jerry Friedman. They and others make up the group of citizens who work year after year at whatever job they are given, and their cooperation is the main reason Whiskey Flat Days has been such a success.

Not only were Whiskey Flat Days set up to bring extra business into the Valley during a slow period, but since the first year the Kernville Chamber of Commerce has endeavored annually to set aside money to be used for the building of a community center. All the organizations and individuals who worked with the Chamber to achieve this goal are too numerous to list here, but two groups that contributed significantly were the Kern River Valley Historical Society and the newly formed Kernville Colonels. Finally, in 1973 the dreams of fifteen years were taking shape and an impressive looking plant was being raised on the corner of Kernville Road and Sierra Way. This building when completed and landscaped would be valued in excess of $75,000.

It has taken a lot of people pulling together to finally achieve this goal. So, even though Old Kernville is covered by Lake Isabella, the same friendly spirit of cooperation still prevails in the town upriver that took its place. It can truly be said that it is the people, not the location, that makes a town.

Tilly Creek

IT WAS on the north bank of where Tilly Creek emptied into the Kern River that one of the greatest atrocities the West has ever known—the Indian massacre of 1863—took place.

Not much has been written by the Indians as to how the settlement of the whites on their hunting grounds affected their lives. Basically a gentle and peace-loving people, they were gradually pushed back from the area they once called home to a land that would not support them and that no one else wanted.

Many of their thoughts and opinions expressed in speeches made at Indian treaties were either lost in the English interpretation or were completely ignored in the white man's blindness by his greed for gold and land. Much of what happened during these bloody years is related in the book, *Bury My Heart At Wounded Knee*, by Dee Brown. It gives the reader some idea of how the tide of civilization gradually smothered the Indian as it spread westward.

Closer to home, the same circumstances surrounded the settlement of the Kern River Valley. Prior to the 1850s, this mountain rimmed valley was home to about two to three hundred of these brown skinned Mongoloids who spoke a Shoshonean language exclusively. They knew nothing of agriculture, stock raising, or metal products. This tribe was known as the Tubatulabal (pronounced Ta-bot-a-lot-al, with a subgroup called the Palagewan. They occupied about 1300 square miles, but much of the area to the north was only visited during a few brief months in the summer. This was the high country of the Kern Plateau and Upper Kern River. The southern third of their territory was the actual center of their activities.

These family groups were generally found in a number of hamlets averaging about 40 to 50 people and consisting of two to six households. While at these hamlets, they lived in thatch or tule mat covered dwelling houses. These were circular, dome-shaped, one-family houses, approximately eight to ten feet high at the top of the dome and 20 feet in diameter. A fire was built in a shallow pit in the center of the house and immediately below a smoke hole.

The Tubatulabals shifted from one locality to another in order to take advantage of the natural resources which the area offered. During the winter and spring they lived in the camps or hamlets on the valley floor, dwelling in the tule houses. In summer and early fall, family groups moved higher into the mountains to fish, hunt small game, and gather piñons. In late fall, groups journeyed westward to harvest their yearly supply of acorns. They then returned to their more or less permanent winter camps. Each season had its food gathering and other economic activities, but winter was the period of greatest leisure time. Stored acorns, piñons and dried meat gathered in other seasons

José Chico, chief of the Kern River Indians, and his wife and child taken on Bull Run Creek. Chico had been a scout for John C. Fremont when he explored the West, and later a scout for the U. S. Army.

allowed for shorter work days. The long winter nights could be whiled away by telling tribal stories or making ingenious string figures representing such well known mythological characters as "hawk flying" or "bat in a house."

In the 1850s the Indians were living basically as they had for centuries, although at this time their lives were becoming increasingly affected by the influx and settlement of the whites.

Nanna Rankin, who was brought to Keysville by her family in 1857, tells of her first contact with the Indians in that year in a writing entitled "Impressions of the Early Days":

José Chico, the chief of the Kern River Indians, was a very fine man and a staunch friend to the whites. His family soon found out our house was a good place to come. They were always satisfied by food and other gifts. They often visited us and named two young daughters after my sister and me.

Then she wrote of the Indians near her home in Walker's Basin:

Our Indians were generally friendly and peaceable. When they came to see us they always expected something to eat and other gifts—clothing, shoes, etc. The soles of their feet, by nature and usage, would outwear any leather but they liked to look dressed up. They had a high standard of integrity and honesty and were honorable men and women. There were men who worked for my father on the farm who were so faithful and efficient that he missed them when they were gone.

In 1863 the Owens River Indians were growing restless. Droves of cattle had come into the country, overrunning their small farming activities, and some of them came over to talk it over with the Kern River Indians at their headquarters in the vicinity of a place called Whiskey Flat (later Old Kernville). Then a call was sent out for all tribes throughout the country to meet at an appointed time. Our chieftain was treacherous and had a hatred for the whites, feeling (perhaps truthfully) that the white people had taken their land from them, forcing the Indians back into the hills, away from the productive land. He was never friendly with the white people. He was camped up at Harmon's hay ground. A white miner also was there mining, washing out gold with a rocker. Old Jesus (our chieftain's name) gathered his trbe together, killed the miner, left him in the ditch by his rocker, and went with his tribe to the council of war.

The Owens River Indians, who had been on the warpath off and on for the past eight years, had just lost their leader, Joaquin Jim, in April of 1863. Joaquin Jim was said to be as brave as a lion. Soldiers ambushed the leader as he was washing his shirt in a creek. Although he ran like a deer, he was soon shot down. It was stated that on his body were found two recent wounds; one in an "advanced state of mortification" in the back, and another across the scalp. Besides these, there were numerous old wounds received in some of his many battles.

Although the war council was held in their territory, the Kern River Indians wanted nothing to do with an uprising. When they became concerned about becoming involved, they went to Joseph Sumner who was living above the Sumner Mill and with whom they had become acquainted when he lived in Keysville. The story of what took place was told by Sumner to his daughter, the late Mrs. Alice Brown, and in 1910 she wrote the following:

In '63 there was trouble with the Owens River Indians. The government had sent a company of soldiers to quell the uprising. Some of our Indians had been out there and come back. Our Indians were peaceful and had no wish to harm the whites but the Captain of the company stationed here was quite a young man and wanted to show his authority. He threatened the Indians. They came to Father and Mr. Caldwell, who was then the Justice of the Peace. Father told the Indians there would be no trouble for them; to bring their guns to him and he would look after them. They brought 18 guns to Mr. Caldwell's house and went back to where the Runyon Ranch is now (the old Tilly Ranch). Captain McLaughlin heard what Father had done and was very angry that he should interfere. He sent some men to get the guns, but Father refused to give them up. Then he came with his company and seized the guns and told Father if he interfered in any way that he would be reported as aiding the Indians in their uprising and would be taken prisoner. Father did all he could but it was no use. One Sunday morning Captain McLaughlin took his company, lined up the Indians, and shot 30 of them, then rode away. He left the squaws to bury the dead, which they did as best they could. It was cold blooded butchery. That same man committed suicide not many years ago in San Luis Obispo.

In her writings, Nanna Rankin went on to tell:

After the killing at Whiskey Flat, the remnant of the Walker's Basin tribe came back to their home near the Lightner place and burned their wigwams and all property belonging to the dead warriors. You could hear the screams and yelps across the valley while the fire was burning. After their funeral exercises were over they came down to our home and sat down in a semi-circle on the ground as evenly as if the places were marked for them. There were about 15 women and they were in full mourning with pine gum and dirt daubed all over their faces, groaning and sighing continuously. Mother was grieved for them and brought out everything edible she could find in the house and gave it to them. The Owens

River Indians were all gathered together and under guard of the United States troops (Capt. McLaughlin in charge), started for the Tejon Reservation—about one thousand Indians, twenty government wagons, cavalry and foot soldiers. It was the longest cavalcade ever passing through the mountains. When in Walker's Basin they reached from the foot of the mountains on the north to the Lightner Ranch near the south end. The Indians were greatly distressed and did not know what their fate would be. One woman left her infant tied in its frame in the willows of South Fork. It was found by some soldiers later, who tried to feed and care for it but it died. Two hundred Indians had escaped when they were counted at the Lightner Ranch. An old Indian came, bringing a little girl on his back from camp to our house; she was just a little shadow, so starved and thin. The old man said he did not know what would become of them, he would like to sell her to Mother for a blanket. He was so distressed Mother gave him a blanket and kept the little girl. I wish you could have seen that child eat and grow. In two weeks she was so fat you would never have known what she had been when she came to our house. She was never sick and grew very fast, marrying very young to Francisco Robles.

The following is a report of Captain Moses A. McLaughlin, Second California Cavalry, dated April 12-24, 1863, regarding his expedition from Camp Babbitt to Keysville, California:

Camp Independence
Owens River Valley, April 24, 1863

COLONEL: I have the honor to report that in obedience to instructions dated Camp Babbitt, near Visalia, Cal., April 10, 1863, and signed Lieut. Col. William Jones, Second Cavalry, California Volunteers, I left Camp Babbitt on Sunday, the 12th instant, in command of twenty-four men of Company D and eighteen men of Company E, accompanied by Lieutenants French and Daley, one 12-pounder howitzer, and four six-mule Government teams, used for the transportation of rations, company property, ammunition and forage, all of which arrived in good condition at Camp Independence, Owen's Valley, on the 24th of the same month. Distance traveled I suppose to be 250 or 275 miles. I had been instructed by Colonel Jones to investigate the Indian troubles on Kern River. On arriving at Keysville I was waited upon by several of the residents of the place, who represented that there was a large body of Indians encamped upon the North Fork of Kern River; that many of these Indians had doubtless been engaged in the war and in the depredations committed in Kern River Valley; that one man had been murdered in Kelsey Canyon; that Roberts and Weldon had lost about 150 head of stock; that many other citizens had lost cattle, horses, and other property; that the roads were unsafe, and finally, that the Indians there congregated were for the most part strangers in the valley, and were

Steban Miranda, who lived to be 107, witnessed the massacre at Tilly Creek where his father and 34 other adult Indians were wantonly slaughtered.

thought to be Tehachapie and Owen's River Indians, who after seeing so many troops pass had endeavored to shield themselves from punishment by seeking the more immediate vicinity of the white settlements. After having the above statements, and learning that José Chico was in the neighborhood, I sent for him and two other chiefs who were known to have been friendly. José Chico is an Owen's River Indian, but resides on Kern River, where he cultivates a farm. He speaks but little English. In Spanish he, however, makes himself well understood. From him I learned that the Tehachapies had endeavored to have him go to the war with them; that many of his own Indians had gone; that some had returned and were now in the valley, sleeping in the camps at night and hiding in the daytime; that there were many Indians there whom he did not know, either Owen's or Tehachapies. I told him to remain in camp with me and dismissed the others. I informed Doctor George, Mr. Herman, and others, citizens, that I would visit the camps early in the morning, and that they might accompany me and vouch for such Indians as they might know. Accordingly at 2 a.m. on the 19th, accompanied by a detail of twenty men of my command

Fredrick Butterbredt, *top left*, Kern River miner, found his wife, Betty (to his right), hiding in the willows with a small baby below Whiskey Flat after the Indian massacre of 1863. Her Indian husband and father had just been killed by the soldiers. To their right are Kathy Butterbredt, Virginia Apalatea Butterbredt, holding Ida Butterbredt Izqerdo and John Butterbredt. *Bottom, left to right,* Fred Butterbredt, Emma Rice Liebel, Ella Skinner Bencoma, Louişe Butterbredt Skinner holding Joe Skinner, *and last,* James Skinner.

and Lieutenant Daley, with José Chico as guide, I left camp, and at dawn surrounded the camp of the Indians, which was situated about ten miles from Keysville, upon the right bank of Kern River. I had the bucks collected together, and informed José Chico and the citizens who that arrived that they might choose out those whom they knew to have been friendly. That was soon done. The boys and old men I sent back to their camps, and the others, to the number of thirty-five, for whom no one could vouch, were either shot or sabered. Their only chance for life being their fleetness, but none escaped, though many of them fought well with knives, sticks, stones, and clubs. This extreme punishment, though I regret it, was necessary, and I feel certain that a few such examples will soon crush the Indians and finish the war in this and adjacent valleys. It is now a well-established fact that no treaty can be entered into with these Indians. They care nothing for pledges given, and have imagined that they could live better by war than peace. They will soon learn that they have been mistaken, as with the forces here they will soon either be killed off, or pushed so far in the surrounding deserts that they will perish by famine.

A Tejon prisoner says the Tejon and Tehachapie Indians (those for whom the Government has done so much) have been engaged in both these wars, and as soon as they are tired, return to the reservation. The Indian agents should be notified of this fact. If I have to send down there I will leave them very little to do, and save the Government some treasure. The route from Visalia by way of Walker's Pass is far preferable to the Los Angeles route, as upon the former there is wood, water, and grass at easy marches. Forage can be purchased in Tulare Valley and forwarded to Keysville, from which point the Government teams can bring it to Camp Independence, having water and grass at intervals upon the road, of not more than fifteen or twenty miles, while upon the Los Angeles road from Tehachapie Cañon by Walker's Pass, a distance of over fifty miles, there is not a blade of grass and the water is unfit to be used.

I have the honor to be, very respectfully, your obedient servant,

M. A. McLAUGHLIN,
Capt., Second Cav. California Vols.,
Comdg. Camp Independence.

COL. R. C. DRUM,
Assistant Adjutant-General, San Francisco, Cal.

* * * * * *

Taken from: *The War of the Rebellion*,
Series I, Vol. 50,
part I, p. 208-210.

All accounts from whites and Indians alike agreed as to the slaughter. José Chico, then chief of the Kern River Indians, was ordered to take all the women and children of all the tribes out of the group that had been corraled. He was also told to take out the men of his tribe. Most of the Owens River warriors were too cautious to be caught in the open and had escaped into the rocks, where they watched the following events. Chico had picked only about four men when Captain Mc-Laughlin told him, "Wait a minute, you have enough Indians in this country." One of those taken out before this occurred was his brother, Old Bill Chico—also called Bill Veijo—who for years had been a scout and interpreter for the Army. The names of the other three have been lost down through the years.

The remaining 35 men were killed, which comprised about all the men in the tribe. Here again, names were not recorded but a few of those butchered were the father of Stephen Miranda the grandfather of Tony Pablo, and the husband of an Indian woman on the South Fork named White Blanket.

An Indian named Quigam, who lived near Cane-brake, was able to escape on the morning of the massacre. Quigam later told Andrew Chico, a grandson of Old Bill Chico, that he and two old squaws had watched the slaughter from across the valley. They were hidden on a rocky point by what was later known as Camp Nine. Quigam told Andrew that he had a blanket draped over his head and every time he would try to ease his head up to take a look, one of the squaws would pull him back down, telling him, "Those soldiers gonna see you." Quigam explained that they could not see him at that distance, to which the squaws answered, "Yes they can; those soldiers got spy glass." They could

The site of the Indian Massacre of 1863 is now used for Easter Sunday services. The worshipers stand on the bedrock mortars, the large rocks in the foreground, that were part of a peaceful Indian camp.

hear the shooting and screams as the soldiers emptied their guns into the helpless natives, then finished them off with their sabers.

Frances Phillips, niece of Quigam, gave the following account in 1933, with her daughter, Legora Tungate, interpreting:

I was born about two years after the soldiers killed all those Indians over at Kernville (1863). My older brother was still being kept in a cradle then and I was born about two years later.

My mother used to tell me about the massacre. José Chico pulled my father out from those men and the soldiers didn't kill him; he ran away. There was one man who was shot in the eye, but he had power and recovered. Lots of men were killed. The fight

Tilly Ranch, later the site of Wofford Heights. Taken in 1900 by Dr. J. H. Johnson. When Lake Isabella became a reality, this old house was moved to the Wofford Ranch north of the airport and became part of the home of John and Gail Wofford.

started over the Indians killing other people's cattle. José Chico interpreted for the white men and the Indians; he was the man who took my father out. There were three men saved when the soldiers shot at the Indians.

One man had an amulet, a bear claw with beads on it. He was running and he got out of breath and dropped the claw; then he was killed. The people found it afterward. If he hadn't lost his power he would have escaped all right. Another man had a rattlesnake for his (supernatural) pet. He was badly hurt; his insides were all cut up. When the people saw him after the massacre there was a rattlesnake lying on top of him and that snake made that man get all right. That man's name was hi-ay-se-l; he was a Monilabal (Yokuts). He got all right again. My father saw him when he was helping bury those dead Indians; he saw the rattlesnake come and help him.

Because of the efforts of Joseph Sumner, the remaining members of the Kern River Tribe were not forced to go to the Tejon Reservation. They were left to pull their shattered lives back together in this country where they were now only tolerated.

In 1893, the Government gave land to the survivors of this tribe in a small attempt to right the injustice. How many acres do you give in reparation for the lives of 35 of their loved ones?

As had been the custom since about 1950, in 1973 the Easter Sunday sunrise services were held south of the town of Old Kernville at the exact location of the 1863 massacre. Among those attending these services could be found descendants of the Indians who died there. They have generally been a race who quickly forgave and forgot, so few people know what took place here better than a century ago.

John Louis Tilly.

TILLY RANCH

The Tilly Ranch, purchased in 1920 by Irven Wofford and used as the Wofford home ranch until 1948, had been the center of social activities on the "North Fork" of the Kern River for 86 years. This site was occupied as a rancheria for one of the local Indian groups until the infamous Indian massacre of 1863.

The first white man to settle on this land was John Louis Tilly. Of Irish and German descent, he was born in Illinois in 1834, and by the time he was 16 he had made his first voyage to California by way of Cape Horn. He was successful in mining but returned to Illinois to be with his widowed mother. In 1853 he again struck out west, this time driving an ox team the entire distance. Arriving in Tuolumne County, he mined and raised cattle there for about nine years, then came to the Kern River Valley.

For the next 28 years he lived in and around the Valley, first settling on land in the South Fork Valley that was flooded in 1862. About that time Indian trouble was developing in the Owens River Valley, so John Tilly joined the Owens River Home Guard, serving as sergeant. His company was

Jane Tilly.

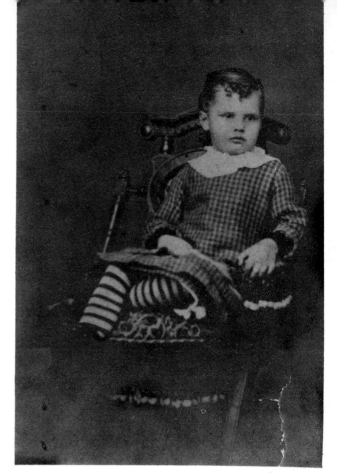

Cleo Tilly Cross—taken in early 1880s.

merged into the Rangers and he remained in this organization until the Indians were subdued. He next settled on land southwest of Old Kernville. The creek that ran through this land was named after him.

His wife, the former Carrie Fisher of Illinois and first schoolteacher in Kernville, died in 1869. In 1876, John Tilly married Jane Prewitt Booth and took her to the Toll House Ranch, located about three miles east of Glennville. Jane's daughter, May, was from a former marriage. In 1877 their first child, Cleo Rebecca, was born. John later sold the Toll House Ranch and returned to his old ranch on Tilly Creek. Here, Carolyn and Cathryn—the first twins delivered in Kernville—were born to the Tillys.

The Tilly Ranch (later called the Beatty Ranch) was the hub of social life around Kernville in the early days. Many times townspeople gathered there for ice cream feeds, and it was a favorite place for sewing circles.

Old-timers told of the Tilly girls running their horses across the suspension bridge to Isabella even though there was a $15.00 fine for being caught at this offense. The girls grew up on the ranch. May Booth married Tom Hooper and, in

1897, Cleo married John Cross, a resident of Kern County since 1866. The five Cross children were Louis, Raymond, Marvin, John J., and Helen, who later became Helen Rankin of Walker's Basin. Cathryn, known as Cassie, first married a pioneer by the name of Dooley and later married Walt Dodenhoff. Carolyn (Carrie) married Newel Beatty in 1894 in a ceremony held at the old Tilly house, with Judge Sumner officiating. When John Tilly died in 1890, his wife, Jane, married John Beatty. This made Jane a double grandmother to Newel and Carrie's children.

The Tilly Ranch was one of a group of ranches the Southern California Edison Company purchased to obtain water rights for the Borel hydroelectric power plant. Water was diverted from the river at Old Kernville and run by flume to the Borel plant 15 miles downstream. The following era of this famous old landmark began when Irven Wofford purchased it along with other ranches.

Irven Wofford, founder of the town of Wofford Heights, was born in July, 1884, in Henderson County, Texas. He came to California in 1909 and was first employed by the U. S. Forest Service at Lone Pine. In 1910 he worked for the Forest Service in Kings County and, in 1911, moved to

59

Early day rodeos were held at the Wofford Ranch on Tilly Creek.

Loraine, a mountain community some 30 miles south of the Kern River Valley.

It was here that he met Naomi Krammes who later became his wife. Naomi, born in Indiana, had moved to San Diego with her family when she was fourteen. There she completed her high school education and attended San Diego State Normal College before coming to Loraine in 1911 to teach school. Irven and Naomi were married on January 31, 1912 and made their home at the Old Indian Creek Ranger Station. While they were living there two children were born to them, John in 1915 and Lucille in 1916. In 1917 Irven was transferred to Old Isabella where he was District Ranger for the U. S. Forest Service.

Irven was a rancher at heart and by 1919 he had left the Forest Service to go into business for himself. He leased from the Edison Company a group of ranches they had acquired to obtain water rights. These ranches included the Beatty (or Tilly), Bennett, Cyrus, Sumner and Page properties. In that same year he applied for a homestead which took up the rest of what was later to be the town of Wofford Heights not covered by the Tilly and Durfuss ranches.

Mr. Wofford had purchased a small herd of cattle from A.D.C. McCay at Loraine and acquired from McCay the O X brand the Wofford family was still using 50 years later. Needing summer range for his stock, he took out his first permit to graze cattle on the Sequoia National Forest in 1921 and was given as his allotment that area known as the "Burnt Country" north of Sherman Peak. For the next four or five years Irvin struggled along with his ranching operations, barely making ends meet.

Then along came Hollywood to his rescue, discovering the Kern River Valley and Irven Wofford at the same time. Movie makers engaged him,

finding not only horses and cattle, but also many needed props such as wagons and stagecoaches. Most of the wagons used in the movies filmed there in the late '20s and '30s came off the ranches in the area. Horse power was being replaced by machine power and he accumulated a vast fleet of horsedrawn vehicles. Some were freight wagons used in freighting tons of equipment in for the Southern California Edison Company power plant at Borel. Others included all types of wagons used on the ranches, from the mammoth freight wagons to the light and fancy buggies used only a few years previously by the ranchers and townspeople. The old Petersen stage, recently retired from its run from Caliente, was also pressed into service by the movie companies.

Nearly every scene made in the Valley included some shots filmed on the Keysville Road. This narrow dirt road was ideal for chase scenes, especially the section of the Keysville Road lying south of the Main Dam Campground after crossing the cattle guard. The rock outcroppings along the river were also used by trick men as they jumped their horses into the Kern River. A swinging bridge for wagons was constructed where there had previously been a foot bridge south of the old Mammoth Mill site on the river. The biggest shot, and the last, was taken of the bridge

Left to right, Cassie and Carrie Tilly—taken 1889.

Irven Wofford not only rented stock and wagons to the movie companies but also played in many of the movies himself. Here he locks actor, Johnny McBrown, behind bars.

when it was blown up with a wagon on it. Some 30 years later the remains of this wagon were visible, and retrieved when the water was down.

In the early days the stock was led from the Wofford Ranch for filming. At first, each man led as many animals as he could handle, up to ten head. After the unions came in, one man could handle only five head of horses. One man was also assigned to each wagon to hook up the team, drive it to location, and then stand on the sidelines in readiness to take over after the cameras stopped grinding. A movie that used a large amount of stock was *Wells Fargo*, starring Joel McCrea. Much of this film was taken at Cap Canyon on the South Fork.

Each company had its head wrangler, and one of the best remembered in later years was Jimmie Phillips. The head wrangler was not only responsible for the stock, but also the wagons, stagecoaches, etc. He had to see that the equipment was rented and on location in time to film. Bert Smith, known to most Valley residents as Red Smith, was blacksmithing for Wofford at that time, and was kept busy keeping the horsedrawn vehicles in shape. John Swett would come down from Kernville to "shrink" wagon wheels—a process when repairing and putting new iron on the outside of the wheels.

Wofford supplied the needed locations as considerable film was shot on his home ranch. He

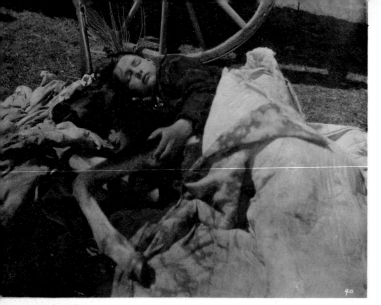

Young Johnny Wofford also took part in the early movies shot in the Valley.

also set up hotel accommodations to become the host and toast of some of the biggest names in movie making. His money worries were over, and as the cameras ground away, Wofford's net worth soared.

The news that "the movies were coming" passed through the town of Old Kernville as if heralded by a town crier. The sleepy little country town was brought to life. This meant extra work, not only for Kernville residents, but for the Valley as a whole. The Mountain Inn, the only hotel in Kernville, was headquarters for the movie companies when in town. The seating capacity in the dining room was stretched to the maximum, and extra people were hired to help the regular cooks and waitresses.

There was always a group of local men, such as Add Cross, Pete Labachote, Charlie Woodard, and Matt Burlando, who were good with stock, and were in demand as cowboys, stand ins, and doubles for western heroes.

Only a few professional actors were brought on location for each picture, as the film companies used local people for extras. One day everyone would be dressed as soldiers and all scenes involving the army would be filmed. The next day the extras would be painted up as Indians and, while using the same stock, the Indian portion of the chase would be shot.

Even the local children were used and, at one time, Margaret Hand, Willard Malone, and Howard Bales went to school on the set for 18 days. A special teacher was brought from Los Angeles, and school was held in a car. Only two scenes were made in the 18 days, but they remembered

that the pay was good. Each received $16.50 per day, and $22.00 for the day they rode in a wagon. Scores of early day stars who visited included Buster Keaton, Ken Maynard, John Boles, and Gloria Swanson.

Movie Street in Old Kernville was a replica of a typical frontier main street. Originally called Granite Street, it was about two blocks long and ran north-south along the hill west of town, which placed it parallel to the main street of Old Kernville. The Methodist Community Church and the grade school were at one end, and a large barn on the A. Brown Company property closed the other end of the street. The first movie set used A. Brown storage sheds and the first school, which was moved back along the hill when the second school was built. Later, as a more complete set was built, the fronts of buildings (the backs of which were only shells) included, on one side, a general store, assay office, jail, and livery stable. On the other side stood a blacksmith shop, saloon, dance hall, hotel, and harness shop. It was hard to realize when walking the street or viewing the set in movies that many of these buildings were only propped up like billboards.

On this street gallons of blood were shed, and from the large old cottonwood trees in the school-yard many a hangman's noose was swung. The heroes hunted down the villains slinking in the shadows, and Indians raided the town and scalped their victims when called for in the movie script. Many happy events were filmed here, which included dances, parades, picnics, fairs and weddings.

East side of Movie Street looking north—note Kernville School in the left background and the Odd Fellows Hall at the far right. Stagecoach is the old Petersen Stage that was used for the run from Caliente to the Kern River.

The west side of Movie Street looking north—note children playing in schoolyard far right. Many times the villains were swung from the cottonwood trees that shaded the schoolyard.

The people who came to town with the movie companies were a friendly lot, and would take part almost as a whole in local community activities. In the summer months, if there were enough men in the visiting company on location who could play ball, they would organize and play the local teams. Roy Rogers could pitch a ball with the same speed and accuracy with which he could fire a six shooter, and Humphrey Bogart did a good job of playing shortstop, while John Huston filled any position. Some of the local boys who played the movie teams were the Witts and the Malones. Other famous movie actors seen in the Valley over the years were Dale Evans, Gabby Hayes, Rita Johnson, Yvonne DeCarlo, Victor Mc-Laglen, Sons of the Pioneers, Audie Murphy, Andy Devine, Rod Cameron, Jack Hoxey, Yakima Canutt, Tom Mix, Hoot Gibson, Bill Fairbanks, Harry Carey, Buck Jones and Gene Autrey.

William Boyd, known to people everywhere as Hopalong Cassidy, was one of the best remembered movie personality. Born in 1895 at Hendryburg, Ohio, the son of a poor farm laborer, he had come to California "to see how things were on the rich side." He recalled, "as a kid, I worked so hard and had so little fun that I couldn't wait to grow up."

Growing up in Hollywood turned out to mean wild spending, gambling, four marriages and divorces. His good looks and brashness made him a romantic star of such films as *The Volga Boatman, King of Kings,* and *Two Arabian Nights."* In the early 1930s, his name became linked with gambling and scandal, and his career seemed

63

South end of Movie Street blocked by A. Brown barn. The Andy Brown home can be seen in the background.

doomed until a Paramount producer offered him a role in what became the Hopalong Cassidy series.

Boyd donned his characteristic black hat, leaped astride his horse, Topper, and rode off on the lucrative and popular "Hopalong" legend. High ethics were part of the Hopalong Cassidy characterization, which ran for 25 years in movies, television, and radio. Hopalong pursued bad guys relentlessly, but he always tried to bring them back alive. If forced into a showdown, he let the villain draw first. Smoking, drinking, swearing or romantic involvement were taboo for Hoppy. His insistence on clean living came rather suddenly for Boyd and, in turn, he credited his fifth wife, Grace, whom he married in 1937, with reforming him.

Boyd became interested in children, preaching the homey virtues to them. "The way I figure it," he said, "if it weren't for the kids, I'd be a bum today—they are the ones who've made my success possible; they're the ones that should benefit from it." Boyd died in 1972, donating part of his fortune from 92 motion pictures and television films to children's hospitals and homes. He also founded a club called "Hoppy's Troopers" which had an idealistic code of conduct.

During World War II, Movie Street was dismantled and moved to the desert, where it was used for Army maneuvers. Motion pictures continued to be made in the Valley, although not as frequently as they had been when Movie Street was still standing.

In 1948, utilizing lands they acquired through the years, the Woffords began developing the Wofford Heights subdivision, which is today the town of Wofford Heights. Many of the first residents of Wofford Heights were a combination of the best from both the town of Old Kernville and Old Isabella.

The first of these old-timers to settle in Wofford Heights was Bertha Converse, a grand old lady who served the town of Kernville as midwife. After her death, her daughter, Doris Moyer, and her husband, Sam, lived there. For Doris it was like moving back home, since her father's ranch, the old Hight place, was located only a mile to the south. Sam also was no stranger to the area. He had worked as an engineer in the Big Blue Mine. Bertha's son, Merle Hight, soon built a home in Wofford Heights for himself and his wife, Helen. Merle met Helen when she was working as a waitress at the Mountain Inn in Old Kernville. After the Hights moved to Wofford Heights, they put up the building that housed the library, post office, and Helen's Gift Shop and Beauty Salon. Helen was the first postmaster in town, a position she still held in 1973.

Clifford and Trudy Cross also bought property in Wofford Heights and built a home. Clifford's father, Ad Cross, came into the Valley in 1879. Clifford chose the cattle business for his vocation, as his father had done before him. Ad Cross married a local girl, Olga Beaty, and together they reared six children. Another of Ad Cross's children to move to Wofford Heights was Nell Graves. Nell's husband, Bill, spent many years as an Edison Company employee. Another retired Edison Company employee who relocated there was Jack Christiansen. Jack and his wife, Zelma, also lived in Old Kernville before he retired.

Jim and Marie Jorgensen continued to live at the Big Blue Mill site for a time until they built a home in Wofford Heights. Marie became the town librarian, a job she held for 15 years. Ole Olsen, a giant of a man, was the Standard Oil representative in Old Kernville. He and his wife, Jesse, also chose Wofford Heights for their home. Joe Hall, who had lived in the Valley since 1918, bought the Wofford Heights Market in 1956. This building, originally Ward's Real Estate Office, was the first building to be put up in Wofford Heights. Joe and Effie Hall operated this until 1973, when they retired and sold to Steve Spradlin.

Eddie and Estella Metz were among the first to build in Wofford's new town. Estella was born in the Valley and spent most of her life there. Eddie came to the Valley in 1947, and his first job was cutting meat in the old A. Brown Store for Charlie Whelden. He next worked for Ken Blomberg after Ken took over the garage at the south end of Old Kernville. When Blomberg went into the gas business with Ole Olsen, Eddie went to work on the dam for Lake Isabella and worked right straight through to its completion. Eddie was very versatile, working on almost every project. He helped rip-rap the Edison Company canals that would be under the lake at times. He ran a motor in the tunnel under the main dam during the construction, and also in the rock plant that crushed rock to use for cementing the completed tunnel. While in the employment of the Willis Company, Eddie helped build the road from Wofford Heights to the Kernville bridge and also to build the Kernville bridge itself. Eddie then spent 22 months as a welder in Morris Knudsen Company's main shop by the dam.

Eddie was a jack-of-all-trades. When he quit construction, he opened a television repair business, which he still operated in 1973. When Eddie and Estella moved their home to Wofford Heights, theirs was the sixth home there. Eddie Metz was one of the unsung heroes of community service in the Kern Valley, seeking only to get every job done that came up and not to gain praise or recognition for himself. Whether it was a project such as getting more doctors into the Valley or only getting a loud speaker system set up for some community function, he worked with the same drive. In the early days of Wofford Heights, some citizens formed a group called the Wofford Heights Improvement Group in order to better solve some of the problems that were coming up as the town grew. Eddie was the first president for this group. When the name was later changed to the Wofford Heights Chamber of Commerce, Eddie was again elected to serve as president. Besides holding many offices in this organization, he served on numerous committees. It was in this capacity that he contributed so much, being a perfect committeeman and always doing more than his share. He also served as president of the chamber in 1973, the year it was disbanded. Under his able direction, the Early California Days Celebration for that year was a huge success as usual.

Left to right, Dick Snyder, assistant to Kent Stacy; Meliss Trumbull; Gus Suhre; Bob Powers, who gave a brief history of the two honorees; and Harry Rogers, at that time President of the Wofford Heights Chamber of Commerce.

Eddie was a Mason for over 30 years, as well as a member of the Odd Fellows for 25 years, in which he held the office of Grand Master. Any community would indeed be fortunate to have more citizens like Eddie Metz.

Wofford Heights had two other residents that were exceptional in their civic contributions; Meliss Trumbull and Gus Suhre. In November of 1969, each was honored by the California Commission on Aging and the California Bicentennial Commission as being the "Oldest Active Member" of the Wofford Heights Chamber of Commerce. They were each awarded an impressive certificate signed by Governor Ronald Reagan of California; Ed Reinecke, Lieutenant Governor; Spencer Williams, Secretary, Human Relations Agency; Mrs. A. M. C. Russell, Chairman for the Commission on Aging; and Chester W. Skoien, Jr., Executive Director for the Commission on Aging.

Meliss Trumbull came to the Valley with her husband, Ross, in 1918, where he worked many years for the Southern California Edison Company. Ross passed away while he and his wife were living in Old Kernville. Meliss's many civic contributions to the Valley are covered in a later chapter so will not be recounted here, but they were many and varied.

When Gus and Gertrude Suhre had to move from the town of Old Isabella, they chose two and one-half acres on the southeast edge of the town of Wofford Heights for their new home. There they built their home nestled in among the oaks overlooking Lake Isabella. Gertrude Suhre was a native from the word go! She was born on the South Fork of the Kern, as was her mother before

Old Odd Fellows Hall is moved to Wofford Heights.
This building later became the Elks Hall.

her. Gus had come from Ohio to visit his sister, Anna Andress, in Old Isabella in 1912. Gus Suhre's life in the Kern River Valley during the 60 years he lived here was chuck full of worthy and dedicated service to his fellow man. He organized the first Boy Scout Troop in the Valley, made a raft of other civic contributions in connection with Veterans' Organizations, historical societies, was an active member of the Odd Fellows Lodge, and worked in the various Chamber of Commerce organizations in the Valley down through the years. Gus would not have been able to perform so efficiently in his many offices if he had not had the help and encouragement of his wife, who attended thousands of meetings with him over the years and also held her share of offices in groups such as the South Fork Womens' Club, Veterans of Foreign Wars Auxiliary, and Rebeccas.

One of the entries for the Epitaph Contest for Whiskey Flat Days read "Gus Suhre, gone to another meeting." That pretty well summed up his life in the Valley. Not just going to meetings, but trying in his small way to make the Valley a better place to live. I would say he had succeeded.

Then, of course, there were Irven and Naomi Wofford. They bought the Dr. Smith home in Old Kernville and had it moved to a spot just north of Wofford Heights Park, overlooking their old ranch which was under the waters of Lake Isabella much of the year. Irven also bought the old Odd Fellows Hall, although at the time he did not know what he would do with it. He finally decided to move it to his new town. It was placed on Wofford Boulevard and became the Wofford Heights Club, later the Elks Hall. In 1961, Irven Wofford died, leaving Naomi to carry on the operation of the club. Through the years Mrs. Wofford was known for her kindness to those around her, and her many civic contributions. In 1965 the Kern River Valley Business and Professional Womens Club, of which she was a charter member, named her "Woman of the Year" in honor of her many activities. Naomi passed away in 1965.

The buildings from the old Tilly Ranch were the last to be moved from the area that would soon be under the waters of Lake Isabella. One of the buildings, a toollhouse, had been on the Tilly Ranch for over 75 years. John Tilly had moved it there from a ranch he owned east of Glennville. This building had been used by the McFarland

Naomi Wofford, Kern River pioneer.

Old Derfus Ranch *looking west*, 1915. This ranch later became the northwest part of Wofford Heights.

brothers to collect tolls on the road they built over Greenhorn Mountain in 1863. The tollhouse was moved less than a mile and located behind Wofford's home, the old Dr. Smith house. The historic Tilly house, as well as implement sheds, barn, granary, bunkhouses, saddle and harness houses, were moved across the Valley to their new location just north of the Kernville Airport on what was formerly the old Sumner ranch. Here John and Gail Wofford were still carrying on their ranching business in 1973.

HIGHT RANCH

On the south side of Tilly Creek was the Hight Ranch. Alfred Davenport Hight and his young wife, Sarah, had started out west from Delaware in 1838. The rugged trip proved too much for the expectant mother, and she died giving birth to a son, Charles Springer Hight. Alfred stopped in St. Louis for several years and, while there, remarried. Continuing on to the Platte River area, he remained until 1850. Then he and his second wife pushed on to California, settling on Greenhorn Mountain at the foot of the Rough and Ready.

Here Alfred Hight cleared land and built a cabin. Besides planting a small crop, he did some placer mining on the side of Greenhorn Mountain that slopes toward Democrat Hot Springs on the Kern River. At the bottom of a 15-foot waterfall he hit a windfall, cleaning up $15,000 in one week. The Hights then moved to San Jose.

However, the call of the mountains was still strong, and when young Charles Hight married

Left to right, **Alice and Nettie Hight dress in clothes that were bought from the gold they found in the old pigeon loft. Photo taken in middle 1870s.**

Sarah Cordelia Cottle in 1863, he headed back for the Greenhorn Mountains. They stopped a few years in Glennville, where their first child, Alice, was born. They lived there until October 1868, when they again set out for the old homestead. They had traveled only a few miles when their second daughter, Nettie, decided to come into the world. Stopping at a small wood-cutter's cabin, Charles rode back to Glennville to get Grandmother Allen, who served as midwife for many of the pioneer women of the Glennville area. They cleaned out the small cabin and lived there for three months. Again loading up for the move back to the home place, they were well on their way when a storm hit with full force. The baby, Nettie, had been placed in with some seed potatoes on the load because the parents thought this spot would be the most protected. The baby was bundled up warmly because when they got to the homestead they took her from her nest, and although the potatoes around her were frozen, the baby was in fine shape.

Born to Charles and Sarah were Les, Herbert, Ida May, Charles Jr., Alice, and Nettie. The Hight

family spent many a happy year at their little cabin on the mountain.

Once Nettie and Alice were cleaning out an old shed that had stood unused for ten years or more since their Grandfather Alfred had used it for a pigeon loft. In the accumulation of droppings, dust, and junk that had been stored in the little building, the girls found some small buckskin pokes which proved to be filled with gold dust. As it appeared to have been there for many years, during the time the Hights were in San Jose, and none of the neighboring miners knew who could have left it, the family decided to use this money to go to San Jose to visit their relatives. They bought a smart little team, a new spring wagon, and also purchased new clothes all around.

In 1879, Charles was having trouble with his back as a result of an old injury, so they moved to Kernville. The family filed on a homestead southwest of Kernville that later became known as the old Hight place, and the children were enrolled in school in Kernville.

Nettie Hight later married Dave Yarbrough, a pioneer teamster. As a lad, Dave had driven one of the 20-mule teams on the trips from the Borax

The Hight family taken in Kernville about 1884,
left to right, **May, Nettie, Lee, Alice, Charles, Bert.**

mines. Because of her knowledge of Whiskey Flat Days, the famous E Clampus Vitus organization initiated Nettie into their organization when they convened in Old Kernville in 1950, making her the only woman member of this organization.

Dave and Nettie lived in Kernville for many years. In their back yard stood the old pine tree which supplied the material for Nettie to make pine needle baskets that were real works of art. In 1934, she wrote the following poem about this old tree:

MY OLD PINE TREE

My dear old pine tree!
If you could but talk to me.
I hear you sigh and moan
As I sit here alone.
You look so beautiful and grand,
I sometimes wonder if you would understand
If I poured out my pent up soul to you.
Are you weeping? No, 'tis only the falling dew.
If you could love me as I love you,
Then I might lay my head on your crest
And sob and cry out the rest.
My broken heart might feel at ease
As you toss and sigh in the gentle breeze.
But we must be content to stand alone
And try to forget to sigh and moan.
You've given me pleasure while here alone,
Picking the rich, sweet nuts from your cone.
I've gathered your needles for my basketry,
I love every hour I've spent with thee.
And when your branches are white with snow
And the sun is sinking low,
No Christmas can be more beautiful to me
Than the one with you, my grand old pine tree.

NETTIE (HIGHT) YARBROUGH,
October 3, 1934.

Dave and Nettie later operated a gas station in Red Rock Canyon, and will long remember the joy they received from visiting with those who dropped by. Nettie would ask if a visitor would eat with them, and then proceeded to serve a seven-course meal. Well laid out on a tray, it was a variety of petrified woods and rocks of different compositions which looked ever so much like food. After she had her fun, Nettie served edible refreshments in gracious style.

The same year the Hight family moved into Kernville, a girl was born there who would one day become Bert's wife. This was Bertha Hooper. Bertha's father, Richard, was born in Cornwall, England in 1825. A carpenter by trade, he immigrated to America in 1856. In Illinois, he married Jane Cox, and their three children, Thomas R., Elizabeth J., and John L. were born in that state. In

Mrs. Baker and two of her children, Albert, Bertha.

1873 he moved his family to California, and the following year to Kernville. There, Bertha and Albert M. were born.

Richard Hooper engaged in the merchandising business in Kernville on a small scale, but he was best known as Kernville's first and only undertaker. A cabinetmaker by trade, he had a large supply of caskets on hand when he died. His wife, who after his death married a Mr. Baker, continued to run the business for many years.

Best known of the Hooper family was John L., known to many in the Valley as "Honest John." John was four years old when he came to Kernville with his family. When he grew up, his first business venture was a grocery store, which he owned and operated until 1896. He had various business interests, including a bottling works in Isabella. John's first loves were mining and milling. He operated one of the first cyanide plants in Kern County, located at the Big Blue Mill. He also built and operated the Keys Mill from 1913 until 1923. During this time he furnished the teams for the construction of the new road which replaced the stage road from Bodfish to the top of the hill going to Havilah.

Bertha Hight and daughter, Doris.

The Wyatts bought the Sumner home at Millville when Judge Sumner moved into Kernville. Built in 1861, this was the second home to be built in the Valley.

In 1895, Bertha Hooper married Bert Hight, joining two of the best known and loved families in Kernville. Bertha and Bert homesteaded land that lay just south of where the town of Wofford Heights was later laid out.

Born to the Hights were Inez in 1901, Merle in 1902, and Doris in 1911. In 1895, Bert was working the Evans Mill above Wagy Flat, farming his ranch, and working various other jobs. For years he worked for the Edison Company. One of his early jobs for this company was that of working on the right-of-way for the proposed power plant just below Fairview in 1909. He camped on a sand flat along the river, now known as Calkins Flat, with another old-timer named Bill Peyton.

In 1915 Bert passed away and Bertha married Jerry Converse, who had worked for the State Highway Department and Edison Company. He proved to be a good father for the three young Hight children, and was affectionately called Daddy Converse by them.

Bertha Converse was truly a person who will be remembered for many years by those who lived in the Kern River Valley. When she passed away in 1965, she had lived her 86 years just a stone's throw from where she was born. While she was still a young woman, she was called on for help when the pains of birth, of living, or of dying were felt. Bertha would appear quietly and take over. Very seldom would she accept any pay. Many residents of the Kern Valley were brought into the world with only Bertha to help their mother when no doctor was available. Some of these were

John built many adobe houses in the Valley, as well as an adobe hall in Isabella. Most of these homes stood until they were removed to make way for Lake Isabella. However, one still stood on the Hanning Ranch on the South Fork of the Kern in 1972. John learned this trade from his father who had constructed some of the finest adobe buildings in the Valley. The elder Hooper had built the structures on the Judge Sumner ranch east of town.

John was well-known for starting the town of Hobo Hot Springs, later changed to Miracle Springs. He started his operation there in 1929, and for ten years was also the postmaster. John married Gwenevere Wyatt in 1894. Gwenevere's father, Mark, had moved to Kernville in 1874, first opening a blacksmith shop and later building and running a sawmill on the slopes of Greenhorn Mountain. He worked at that business until his death in 1890. A clipping from a Bakersfield paper reads as follows:

Early last week Mark Wyatt of Kernville, who was feeling a little indisposed, remarked to a man in his employ, "Well, I will haul just one more load of lumber to the Valley, and it will be the last." Truly it was, for shortly after reaching here Mr. Wyatt took to his bed at the residence of his friend, Alvin Fay, Esq., and on Sunday last he died.

Bertha and Bert Hight, *to left*, on the Hight homestead south of Tilly Creek. Others unidentified.

70

Clyde Barbeau, Virginia and Evelyn Palmer, and several of the Art Malone children. Bertha also delivered four of her grandchildren. Although just a "practical" nurse, she had the natural ability and love for her neighbors that made up for lack of formal training.

When Bertha's mother, Mrs. Baker, passed away, she inherited the undertaking business along with a supply of caskets. She reserved a room at the rear of her house for this purpose. Her daughter, Doris, remembered that there was a child's coffin stored there that she used as a cradle for her dolls. Bertha continued to care for the deceased until a law was passed which required a license. This Bertha was unable to obtain. Having someone like Bertha Converse for a neighbor was one of the things that made Old Kernville such a wonderful place in which to live.

Bertha's only son, Merle Hight, lived all his life on the Kern River. For many years he worked for the County Road Department. He served as constable of Kernville, filling the period between Clarence Pascoe and his son, Cecil. Merle's only daughter, Phyllis Beatty, also chose to remain in the Valley, as did her son, Jerry (Red) Beatty, Jr.

The youngest Hight girl, Doris, had a son, Jack Ellis, by her first marriage. Jack moved away from the Valley, as did Doris, for 25 years. After the death of her mother, she came back to the Valley and moved into her mother's home in Wofford Heights.

Inez Hight married Clare A. Tuttle while she was going to school in San Jose in 1918. After their marriage they returned to the Valley and moved into the old Hight place. Clare Tuttle was a carpenter and built many of the homes that still stood in 1973, including the Silicz home on the Prince Ranch in the South Fork Valley. Clare and Inez also owned and operated the Mountain View Dairy which was located on the Hight Ranch from 1930 until 1937.

This couple had one son. Born in 1922, Alan R. Tuttle worked for the Edison Company as an operating lineman. In 1973 he had completed 27 years with the Company, serving solely in the Kernville area. Alan and his wife, Ann, also have children and grandchildren living in the Valley, so the Hight lineage still remains.

Kern River Fish Hatchery

LOCATED just a mile above Kernville is a 12½ acre site that has had more of an economic impact on the Kern River Valley than any parcel of ground in the Valley. This is the Kern River State Fish Hatchery. In 1972 it reached its full capacity of over one million catchable trout produced in a year. This hatchery is responsible for stocking 72 miles of roadside river from the mouth of the Kern Canyon near Bakersfield to Johnsondale Bridge, plus the Kern's tributaries and streams on the west side of Greenhorn Mountains.

This project had its beginning in 1928 when the Kern County Sportsmen—wanting to increase the survival rate of planted fish by holding them to a larger size before release—built their first rearing ponds at Kernville. These first concrete tanks were built on the old Burlando Ranch and can still be found in Kernville adjacent to Sirretta Street, where they have been filled with soil and are now being used to grow gardens. These tanks were supplied with water from the irrigation ditch for the Burlando Ranch, which in later years became the town ditch. It was discovered that water temperature could not be controlled along the ditch, so the next year four rearing tanks were built at the present location. The Kern County Sportsmen supplied the material, and it was made a W.P.A. (Works Progress Administration) project.

The California Department of Fish and Game delivered fingerling trout from the Kaweah Hatchery, as well as periodically checking the project's progress to the time of planting. At planting time, a Fish and Game employee was on hand to weigh and record the rate of growth, and to generally supervise. Planting during this period was done

Trout rearing ponds, Kern State Fish Hatchery.

Dedication of Kern State Fish Hatchery, June 1942. *Left to right*, Cecil Ray, John Loustalot, a Congressman from Santa Barbara, Kern County Supervisor Roy Woollomes and Vince Clerou.

with the help of the Kern County Fire Department and boys from one of the local C.C.C. (Civilian Conservation Corps) camps. The continued cooperation of the Kern County Board of Supervisors since the early years of the catchable trout program has been one of the secrets of its success, as down through the years Kern County contributed much of the labor. During the time that the County Road Camp was located at Kernville, the work crews contributed untold hours at the hatchery. Also under Kern County jurisdiction, Camp Owens as well furnished crews for over 35 years.

A tent was put up at the hatchery site and one of the local residents was hired to keep a day and night vigil over the trout ponds. Merle Hight was one of those to spend several summers on this job. The Kern County Sportsmen also built the first residence on the site, this being the second dwelling as you come up river.

In 1941 the State of California Department of Fish and Game took over operation of the rearing ponds and started the expansion that continued up through 1972. The Kern River Hatchery was the first of 23 hatcheries scattered throughout the State, and down through the years it continued as a leader in improved hatchery practices.

When the Kern River State Fish Hatchery began, Cecil Ray took the job of Fisheries Manager for the Kernville plant, a job he continued in for over 30 years. Ray was no newcomer to the project, as in 1929 he not only hauled trout in for the initial development, but had further supervised the job during the growing and planting periods. The Kern River Hatchery was designed to be operated with a minimum number of employees, and

a production of over 200,000 pounds of fish. Only five permanent and two seasonal personnel staff the operation.

Each step from incubation of the eggs to the actual planting of catchable trout is closely controlled and supervised. In April, hatchery employees strip eggs from brood stock that are kept on hand. The eggs are then placed in wire mesh baskets in the hatchery house. If the water is kept at around 54°, in thirty days the eggs will hatch and the small fish will fall through the mesh to the bottom of the tanks. From the tank they are moved to one of eight rearing ponds before transferring to one of the natural raceways located along the river. These raceways have been ingeniously engineered to reproduce the natural habitat of the trout. A total of 3,300 linear feet of raceways are separated in 100 feet length sections with a specially designed screen barrier between each. These revolving screened drums allows the water to pass while keeping the fish separated and screen free of trash. The ingenious revolving design, although very simple, was self-cleansing of clogging debris.

The feeding of the trout at the hatchery is one of the most important aspects of the project. Fed twice daily, each trout consumes about 2% of their body weight daily. Feeding is done in pellet form which is delivered in graduated sizes for the various size trout and stored in overhead bins at the hatchery. This pelletized food furnishes all the needed protein, fats, carbohydrates, and minerals needed for the most rapid growth of these trout.

In this day when a dollar doesn't buy much, the Department of Fish and Game is still able to grow and plant trout for 91 cents per pound

(1972). All costs are included in this figure, and the total amount spent for the operation of each hatchery comes from the $2 trout stamp that each fisherman buys. Probably the best buy for a dollar today!

When the Trophy Trout Program was first implemented in 1969 at Lake Isabella, the first year's plant came from the San Joaquin Hatchery. Thereafter, they were planted from the Kern River Hatchery stock. With the exception of a dry year that makes Lake Isabella abnormally low, good feed conditions will allow these trophy trout to grow up to four or five pounds in one year.

The Kern River Hatchery takes part in planting the high country lakes by airplane and, with an improved airport, would play an even bigger part as it is only ten minutes from hatchery to airport. A plane can reach most of the lakes in the southern High Sierras in thirty minutes. The fingerling trout are loaded into a tank with a bottom fitted with flaps that release the full load. As the pilot locates the lake to be planted in his bomb sight, he releases the contents. Fish, water, and all fall uninjured into lakes that previously took days to pack fish into with stock.

Except for a period after the 1966 flood, when there was a 27 month setback in hatchery expan-

Cecil Ray weighing and loading fish with the help of two Camp Owen boys, 1944.

Cecil and Ida Ray and their family. *Left to right,* children are Stan, Fred, Louise, and Roberta.

sion, this hatchery has continued to grow and improve. In 1941 they produced 35,000 trout. Since then the hatchery has increased the yearly plant nearly thirty fold. It has been estimated that 87% of the planted trout are caught within ten days, so this makes fishing along the Kern some of the best in the nation.

A stay in the Kern River Valley is not complete without a visit to the Kern River Hatchery, where the State of California, with the cooperation of Kern County government and sportsmen, have made one of the biggest and best production complexes to be found. And, best of all, at no added cost to the taxpayer.

Camp Owen

Erwin W. Owen Boys Camp, located a mile north of Kernville, has served as a temporary home for as many as eighty boys from Kern County and eight other California counties. Most of these boys have had long histories of arrests and have been taken from their homes by the Juvenile Court and placed in Camp Owen for their own welfare and for the safety of the community. Their offenses have run the whole gamut of problem behavior including petty theft, runaway, burglary, assault, drunkenness, and various types of drug abuse.

But Camp Owen is not a jail, and most boys placed there like the rural-setting. It is not an ordinary boys' camp. Down through the years it has been the start of a new way of life for many of the boys.

Camp Owen had its beginning in July of 1938, and unlike many state and county projects today, it started on a shoestring. There was not much to go on during the early years except for a lot of good ideas and strong determination. Roy Woollomes was one of the county supervisors who pushed the idea of Camp Owen the most. When someone was needed to pioneer the project, Mr. Woollomes thought of Leland Scott, who was then working for the County Road Department. Mr. Woollomes found Scott working on the Old State Road that came down off Greenhorn, and asked him how he would like to go to Kernville and start a boys' camp. Scott accepted, and within a few days he was in Kernville with forty boys and a terribly big job on his hands.

This was July 10, 1938. C. C. Keen was sent as interim camp director. Due to poor health, though, he was not able to be of much help. The County had applied for a special use permit on Forest Service land later occupied by Camp Owen, but the permit had not as yet been approved. A tem-porary camp was, therefore, established north of the Kern County Fire Station in Old Kernville.

To get the project started, Scott took some of the boys to Poso Flat where a few temporary buildings had been set up during the depression. The group moved these structures over to serve as kitchen and mess hall, while tents were used for sleeping space and offices.

The County gave Scott a ton-and-a-half G.M.C. truck. For the next several months he and the boys drove up to work at the campgrounds on Greenhorn Summit. They made forms and poured concrete picnic tables, doing such a good job that the tables were in excellent shape some 35 years later. The boys also cut 100 cords of wood that summer, some of which was used to heat their barracks the following winter. The balance was used for the County facilities on Greenhorn.

Just after Labor Day they were finally given permission to start building the camp. A road was

Camp Owen—a home away from home.

constructed into the property and brush cleared. The location was one big brush patch with a rock to match every bush. Rocks that could not be moved by hand or dragged out of the way with the truck had to be drilled and blasted. Did the boys learn to run jackhammers? Not hardly. As no money was available to buy or rent a compressor, all drilling had to be done by hand.

On week-ends, Scott and the boys went on field trips to visit old mines in the area, picking up discarded steel. As they did not have the money to buy new steel, these old bits of steel were sharpened on a forge at the fish hatchery and pressed into service. With one boy holding the steel and another swinging the hammer, the holes were drilled. A little powder was borrowed from the County Road Department, the rocks dynamited, and the pieces moved out of the way by the boys.

They finally moved to their permanent location on December 2, 1938. Their two buildings had been moved from Old Kernville, and five more temporary structures had been moved from Poso Flat. The kitchen and mess hall were put up first, then the barracks and a 20-foot by 20-foot office. Leland Scott also slept in this office. Because of the personnel shortage, he was required to be on the job twenty-four hours a day. In 1939, Scott and his wife, Leila, moved into the house in front of the rearing ponds at the fish hatchery, built by the Kern County Sportsmen.

Scott organized the boys into a system that proved to be successful up through the 1970s. In all aspects of camp life, including work programs, a corporal was put in charge of each squad of boys, with a sergeant in charge of all the corporals. The honor of these ranks were earned, and working on a point system, court was held each night. Each boy had to earn 1,500 points in order to gain his release. Points or credits were received each day, and could be reduced for improper behavior.

Many problems had to be faced in those first few years when funds were so short. The first cook stove burned stove oil fed by gravity, and smoked so much that most of the cooking had to be done outside. Finally, at Scott's recommendation, a new forced air oil burner was installed which ended the cook stove problem.

The first of a long line of men called group supervisors or counselors began with Jerry Sanders. Scott said that Sanders was the best hand with the boys of any of the men he later employed. Jerry had a special way of meeting the boys on their

level, and equally as important was his ability to do a multitude of things with his hands. He was able to transmit his skills in building and maintenance to the boys, giving them—often for the first time—a feeling of accomplishment. When they looked at the tool room, it was more than just a building, because they had helped make the adobe bricks, one by one, and put them in place. This also gave them a feeling of pride in their camp.

In the beginning, Sanders worked part time for the Kern County Park Service and part time for the County Road Department. He took different crews out for full days. Part of the time they drove to Greenhorn Summit where they hauled the garbage and cleaned the toilets in the County campgrounds, as well as doing a variety of maintenance and construction jobs. The time spent patching blacktop and various other jobs on the County roads furnished the County with inexpensive labor and gave the boys the same sense of accomplishment as did their work in the campgrounds. They developed a pride in their jobs, no matter how humble.

The first schoolteacher, Charles Smalley, joined the staff at Camp Owen and stayed three years. After being part of the Kern High School District for many years, in 1972 the instructional staff at Camp Owen was operated directly out of the office of the Kern County Superintendent of Schools. The boys alternated going to school one day and working the next. Giving them a full day in the work crews was necessary because of the lengthy travel to their jobs.

A shop teacher was also added, and the different men who have since filled this job have contributed greatly to the overall rehabilitation program. Hopefully, in learning to work wood and metal, the boys will acquire skills they are able to use for the rest of their lives.

Scott made a statement about counselors that many people may not agree with. He found that the more education a man had, the more trouble he had meeting the boys on their level. And, that a man with considerable education tended to talk down to them. He also stated that what the men could do was more important than what they knew, and there was no education gap. In other words, the boys seemed to to identify more quickly with a person who could do a physical job well, especially a construction job. These men, in turn, transferred their skills to the boys, as the boys did

The first dwelling completed in 1941. Built by Camp Owen boys for one dollar per square foot.

all the work and the men only supervised. Of course, a world of patience was also required in order to be able to stick with the boys until each one learned his individual job.

Many men in addition to Jerry Sanders were able to reach a place of trust with the boys at Camp Owen. Such men were Lew Sergent and many more over the years who became personally involved and lived with these youths and their problems twenty-four hours a day. In many cases they took the place of parents the boys never had.

The building program occupied a large part of camp life those first few years, as it continued to do into the 1970s. The difference was the budget. In 1939 the yearly budget was $11,000 to cover building and operating expenses, including salaries. The building program was greatly assisted by boys' handmade adobe brick used in the construction of many buildings.

Jerry Sanders worked closely with the boys on this project. Finding the right type of clay soil just north of the cow barn, they experimented with adding to the clay the proper amount of sand and, of course, straw to get the desired proportions. The bricks were dried in forms in the sun, and

were then used for the walls of most of the first structures built. The first bricks were used to construct the wall around the old water tank, followed by the tool shed and the old cow barn.

Leland Scott and his wife moved into the first building, completed in 1941. This is the house near the baseball diamond that has always been used for the Camp Director's living quarters. The total of 1,600 feet of floor space cost the county $1,600, or $1 per foot; the type of construction that would cost $25 per foot in 1973.

A favorite part of camp life was, of course, the meals. Many expert cooks are remembered, beginning with a Chinese who baked bread every day and was an all-around culinary expert. Another excellent cook was Lew Blaney.

Since the beginning, Camp Owen has raised much of their own food. This not only helped keep the cost down, but also made it possible to serve far better quality food than would have otherwise been obtained. They raised all their own pork, and much of the beef, chicken, and rabbits. A large flock of laying hens furnished eggs, and a large, diversified garden produced an abundance of vegetables. The first five heifer

A typical group of Camp Owen personnel taken in 1961. Also the number of years some of the old-timers worked at Camp Owen. *Top, left to right*, Ed Kuhnly, Tom Gribbins, Al Smith, Clarence Miller, Kenneth Watts, and John Robinson. *Middle row*, Lew Blaney, cook, 20 years; Clifford Cross; Mildred Beatty, secretary, 24 years; Cliff Baumeister, camp director, 20 years; and Phil Strauck. *Bottom row*, Warren Ripley; Lew Sargent, 15 years; Bill Stephens, 24 years; Stan Whiteside, 12 years; Tom McCambridge; and Wilbur Molitor.

calves came from the County Road Camp in Bakersfield, the beginning of the dairy herd that still exists.

The privilege of working in the cow barn had to be earned, and many of the boys would remember this experience the rest of their lives. Many had never been around animals before, so humorous events occasionally took place around the cow barn. The boys who were interested were taught to milk the cows. One boy, named Tom, was bound and determined that he would learn. He must have had an overwhelming desire, because he was deathly afraid of the cows. Assigned to begin his lessons on Old Mary, he was given instructions while observing from a safe distance. Then he was allowed to try it himself, and he began to stalk. He would try to sneak up on Mary from one angle, then from another. His eyes were

wide with terror and he was trembling like a leaf, but he would not give up. Mary was a veteran at this sort of business and calmly ate her grain. After about half an hour, Tom got up his nerve and was able to touch her. It took many more similar sessions before he lost all fear and started to become an expert milker. At first Mary would pull such things with Tom as stepping right in the middle of a bucket and refusing to remove her foot.

Work with the animals was just the tonic needed by some of the boys, and in many cases, the old cows broke down a barrier of pretended toughness that was only a front. The work habits they had to learn were to become invaluable in later life, as well as the pride they felt in having a part of something worthwhile.

When Leland Scott left Camp Owen in July of

1943, his job as Camp Director was taken over by Bill Steward, who had been a counselor. When Steward later became the Kernville postmaster, Walt Marks followed him as Camp Director. Cliff Baumeister then filled the position for 15 years, followed by Ken Durant, who still was there in 1973.

Regular hours of sleep, a well-rounded diet, and enforcement of the rules and regulations of the camp have resulted in boys being returned to the community as an asset. The success of Camp Owen has been due to a sound program including physical work, classes to raise the level of a boy's education, a good sports program, and the encouragement for each boy to follow the religion of his choice. Any youth program, no matter how well planned, is only as good as the personnel who carry it out. At Camp Owen, the counselors had personal contact with the boys, and so were most integral in rehabilitation of these youths. Lew Sergent devoted his every waking hour to the welfare of his charges and will long be remembered by those placed there, as will other counselors like Harry Kessler.

Camp Owen has a lower rate of released boys being rearrested and appearing again in juvenile court than any similar camp in the State, which gives strong support to the effectiveness of their program. Regardless of how good a program, it can only be successful when each boy comes to the point where he wants to improve himself and solve his problems in a constructive manner. Not all of them will succeed in keeping out of trouble with the law, but they are given some of the best available training at this youth facility. A "temporary home away from home" seems to appropriately fit Camp Owen.

Harley Mine

ONE OF THE most amazing feats of engineering attempted in the early West had its origin in a fight between a newcomer to Kernville and the town bully. It began in 1876. Charles Harley was the name of the young man newly arrived in the Kern River Valley. The bully is remembered only as Big Bill. From all accounts, Big Bill had pretty much his own way around Kernville. Anyone who had lived there for any length of time knew better than to tangle with him. Strangers in town who took offense at Big Bill's unrestrained behavior soon learned the same lesson. Sometimes they learned permanently, and always to their sorrow.

Maybe young Harley just didn't realize who he was dealing with. Or maybe he did, and chose to fight anyway. The details are obscure. At any rate, Harley and Big Bill did have a go-around which resulted, surprisingly, in the bully being shot by the newcomer.

Feeling that killing a local resident, of whatever reputation, was not the most auspicious way to introduce himself to a new community, young Harley lit out for the hills northeast of town. Discretion, as they say, is the better part of valor. One of the happy accidents that figure so often in stories of the early settlers occurred as Harley wandered the hills on what was then called Mineral Mountain, fleeing, he thought, from justice, when he stumbled on a good sized deposit of gold-bearing quartz.

Imagine his dismay. All that quartz and nowhere to go with it. No one to tell about it. No way to get it down from the peak where he had found it. What to do? After a good deal of soul searching, self-reproach, and probably more than a few swear-words, Harley realized that the only answer was to return to Kernville, take his medicine if he had to, and do something constructive about that quartz.

Harley slipped into town as inconspicuously as possible, only to learn that Big Bill's injuries were so minor as to cast considerable doubt on the shooting ability of one Charles Harley. The combination of relief and remorse on Harley's part, and respect for anyone with nerve enough to come at him with a gun on the part of Big Bill, resulted in firm friendship between the two former adversaries. Big Bill became Harley's foreman, and the unlikely pair set out to find a way to bring the quartz down the mountain.

The ore was located 5,500 feet up what is now Harley Mountain. It would have to drop 2,000 feet in 1.5 miles to the site selected for the mill through some of the most rugged terrain in the West. This site for the mill was by the Kern River on the little flat later named Gilbert Campground. Development began in 1877 and had shut down by 1882, with actual operation limited to three years out of the five. One of the first methods of getting the ore down the mountain was by pack mules. However, this was a seven-hour round trip, and even with three strings of ten mules each, they could only pack out about 4,500 pounds each shift. This was very time consuming for the amount hauled out. The final solution was as beautifully simple in conception as it was staggeringly difficult in execution.

They decided to build an aerial tramway. The difficulty lay in the stark steepness of terrain. The

Dry masonry trails cling to the mountain side on the way up to the Harley Mine.

The hearth of the blacksmith shop where the steel was reshaped and sharpened.

mill site was located on the boundary of the Sequoia National Forest and just across the road and east of where Camp Owen now exists. Andrew Smith Hallidie of San Francisco was contacted to build the tramway. Hallidie was a native of Scotland, who immigrated to the United States when he was seventeen, and was the inventor of the cable car. A brilliant man, he was the first to conceive of this "wire ropeway," as his aerial tram was called. He built his first tramway in 1856 to bring ore to a mill on the American River.

The pincipal feature of Hallidie's tramway was an endless wire cable passing tround two horizontal iron wheels, each of which were six feet in diameter. One iron wheel was located at the mill and the other at the mine some 2,000 feet above. About every 100 yards, depending on the terrain, a support or "way station" was located. These stations were A-frames that stood between fifteen and twenty feet high and were constructed of tree trunks cut to the proper height, or of four 10-inch timbers leaned together. On top of these supports stood a horizonal beam. This beam supported a 2-inch shaft whose ends were fitted 18-inch grooved iron wheels, over which the ascending and descending cable passed.

The wire cable on the tramway was ¾-inch in diameter and over three miles long. Attached to this cable at approximately 100 foot intervals were 145 iron buckets, each large enough to carry 100 pounds of ore. Also attached to the cable were iron extension bars which had been shaped to carry lumber, water, and other needed supplies,

Bullwheel that was located on top Harley Mountain. Those that made the three hour hike are *left to right* Judy and Rocky Stone, Marj and Bob Powers, and, *in front*, Ted Martin.

and also a special car which could safely carry two people. This car, when filled, weighed nearly 500 pounds. The ore buckets, iron bars, and passenger car were all hung from rods which easily passed over the wheels of the supports or way stations. The weight of the loaded buckets provided the power which carried up the empty buckets, supplies or passengers.

The dumping of the ore bucket was accomplished by a simple contrivance which enabled the bottom to "drop out" as it passed around the large horizontal wheel at the mill. The cost of delivering 20 tons of ore per day from the mine to the mill was only about twenty cents per ton and was a tremendous saving over delivery by muleback.

Another famous Hallidie ropeway was constructed for the Standard Mill at Bodie' and had worked quite well. An aerial tramway is not too difficult to build if you are able to pick your site. However, to come straight to Harley's mill would have been impossible because of insurmountable bluffs. So the tram was routed south about a half mile, then turned southwest, making a 45-degree turn which was near impossible with an aerial tram.

Many strong backs were needed, and Chinese laborers who had worked on the Tehachapi railroad job provided the manpower. The three miles of endless cable and the huge bullwheels were freighted by ox team from Visalia. Williams, of Granite Station, hauled the material over the McFarland Toll Road.

In construction over normal terrain a support or "way station" would be spaced about every 200 feet, but in one place just before the tramway made the 45-degree turn, it crossed a great chasm. The supports at this point were placed more than 900 feet apart. The foundations for these supports were built by the method known as dry masonry. No cement was used and each rock had to be placed in exactly the right spot so that all the rocks would fit together to make a substantial base for the support. Just west of Camp Owen in a small draw back of a telephone repeater stands the lowest of the remaining bases for the station. A five-minute walk up the dirt road towards Cannell Creek from the Johnsondale Highway will give an idea of the quality of work done on this job, as this last station is in the draw above the road. From this point, the tramway headed northeast to the top of the ridge, again a span of some 600 feet. In one spot a huge boulder was scaled, and after four holes were drilled into the top surface with hand steel, anchors were installed to support a station on top.

The construction of the way stations were no easy chore. As it was too costly to construct a trail up the route of the tramway, the twenty-foot 10"x10" had to be hauled up the mountain by brute strength, using block and tackle in many places. These huge timbers were freighted in from Senator Jones' mill above Wagy Flat and, being of green lumber, made them even heavier and more awkward. The seven-foot 8"x8" also had to be carried in, usually on the backs of two men.

The only A-frame left on any of the "way stations," built in 1878, as it appeared in 1970.

The six-foot bullwheels, even after being taken apart in sections, still weighed too much to haul in on one animal. So these heavy pieces were sledded up the trail, pulled by mules working in tandem, or carried on the backs of two mules. A swivel support was constructed above the pack boxes on each mule and one end of the load was fastened onto each support. With the mule on each end supporting half the weight and going up the trail one behind the other, they could be used to transport sizeable loads. The seven-foot shaft for the bullwheel at the upper terminus of the tramway and 20-foot timbers for the stations were transported in this manner.

A dry camp was set up on the top, which meant that all water either had to be carried up the tramway in five-gallon containers or by muleback from Tunnel Spring, a half mile to the southeast. Because space was limited, the only buildings erected were the cook's shack and a house for the foreman. The other men slept in tents erected on small benches of level ground.

One of the rugged individualists who camped out on top of Harley Mountain was James Morris. In 1888, Morris told William Ireland, Jr., State Mineralogist, that the "pay streak" was at first three to four feet thick. He said that the tunnel driven northeasterly on the vein had daylighted through the mountain (coming out high on the saddle between Cannell Creek and Caldwell Creek), and that it passed some 75 feet beneath the peak. He also stated that the mine had been worked to a depth of 150 feet below this with some very rich ore having been taken out.

The upper landing on the Harley tramway after the bullwheel was moved to Kernville affords a spectacular view of Kernville.

All that remains of any of the buildings used for the Harley Mine is this rock fireplace.

The rails for ore cars in this main tunnel were unusual. To cut down on the weight being hauled up the mountain, they were constructed of 4″x4″ oak. Metal strips were fastened on top where they came into contact with the wheels of the ore car.

Of the buildings that were erected on the mountain, all that remained in 1973 was the chimney of the foreman's house which stands as a lonely sentinel on the ridge. The only other part of the tramway remaining were several rock platforms that supported the way stations. One station which survived nearly a century of weathering as well as several wild fires, stands one-fourth mile below the mine.

The blacksmith "shop" on Harley Mountain was nothing more than a crude, altar type hearth on a little ridge close to the mine entrance. It stood intact for some 90 years until, in 1970, vandals almost completely pulled it apart, rock by rock. Their reason will probably never be known. The same type energetic individuals had also attempted to roll the six-foot bullwheel over the edge and down the cliffs where it would never be seen again. However, a local resident, wanting to save it for posterity, took it apart and built a heliport out of the upper landing of the tramway. The pieces were flown down to the old mill site by the Kern River. It was reassembled and stored for later use as a historical display.

The discovery and development of the mine came about by accident, and a tragic accident brought its operation to a close. One day in 1882 the tramway cable broke, and the ore buckets and cable came screeching down the mountain, banging and scraping against the rocks, emitting a stream of sparks that could be seen in Kernville even though it was broad daylight. Two men working near the tramway were killed, cut to pieces by the madly whiplashing cable.

The project had been beset by breakdowns, accidents, and general bad luck for some time. They had to face it—Harley Mountain was too rugged for even Hallidie's superior engineering skills. This latest occurrence, although accidental, was the straw that broke the back of the backers. The Harley Mine was shut down; the metal portions of the tramway that were readily accessible, including the cable, were sold for scrap during World War I.

The remains of the Harley Mine can be viewed by walking or riding horseback up the Cannell Trail to the saddle above Caldwell Creek, then turning west up the ridge where one can find the east end of the main tunnel, and on the ridge further west, the old chimney. The upper terminus of the tramway is located just over the crest. Or the trip can be made by locating the old trail up the south slope of Harley Mountain where it starts in the canyon back of James Store. This trail built to haul ore out by muleback was later used to transport lumber and other needed supplies up to the mine. This is a rough ride, but in 1972 Ernie Knowles and a group of local equestrians were able to make it all the way to the mine dump.

Anyone with enough stamina and love of history to make this three-hour walk up the mountain can get some small idea of what 100 Chinese saw as they sweated and toiled to accomplish the nearly impossible.

Southern California Edison Co.

THE Southern California Edison Company has played an important role in the settlement and continued prosperity of the Kern River Valley since the year 1900. In 1972, over two million dollars in property taxes were paid into the Kern County treasury by the Edison Company, half of which was used exclusively for schools and roads. Even outweighing the financial stability to this area are the contributions made by the Company's employees and their families as they lived and worked here on the Kern.

It might be interesting, therefore, to look at the early development of the Southern California Edison Company. An overview of the Company's success in California as a whole is necessary to better understand their accomplishments here. A good place to begin would be the year 1879 when Thomas Alva Edison perfected his incandescent lamp. Three years later he officiated at the opening of the first central power plant, located on Pearl Street in downtown New York. Among Edison's first 59 customers was the *New York Times*, where workmen had rigged 25 lights in the editorial office. When the incandescent lights came on for the first time at 5 p.m., September 4, 1882, a veteran reporter summed up the history-making occasion with these words:

It seemed almost like writing by daylight to have a light without a particle of a flicker—and scarcely any heat to make the head ache.

That was the beginning of America's electric utility industry. Before this, isolated plants had served individual users, but Edison's Pearl Street Station was the first attempt at extensive and continuing distribution of bulk electrical power. Within four years the demand for this new kind of power had spread across the United States. In 1887, some 600 electric light companies were in operation, although few of these made a serious effort to provide electricity on a round-the-clock basis.

In that year, two such small companies began service in Southern California, one at the community of Highgrove near Riverside, and the other at Santa Barbara. At Highgrove, the first commercial service from a hydro-electric generating plant in California became a reality as the result of quiet negotiations between Charles R. Lloyd of

San Francisco and the Riverside Water Company, owners of a canal under construction near Highgrove.

Lloyd was a "behind-the-scenes" type entrepreneur who, throughout the earliest days of hydro electric development, was likely to be found involved in many deals in which commissions were to be made. Near Highgrove the Riverside Water Company's canal dropped 50 feet, and Lloyd saw an opportunity to build a small hydro plant to provide lights for Colton and Riverside. On May 8, 1886, Lloyd concluded a tentative lease agreement with the water company to install a 12 horsepower waterwheel at the drop in the canal, at a lease price of $1 per H.P. per month. However, water was not let through the canal until April of 1887, and as other developers also wanted to use the drop, Lloyd finally had to up his bid to $250 per month.

When the lease was concluded, Lloyd engaged Gustavus O. Newman, Chief Engineer of the Riverside Water Company, to design and build the Highgrove plant. (Newman later became Chief Engineer of the Pacific Light and Power Corporation.) The plant, as originally built, was a wooden building containing a single waterwheel driving a direct current dynamo. The plant went into service in September 1887, supplying power for 15 arc lights in Colton and 15 in Riverside.

In 1888, Lloyd organized the San Bernardino Electric Light and Power Company, and its principal property was the Highgrove plant into which several additional dynamos were installed as demand picked up. In 1896, Highgrove was extensively rebuilt in order to provide electricity for street-cars in nearby San Bernardino. A steel penstock replaced the wooden flume, and the original

The first Edison Company construction on the upper Kern River was the diversion dam for the Borel Canal, *lower front.* This photo, taken in 1903, also shows the foot bridge that crossed the Kern River at the end of Nellie Dent Street in Old Kernville.
Southern California Edison Company Photo.

arc machinery was replaced by a General Electric 150kw, 3-phase, 2,200-volt alternator, operated by two water turbines connected by belting. Power was stepped up to 15,000 volts for delivery to Colton and San Bernardino.

In 1903, the Highgrove hydro plant became a property of the Pacific Light and Power Corporation, a predecessor of the Southern California Edison Company. The last important power delivery from Highgrove was made in December 1914. The plant burned down in March 1915. However, a substantial part of the plant remained in 1973: the stone and concrete forebay, the penstock that still carries water beneath Iowa Avenue, and the concrete piers of the plant—all are in a lot surrounded by eucalyptus trees. And, until 1952, the Edison Company leased power privileges on the site from the Riverside Water Company at $250 per month.

The first steam central station to operate in what became the service territory of the Southern California Edison Company was located in Santa Barbara. Unlike the Highgrove venture, which was a personal speculation by C. R. Lloyd, the Santa Barbara plant was planned as a project for civic betterment and enjoyed full public and subscriber backing from the start.

General Samuel W. Backus moved to Santa Barbara in 1886 and immediately began plans for a plant to provide electric lighting for the pueblo town. In October 1886 a meeting of backers was

Highgrove hydroelectric generating plant near Riverside, built in 1886.
Southern California Edison Company Photo.

held in the City Hall, out of which came the Santa Barbara Electric Light Company. A 100 x 250 foot lot on Ortega Street was purchased for $2,000. Although it was first thought that steam purchased from an adjacent lumber mill could run a dynamo, General Backus soon decided to provide electricity not only for arc lights at night, but to provide power for daytime use—and to allow for future expansion. Accordingly, a 45 x 35 foot wooden building, with an iron roof, was erected on the lot to house the boiler, engine and dynamos.

Finally, on March 19, 1887, the plant, containing two Thompson-Houston direct current dynamos powered by a direct connected 80 horsepower buckeye engine, went into operation. The plant operated two circuits. One provided electricity for 15 arc lights of a total 2,000 candlepower, the lights being mounted on 40 and 60 foot high steel masts along State Street. The other circuit provided electricity for 45 Edison incandescent lamps, totaling 1500 candle-power, located in various stores, hotels and residences downtown. At the first stockholders' meeting held after the system went into operation, it was reported that the "works" had cost $21,917 and the company was making a "handsome" profit of $153.50 a month.

In 1895, the plant was modernized with the addition of a 150 kw, 3-phase alternator to provide electricity for lights and motors. As rebuilt, the plant had a total of four generators belted to a jack-shaft driven by a single steam engine.

In June 1901 the United Electric, Gas and Power Company took over the Santa Barbara Electric Company, and in November of that year put a new "modern" steam plant into service. The old plant was abandoned in 1902 and its largest generator moved into the new plant. In 1903 the Edison Electric Company, corporate predecessor of the Southern California Edison Company, took over the U. E. G. & P. system. In 1973 all traces of the earliest steam power plant on the Edison system are obliterated, the site being now a Coca-Cola bottling works.

Other pioneer electric generating plants, later to become part of the Southern California Edison Company, quickly sprang up in the late 1880s: Visalia—1887, and San Pedro, Ventura, San Bernardino and Pasadena, all in 1888. All through the 1890s demand for electricity grew steadily. Additional steam and hydro electric plants were put

into service in many places—Pomona, Santa Ana, Santa Monica, San Bernardino, Upland, Long Beach, San Pedro, Redlands, and Hanford. Unfortunately, all these plants shared a common problem: because they generated low-voltage direct current, they could not transmit their electricity more than about three miles.

It was the engineers of Edison's predecessor companies who solved the problem of "long distance" electrical transmission. In 1890, Dr. Cyrus G. Baldwin, President of Pomona College, organized the San Antonio Light and Power Company to harness a waterfall in San Antonio Canyon to generate electricity for the benefit of the nearby town of Pomona. Dr. Baldwin's engineer, Almarian W. Decker, built a generating plant and a transmission system that was the first commercial application of the principle of step-up and step-down transformation of electrical current, utilizing special transformers (then called "converters") manufactured by William Stanley. The "Pomona Plant" went into operation on November 28, 1892, when to the surprise of many "experts" electricity was successfully sent 14 miles into Pomona.

After this success, Decker promptly went to work designing another plant for Henry Sinclair's new Redlands Electric Light and Power Company, this new generating plant to be located in Mill Creek just east of Redlands in San Bernardino County. For this plant, Decker designed a revolutionary new generating system that produced alternating current at three phase—the first utilization of the type of electricity most commonly in use today. Although the original generators were replaced in 1934, most of the machinery in Mill Creek No. 1 hydro plant has been in service since 1893, making the plant the oldest still active on the Edison System.

Decker, who also designed the electrical system for the world famous Mount Lowe Railway in Pasadena, died at the age of 41, soon after the completion of the Mill Creek Plant. He was the first of a long line of Edison engineers who pioneered electrical development in the United States.

While these developments were happening around Southern California, the direct corporate ancestor of the Edison Company was developing in the City of Los Angeles. Walter S. Wright of Pasadena and E. E. Peck formed a partnership to buy a miniature electric light plant located in San Pedro, then a fishing village which had just been disappointed in its expectations of a government breakwater and other improvements to the harbor. The city fathers cancelled their street lighting contract and left the fledgling company without sufficient business to warrant the operation of the "large plant," and it was shut down. Later, in the absence of Peck, the unit was sold to a junk dealer. On his return, Peck again came into possession of the plant and attempted to obtain a franchise from the city of Los Angeles. He was unsuccessful, but did manage to obtain a franchise from the county supervisors to build and operate a power plant outside the city limits.

The plant, consisting of an 80 horsepower boiler and a 30 arc lighting dynamo, was installed in a small frame building on 22nd Street east of Vermont Avenue, then outside the city limits of Los Angeles. It began operation in December 1895, with a total connected load of five commercial arc lights and three street arcs. The total investment was $11,000.

The firm then was known as the Walter S. Wright Electric Company and consisted of Wright, Peck, William R. Staats, and G. H. Barker (of Barker Brothers fame). Staats, who also was the owner of a national investment firm bearing his name, played an important part in the financial arrangements of the new company. The founders did not relax their attempts to gain a franchise in the city of Los Angeles, nor did they confine their business to the county territory. They extended their lines into the city by setting their poles on private property.

Wright discovered an old franchise which had been granted by the Los Angeles City Council some years previously, but which had never been used. He bought it and then found the one "catch" to the franchise—a provision that the company would furnish lighting at the city hall by April 1, 1896—and that date was only two weeks away.

Every man in the company went to work and, by toiling days and nights, succeeded in building the line as far as Third and Hill Streets by stringing the lines on the poles of the Los Angeles Traction Company. The poles ended at that point, but this did not stop the Wright Electric Company. Wright got permission from the owner of the Byrne Building at Third and Broadway to set a wooden sawhorse on the roof to which they could attach the wires. From this point the lines were draped across the street to the tower of the city hall. And, dramatically, on the night before the day the franchise would have expired, an electric

John B. Miller, founder of the Edison Company.
Southern California Edison Company Photo.

light—albeit only one—was burning in the city hall tower.

With this victory, Wright and Peck, on June 5, 1896, incorporated the West Side Lighting Company. The demand for electric power developed rapidly, outgrowing the small plant at 22nd and Vermont. The directors, in a bold move, decided to "build for all time." A modern plant was constructed at Second and Boyleston inside a brick building formerly used as a powerhouse for the Second Street Cable Railway Company. It was placed in operation in December 1896, but within a month was enlarged with additional generating machinery. Still more was added in the fall of 1897.

The West Side Lighting Company was to last only 17 months. In December 1897 the Edison Electric Company of Los Angeles was formed. This company took over the properties of the West Side Lighting Company. The inclusion of "Edison" in its corporate title occurred as it was the Southern California franchise to use Thomas Edison's patented system of underground distribution.

W. G. Kerckhoff.
Southern California Edison Company Photo.

The money required to carry out the rapid development of the new company was "risk capital," and not easy to acquire. Fortunately, John B. Miller became associated with the Company as its Treasurer and a member of the Board of Directors. From the beginning, his presence was an important factor in its growth. He became its financial foundation, a genius in money affairs, and continued to hold this distinction until his death in 1932.

Miller now is considered to have been the founder of the Company. Through his farsightedness, courage, and exceptional promotional ability, he consolidated the numerous small companies which were then springing up in the territory into a large, effective organization. Russell H. Ballard, another outstanding leader, also became affiliated with the Company about that time as its only bookkeeper.

The Edison Electric Company was still having great difficulty finding a power supply equal to the quickly increasing growth in its service territory. Harry Sinclair's Redlands Electric Light and Power Company, on the other hand, was looking for new markets for its surplus power. Thanks to this fortunate situation, John Miller was able in 1898 to engineer the first of his many successful mergers.

One result of this merger was the acquisition by Edison of an unfinished power plant on the Santa Ana River not far from the old Mill Creek Plant. A young engineer named James A. Lighthipe, then the West Coast representative of Thomas Edison's General Electric Company, was consulted concerning the best method of transmitting electricity into downtown Los Angeles some 83 miles away. Lighthipe designed a novel 33,000-volt transmission system. When the new system went into service, so successful was it that President Miller on the spot hired Lighthipe as Chief Engineer.

Also in 1898, the Edison Electric Company acquired the properties of Pasadena Electric Light and Power Company, followed in 1899 by the purchase of the gas* and electric properties of the Santa Ana Gas and Electric Company. Several smaller companies also were absorbed during this time, mostly for water rights. The merger of these properties and companies made necessary further expansion of the capitalization, and the Edison Electric Company was reorganized, taking over all properties on September 1, 1902.

Edison Electric and the United Electric, Gas and Power Company were consolidated in 1903, bringing into the system the gas and electric properties at Santa Barbara, Santa Monica, and Long Beach, and electric properties at Redondo, San Pedro, and Monrovia. Interestingly, this consolidation also brought into the system a street railway in Santa Barbara, a 224 kw steam plant at Santa Monica—and bathhouses in both beach cities.

In 1902 a company was formed that grew almost to the same size as the Southern California Edison Company by the time they merged in 1917. This was the Pacific Light and Power Company, forged from several small companies along the coastal side of the Sierra Madre and San Bernardino Mountains, chief of which was the San Gabriel Electric Company organized in 1897 by William G. Kerckhoff and Allan C. Balch. Its hydro plant along the banks of the San Gabriel River near Azusa provided electricity for manufacturing

*All gas properties of the Edison Company were turned over to a wholly-owned subsidiary company, the Southern California Gas Company. After Edison's 1917 merger with Pacific Light and Power, the Gas Company was made independent. Ironically, in the 1950's and '60s, the Gas Company became a major competitor with its former parent.

companies and street railways in Los Angeles. Other early companies which were absorbed into what later became the Pacific Light and Power Company were the San Antonio Light and Power Company, formed in 1891; Riverside Power Company, 1901; Mentone Power Company, 1901; San Bernardino Gas and Electric Company, 1900; and the Kern River Company, 1897.

Kerckhoff was a key figure in the San Gabriel Electric Company, but when P. L. & P. was organized he was overshadowed by Henry E. Huntington, a name linked with the light and power industry and also with railroads, ship building, and land holdings. By 1902, Huntington was said to have been the wealthiest man in Southern California, with holdings in more than 60 companies.

In July 1909, Edison Electric, in order to reflect its establishment as a regional public utility, changed its name to the Southern California Edison Company.

Less than a year later, Edison broke ground for the Long Beach Steam Station. This station was to become the showcase of the industry—the latest in design and efficiency. Unit 1, with a capacity of 12,000 kw, went into operation in August 1911; Unit 2, with 15,000 kw, in February 1913; and Unit 3, with 20,000 kw, in April 1914. These were the first three units of what was to become an eleven-unit power installation without parallel in the industry.

BIG CREEK

Even this new plant was not enough to meet the rapidly growing demand for power in Southern California. In 1916, confronted with the specter of a short power supply, the Edison Company began negotiating with Henry E. Huntington to purchase the franchises, property, and business of the Pacific Light and Power Corporation. An agreement was reached in May 1917 to bring into the Edison System six hydroelectric plants, including the famed Big Creek complex, a large steam plant at Redondo (abandoned in 1934), and several smaller steam plants. The additions more than doubled the Company's power supply, as well as adding considerable water rights for further hydroelectric development. The service area of the Mt. Whitney Power and Electric Company in the San Joaquin Valley, the Ventura, Santa Paula, and Oxnard districts of the Ventura Power Company, plus electric railways and certain service franchises and businesses in and around Los

Henry E. Huntington.

Southern California Edison Company Photo.

Angeles were also included. Thus, came into being the nucleus of today's Southern California Edison Company.

Work was immediately initiated to expand the Big Creek Project's capacity. Dams at Huntington Lake were raised and new dams at Florence and Shaver were built, providing for greater water storage. A key achievement was the digging of the Florence Lake tunnel through the granite heart of Kaiser Ridge. Upon completion, it was given the distinction as being the longest water tunnel in the world. The tunnel was renamed Ward Tunnel in 1928 to honor Edison Vice President George C. Ward. Big Creek Powerhouses No. 1 and No. 2 were enlarged and Powerhouses No. 8, No. 3, and No. 2A were built.

Again under the direction of Chief Electric Engineer Jim Lighthipe, Big Creek's 150,000-volt transmission lines to Los Angeles were modified and the towers raised to handle an increased load of 200,000 volts. For this achievement, done while the lines were energized, the Southern California Edison Company in 1923 became the first recipient of the Charles A. Coffin medal, created by the

John S. Eastwood.
Southern California Edison Company Photo.

General Electric Company for outstanding accomplishments in the electrical industry.

By 1929 the Big Creek-San Joaquin River Hydroelectric Project was essentially complete. Water descends from Florence Lake, at 7,328 feet elevation, through a chain of reservoirs and conduits to turn the generators at five Edison power plants. This water produces more power per unit than anywhere else on earth. Or, as has been said, "Big Creek is the hardest working water in .the world."

In 1910 the P. L. & P. turned its attention to the Big Creek-San Joaquin River watershed and bought the Mammoth Power Company which, until then, was a company existing on paper only and consisting mainly of maps and survey data in the Big Creek area preparatory to setting up dams and powerhouses. Much of this data was collected by John S. Eastwood, one of the first engineers who dreamed of converting the Sierra snow into "white coal"—making electric energy out of falling water. Eastwood was a Minnesota mining engineer who found his way into the Sierra in 1880 and conceived a complex of dams, penstocks, and powerhouses that would repeatedly use the falling waters of Big Creek and the San Joaquin River. A man ahead of his time, his plan was put down on paper in the early 1900s and gathered dust until the right technology and leadership came along.

By 1911, Pacific Light and Power, now reorganized as a corporation, was ready to begin the initial development of Big Creek. Henry E. Huntington, then president, found the first big problem in transportation of men and materials to the job. His solution was to build a railroad. So was born the San Joaquin and Eastern Railroad, a 56-mile standard gauge line which had a 5.2% maximum grade and a sharp 60° curvature for many of its 1100 twists and turns. The railroad was often referred to as the "Slow, Jerky, and Expensive." The SJ&E hauled 60,000 tons of supplies, food and equipment, and thousands of laborers to the job at Big Creek. By 1913, three dams, two powerhouses, and a 240-mile transmission line to Los Angeles had been completed.

In 1917, the Pacific Light and Power Corporation merged into Southern California Edison Company, and the Big Creek program was expanded. This was America's first large-scale progressive hydroelectric development and one of the largest construction jobs of its kind ever attempted, comparable in scope with the Panama Canal. But that is getting ahead of the story!

When we left the Edison Electric Company, it had just absorbed the United Electric Gas and Power Company. Thus, in 1903, there were two major electric utility companies serving Southern California: Edison Electric and P. L. & P. The latter supplied most of the power for the Pacific Electric and Los Angeles Railways. Edison Electric, on the other hand, with a larger number of customers, was still relying on the many small steam and hydro plants it had scattered throughout its system.

This train, dubbed the Slow, Jerky, and Expensive, was used on the Big Creek job. S. J. & E.'s conductor, William A. Barnett, is shown second from right.
Southern California Edison Company Photo.

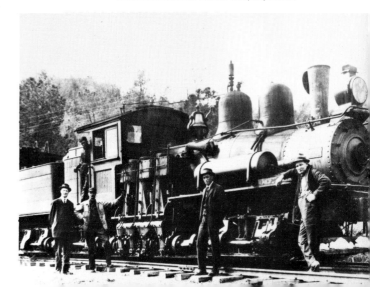

Big Creek Construction clearing site for Plant No. 1 at Cascade. *In right foreground* is the trestle for the S. J. & E. R.R., and Kerckhoff Dome looms in the background.

Southern California Edison Company Photo.

Jerk-line team driven by Percy Bubar hauls the armatures for one of the four generators used at K. R. No. 1. This plant that went into service on May 19, 1907 was at that time the largest hydroelectric plant in the United States.

Southern California Edison Company Photo.

In 1895, Kerckhoff and a partner, Charles Foreman, formed the Kern River and Los Angeles Electric Power Company, later to become part of the P. L. & P. for the purpose of locating a good site for a hydro power plant on the Kern River. Immediately following incorporation, surveyors were sent out to the Kern. An August 1895 entry in the *Journal of Electricity* states:

Los Angeles, Cal. H. Hawgood, Consulting Engineer of the Kern River and Los Angeles Electric Power Company, has sent out a party under F. H. Olmstead to locate a route for the transmission line from the point where power is to be generated to this city, a distance of almost 105 miles. The work of the surveying party will occupy about a month and in the meantime work on the canal is progressing rapidly. From the report of W. D. Larrabee, C.E., it appears that 10,000 horsepower at 200 feet fall, or 50,000 horsepower at 1,000 feet fall can readily be developed. It is expected to develop and transmit to Los Angeles

40,000 horsepower which can be done at a cost of $125 per horsepower.

Franchises to construct transmission lines in Kern and Los Angeles Counties were quickly obtained, but little more was done on this project for several years. One suspects that the engineering problems associated with a hundred mile transmission line caused this lengthy delay in the project. (This was still three years before the successful installation of the 83 mile long Santa Ana River line.)

In 1897, the Kern River and Los Angeles Electric Power Company was reorganized as the Kern River Company. But it was not until 1901 that work was seriously begun. This plant was later known as "Borel," named after Antoine Borel, one

Jerk-line teams stop in front of the Hot Springs House in 1904 on their way back to Caliente to pick up another load of cement for the Kern River Canal (Borel Canal).

A tour of the tunnels on the Kern River No. 1 job in 1906.

Southern California Edison Company Photo.

Construction under way on K. R. 3 Plant—1919. Note Bulldog Mack trucks with hard rubber tires. Yellowjacket Mountain looms in the center background.

Southern California Edison Company Photo.

of Henry Huntington's partners in forming the Pacific Electric Railway. In 1902, soon after the plant was completed, the Kern River Company was absorbed into Pacific Light and Power Company. The earliest filing on the upper Kern, in 1900, was for 25,000 miner's inches just above Fairview by Henry Sinclair, then President of the Redlands Company. This later became the headworks site for Edison's Kern River No. 3 plant. Another filing was made in the Kern River Canyon just a few miles above where the river empties out of the mouth. At this place Edison constructed what was at that time the largest hydroelectric plant in the United States. The four generators at Kern River No. 1, producing 24,800 kilowatts (33,256 h.p.), went into service May 19, 1907. The transmission line from this plant to Los Angeles was rated at 66,000 volts, a new world's high, and was the first high-voltage transmission line to be supported entirely upon steel towers. Once again, Jim Lighthipe's engineering had made Edison a pioneer in the electrical industry.

Then, in the early twenties, Edison returned to the Kern. Henry Sinclair's water rights for 25,000 miner's inches at Fairview had remained unused for years, although in 1906 Edison obtained a permit from the U. S. Department of Agriculture, signed by Thomas B. Sherwood, Acting Forester, to build a wagon road from the proposed Kern

"Kern River" plant, later known as "Borel."

90

Intake

Camp 8
later Roads End

0.1

Adit 1-4

0.1

Fairview

Adit 4-6

2.3

Camp 7½

1.0

Salmon Creek

Camp 6

1.0

Adit 12-15

2.3

Adit 16-17

Corral Creek

Camp 5

flume

0.5

Adit 18-19

Camp 4

Adit 19-20

Hospital Flats

1.3

1.6

Adit 20-21

Camp 3

1.0

Headquarters
Camp

Camp 2

Adit 21-22

Cannell Creek

Syphon

1.3

Tramway

0.3

KR3
Powerhouse

Kern River 3
Edison Co.
Project

HEADQUARTERS CAMP — JUNE 1919.

Southern California Edison Company Photo.

Trucks hauling a 40,000 pound section of the crane used in the construction of K. R. No. 3 pulls over to let Phil Hand and his mail stage by.

River No. 3 intake to the forks of the Kern. This was in preparation for a plant to be called Kern River No. 4, which never materialized. Also planned was a Kern River No. 5 further upriver.

Part of Southern California Edison's planned development was a reservoir at Big Meadow, northeast of Kernville on the Kern Plateau. The proposed water storage was to be released through Salmon Creek and tie into the K. R. 3

K. R. No. 3 Power Plant site in 1919 before construction commenced.

Southern California Edison Company Photo.

flume above the Kern River. The small dam and pool at Big Meadow never became a reality although a road was started that can still be traced. This road ran from what is now the north shore of Lake Isabella, crossing above Hanning Flat, and finally ends near the Fay Ranch.

Although work had been in process on the upper Kern ever since the first survey was made in 1901, not much progress had been made until after 1909, except for token work along the right of way to retain their rights. By the last part of 1910, the Edison Company had a rough wagon road upriver as far as what is now known as Road's End. They had a camp set up at this spot that later became Camp 8, as it was the uppermost in a series of camps to be used in construction of the Kern River No. 3 Hydroelectric Plant.

This powerhouse, known as K. R. 3, is located two miles north of Kernville on the Johnsondale Road. Even though the project had been in progress for many years, it was not until March of 1919 that construction work commenced on the actual power plant site. After the foundation was in, the major construction of the plant—including

93

Construction of the K. R. No. 3 Power Plant.

K. R. No. 3 Power Plant and living quarters for the company employees—taken in 1923.

installation of the generators—centered around a Shaw crane rated at 65 tons. The main arm for this crane weighed 20 tons, and it was quite a job to haul it over the rough dirt roads from Caliente and get it installed at the powerhouse.

After completion of K. R. 3 in March of 1921, the Edison Company with teams and scrapers carved out a number of flat spots for dwellings on the small ridges just north and east of the power

plant. On these niches above the river the Company built homes for its employees who were to operate and maintain the plant. The Company had kept the houses in good repair, and some 50 years later. Edison employees were still living in these same houses.

Also part of the K. R. 3 complex was a school built for the children living in that part of the Valley. Some were children of Edison employees who either lived in Headquarters Camp or in the homes built above the plant. Others included the Diltz children who lived on the Gilbert Ranch adjacent to where the Standard Oil Bulk Plant in Kernville was later built. There was no bus system for the schools in those days. Children either walked or rode horseback to school. In the case of

Johnny and Betsy Burlando start for school.

The swinging bridge across the Kern River just above the powerhouse, and the Burlando children crossing the bridge on their way to school.

Edison Camp at Caliente, 1920. It was here that all the materials for the K. R. 3 job were unloaded from the train and loaded on a fleet of trucks. *Upper left* is the generator building set into the hill. *To the right* of this is the garage where a crew of mechanics kept the Mack trucks and other vehicles used for the job in running condition. Above the third building which was used for storage of materials can be seen the A-frame that unloaded the large sections of pipe to be used for the siphon and penstocks from the flat cars and on to the trucks. The last building, *at top*, was used to store cement after it was unloaded from the railroad. Long building that runs into the trees was the cookhouse with the office to the left of it. A number of small bunkhouses for the men made up the rest of the camp. *At the far right* are some of the buildings of the northeast part of town.

K. R. No. 3 School about 1922. *Back row*—Edith Schuetze, Betsy Burlando, Zetta Garris, Gloria Kemmer. *Front row* — Johnny Ridgeway, Johnny Burlando, Dick Price, and Johnny Price.

Two of the Edison Company's Holt 75 Caterpillars tow a 25-ton generator section to the K. R. 3 job. This load was too heavy for the bridges, so the South Fork of the Kern River was forded at Old Isabella and the generator was towed up through the river-bottom to the job site. Date is Nov. 1920.

Southern California Edison Company Photo.

Hoist that pulled cars loaded with material for the forebay and penstocks. The flat along the river is the site of the Lazy River Lodge Motel.

tedly the milk was not quite as pure as when it had left the cow.

The site of the old school can easily be relocated by three large evergreen trees growing along the lower road into the power plant. Beside these trees on the spot the school once stood, the State Fish and Game built a garage for their uppermost dwelling. These trees date back to Arbor Day, 1922. On that day, three of the K. R. 3 students were given the honor of each planting a tree in front of the school. One of these was Johnny Price, then only a lad of seven. Johnny had heard somewhere that if you cut the top out of a tree when it is small it would branch out and make a bigger tree. Well, Johnny wanted his tree to be the biggest, so he borrowed a coping saw from the school woodworking set and proceeded to crop the top. He remembered receiving a pretty good whipping for it, but admitted that this was a regular occurrence for him in those days. Young Price's tree— the one on the east end—was different from the other two. It spread out while the others grew straight and tall. Then in the early 1970s, the tree on the west end also had to be topped. It kind of spoiled the story, but you can still tell which was Johnny's tree.

As soon as the major portion of the powerhouse was constructed, the forebay and penstocks were constructed. A hoist that pulled cars loaded with materials and supplies, located one-half mile above the plant, played a big part in this phase of construction. Another big job was the installation of the inverted syphon that connected tunnels 23 and 24 across Cannell Creek.

The hub of Edison's K. R. 3 job was located one-half mile above the town of Riverkern and was known as Headquarters Camp. The U. S. Forest Service later built a campground there, keeping the same site name for their campground.

Although most of the people who worked on the K. R. 3 project have since passed away, some still remain. Without question, the success of the Southern California Edison Company throughout California has been due mainly to the quality of its leaders and employees. Their operation on the Kern River is no exception.

Some of these outstanding employees worked on the Kern River only a short time. Such was the case of Edward R. Meyers, as he only worked on the K. R. 3 project for two years. Stationed at Headquarters Camp, he was first paymaster and later chief accountant. Meyers had joined the

the Matt Burlando children, they rode burros to school. They would travel up canyon about a mile above their father's ranch and cross the river on a suspension bridge the Company had built just above the powerhouse. Each day when the Burlando children came to school they delivered milk to many of the Edison employees. Although it was not pasteurized or homogenized, the milk certainly was well mixed by time of delivery. Several times there were accidents that caused the milk to be spilt, but luckily it spilled into the pack boxes. Most of the spillage was saved, although admit-

Company in 1913 and progressed to chief accountant for the entire Edison Company, the job he held when he retired in 1948 after 35 years of service. In 1972, Meyers returned to the Valley with his daughters and Mr. and Mrs. Emmett Barry. They walked over the old construction site, recalling the many friends and good times of 53 years ago. He reminisced about marrying and coming to the K. R. 3 job in 1913, and about the Company building them a home on Cannell Creek. He talked of learning to drive on mountain roads that were little more than cow paths. His first attempt to drive was made downriver from Camp 8 (now Road's End) alone. Driving off the road twice, he had to wait a while until a crew of men came along to push the car back onto the road. He also reminisced about jumping into one of the Company's Fords in the evenings and driving over dirt roads to take hot baths at the natural mineral springs in Bathhouse Canyon just east of the present Kernville airport.

Another young couple who were living in Headquarters Camp at the time were Ross and Meliss Trumbull. The Trumbulls were among the first to move into the Edison Company's Headquarters Camp in August of 1918. It was there they lived when their son, Kern, was born in May 1919, and named for the river that ran past their doorway. Ross had come to the Valley as an electrician for the Edison Company. When the K. R. No. 3 plant was finished, he and Meliss moved into one of the homes the Company had just completed on the hill near the power plant. They lived there until 1937, when they moved to Old Kernville. Other Edison employees who worked for a long time on the Kern River were Jack Price, Harvey

A crew does it the hard way as they open up one of the adits on the K. R. 3 job. Date is September 1914.
Southern California Edison Company Photo.

Malone, Howard Fulton, Elmer Bond, and Al Apalatea.

While the men working for the Edison Company have contributed much to the Valley through the years, many of the Edison wives, too, have carried more than their share of community and civic jobs. Meliss Trumbull was an outstanding example of one of these women. Formerly an Illinois schoolteacher, she was honored in 1965 by the Kern River Valley Business and Professional Women's Club as one of their charter members, being the Woman of the Year. The *Bakersfield Californian*, for which she had acted as correspondent for several years, carried the story of the dinner where friends and well-wishers gathered to pay tribute to a woman who has served the Valley for almost 50 years.

Some of her accomplishments include serving as clerk of the North Fork School Board until it consolidated with the Kernville School to become the Kernville Union Elementary School District. She was a member of the Kernville Rebekah Lodge, a past Noble Grand, and served as financial secretary to the order for 30 years. She also was a charter member of the Past Noble Grands Association and had served that organization as president and secretary on a number of occasions. In addition, she was past District Deputy President of the Rebekah Assembly of California. A member of the South Fork Women's Club for over 40 years, she served as president, secretary, treasurer, and parliamentarian. A charter member of the Wofford Heights Chamber of Commerce, Meliss was a past president of this organization and served many years as its secretary. She was

Men work on the drills at heading of lower 21 above Camp 2 on the K. R. 3 job.
Southern California Edison Company Photo.

General view of Camp 2. November 10, 1915.

Southern California Edison Company Photo.

the first librarian of the Wofford Heights Branch Library and was the first inspector named to the Wofford Heights precinct election board. Meliss held various offices in her many years with the Kern River Valley Business and Professional Women's Club. She served as director and secretary of the Kern River Valley Chamber of Commerce and, also, was director of the Kern River Valley Community Chest. For all of the organizations she has served as entertainment and public relations chairman at various times. She was clerk of the Kern River Valley Cemetery District 18 years, a job she held until 1972.

Others who lived or worked at Headquarters Camp in 1919 and still living in the Valley in 1973 were Merle Hight, Ethel Kerr, Bert James, and Elmo and Esther Day. Elmo had gone to work for the Company in 1915 at Borel, and in 1919 he transferred to K. R. 3 as maintenance line boss. The Days were newlyweds when they came to K. R. 3, and their home was one of those that stood on the east side of Yellow Jacket Mountain, above the cookhouse.

The Edison Company built the first buildings at their Headquarters Camp in 1915. There were a number of bunkhouses, and along the bank that dropped off to the river were the camp office, the commissary, and furthest downriver, the cookhouse.

An interesting story was related about the Chinese cook who plied his culinary skills there along the Kern. The Bulldog Mack trucks were starting to replace the jerk-line teams to haul from the railhead at Caliente, and a fleet of these trucks with hard rubber tires had pulled into the Head-

quarters Camp after the dinner hour. With a cook's traditional stubbornness, the Chinaman refused to feed the truck drivers because they had not arrived in time for dinner. A truck driver who was an even match for the cook backed his Mack truck against the corner of the cookhouse and told the cook to trot out the grub or he would find his cookhouse in the river. As the timbers started to creak, the cook, with his pigtail popping, hurriedly set out a feast fit for a king.

Adit L21-W22 was one of the first tunnels opened, and a camp (Camp 2) was set up on Cannell Creek, then called Little Brush Creek. One of the local citizens who worked in the tunnels out of Camp 2 was Roswell Tibbetts, and he and his wife, Edith, first set up housekeeping in this camp after being married in 1915.

In 1915, the Edison Company also had a construction camp known as Camp 3. With a crew working steadily through adit 20, by 1919 the work was completed and the camp closed down. But the name Camp 3 stuck, and the Forest Service used the site name for a campground later located there.

In the same year up the highway from Camp 3, the Company built a hospital. Although they removed the buildings in 1921 when the K. R. 3 project was completed, that spot along the river retained the name Hospital Flat and was again used by the Forest Service when they located a campground there.

One day when Merle Hight was going up the road past the Hospital in the Candy Wagon—a truck he drove to make daily deliveries between camps—he glanced over at the Hospital at just

Taken in Headquarters Camp, January 10, 1915. Overlooking the river *to the left* are the cookhouse where the Chinese cook plied his trade, the commissary, and *to the right* the job office.

Southern California Edison Company Photo.

Home of Lewis Schuetze, first chief of the K. R. 3 powerhouse, located in the Headquarters Camp.

the moment the Edison doctor lifted a man's leg out the window onto the porch. The patient had been hurt in a blasting accident and had to have his leg amputated above the knee. Dr. Smith, a longtime Kernville physician, visited the Edison Hospital regularly after the Company doctor transferred back to the Big Creek job.

A mile upriver from Hospital Flat, the road that went to Camp 4 turns sharply to the right. It takes a country vehicle to negotiate the steep, rocky road. As you get to the first hairpin turn, you can see portions of the old Edison road that until 1936 was the only road up canyon. As you continue, and just before you get to the end of the right fork of this road, you will find the remains of Camp 4. All that is left are a few chunks of concrete, the pit where the air compressor house sat, and the remnants of the monument that sat in front of the Camp Superintendent's office. Tunnel Upper 20 had been excavated to the depth of 80 feet by hand before the actual opening of Camp 4 in 1919. The men drove back and forth from Camp 3 each day. When Camp 4 opened, young Bruce Mills, son of Captain Mills,

Some of the Edison Company old-timers of the Kern River, taken in April of 1951. *Left to right,* Joe Strain, Ben Werth, Mr. Stavert, Clayton Landry, Luther Godby, and Sedrick Hackley. At this time, **all these men had their 25-year pins.**

All that remained of the Edison Headquarters Camp in 1974 was the chimney of Captain Mills' home. Captain Mills was in charge of the major part of the construction of K. R. 3 project. It was to this home that Mrs. Mills would invite the other ladies of the camp for tea. A high point of their week.

boss of the entire K. R. 3 project, was placed in charge of the Camp.

There was a variety of other work to be completed from Camps 4 and 5, as an open cut had to be made with teams and scrapers, which was later formed in, lined, and roofed with concrete. A flume also had to be constructed over Corral Creek, and a good sized camp was established at Camp 5. Rettinger, who later became chief engineer on the Big Creek Project, directed operations here. The home Edison Company built him was left intact when they dismantled Camp 5. It was set up as part of a special use permit, and in 1973 was still leased by Stan and Joan Whitesides. This spot along Corral Creek is far enough from the

Edison Company hospital at what was later the
U.S.F.S. Hospital Flat Campground. Taken in 1915.
Southern California Edison Company Photo.

Edison Company Camp 4.

main stream of traffic that the peace and quiet has
not been affected by the increasing influx of
recreationists to the upper Kern each year.

There were several small shoestring camps set
up where the adits daylighted, but the next major
camp was Camp 6. Setting just east of Salmon
Creek, the old camp site can be reached by driving up a mile of dirt road. Portions of this road
follow the old original route that Edison built.

The main thing remembered about Camp 6 by
Merle Hight was the cook. One day, as he was
making his daily round of the camps, Merle
stepped into the cookhouse just as a big heavy
crockery cup hit the doorframe by his head. He
had already shut the door and was moving inside
when a steady stream of the heavy projectiles
started coming his way. He said he was under the
table and all over the cookhouse trying to keep
from getting clobbered. As Merle put it, if any
one of the two dozen heavy cups would have hit
him in the head, they could have killed him. All at
once the onslaught ceased as abruptly as it had
started. The cook roared with laughter. It seemed
there was no reason for the attack except the cook
had drank too much of his own home-brew. Every
time he ordered a new load of staple goods, he
put a large amount of Green Gage plums on order.
They were shipped in small crocks with a seal on
the top, and were the main ingredient for the
cook's potent brew. Merle said he was expected to
haul a supply of this White Lightning to the cook's
friends down at the Headquarters Camp.

During construction there was a bridge over
Salmon Creek just north of Camp 6 and the road
continued around to Camp 7½. Here again, not
much remained in 1973 to even give a hint of the

large camp that was located there over a half
century ago. A hole dug in the mountain, used as
a powder magazine, the cement foundation for the
air compressor, and miscellaneous camp midden—
such as broken glass and bent, rusty metal—repre-
sents the few remains.

After the Edison road left Camp 7½, it went
through what was later called Calkins Flat,
around a sharp, rocky bend, and on upriver. Located on the little flat, which láter became Road's
End, was the Edison Company's Camp 8, the uppermost of their camps along the river. The Edison Company had a camp set up there since 1910.
It served not only the men who worked on the
upper tunnels but also the crew who constructed
the intake.

Construction of the intake started in 1914, but
went rather slowly until 1918. At that time the
rate of progress picked up, and the intake, with
headgates for controlling the flow of water into
the tunnel and traps for collecting and flushing
sand out before it went into the tunnel system,
were completed.

The Edison Company built a dwelling across
the road from the intake. One of the first couples
to live there was Billy and Ava James, as Billy was
the caretaker. Ted and Lila Lofberg were the
last.

Edison Company Camp 5.

Edison Company Camp 7½.
Southern California Edison Company Photo.

Edison Company Camp 6. To the far left is the cook-house where the cook made the home brew out of Green Gage plums.
Southern California Edison Company Photo.

A home was also constructed across the river and below the intake in 1921. This structure was built in part with form lumber and timbers used on the intake. In 1973, Skeets and Mildred Byers, who operated the Road's End Store for years, still made this their residence.

Although K. R. 4 and K. R. 5 that were planned on the upper Kern never materialized, two additional plants were built in the Edison Company system later; Portal at Bishp in 1956; Mammoth Pool on the San Joaquin in 1960.

Since World War II the Edison Company has grown to become the fourth largest operating electric utility company in the United States. In 1964 came the merger with the California Electric Power Company which more than doubled the area of its service territory. At the end of 1971 the Southern California Edison Company was an enterprise of 112,831 employees, having shareholders numbering 144,252, a total utility plant investment of four billion dollars, and serving over 7.3 million people in an area of 50,000 square miles. Operating capacity in 1972 totaled over 12.5 million kilowatts.

After almost 70 years in the Kern River Valley, the canals, dams, and powerhouses seem to blend into the scenery and have become an important part of the colorful history of the area. Notwithstanding, the financial support and stability that the Edison Company has contributed to Kern County and the Valley as a whole down through the years is unequaled. The most outstanding contribution, though, has been and will continue to be the civic help and friendship extended from its employees to their neighbors in the Valley.

J. K. Horton, president of the Southern California Edison Company in the 1960s and '70s. Chairman of the board in 1973.
Southern California Edison Company Photo.

Edison Company Camp 8, later Road's End.
Southern California Edison Company Photo.

101

Edison Company's First Lady

Lila McKinley Lofberg, Edison Company's first lady. Taken in the 1920s.

THE KERN RIVER VALLEY has had more than its share of unusual people. They will long live in the memory of their Valley neighbors and those countless thousands who came in contact with them, if only briefly.

One of those most loved and best remembered was Lila Lofberg. Lila McKinley Lofberg came to the Kern River in the early 1920s as a feature writer for the *Los Angeles Times.* Having become disenchanted with the hustle and bustle of city living, she had already decided to stay in the Valley prior to meeting Ted, her future spouse. He was at that time employed as an engineer for the Southern California Edison Company during the construction of their K. R. 3 hydroelectric plant.

Ted and Lila were married while he was working on the Kern River; and after a time there, he was transferred to the Company's Big Creek hydroelectric plant.

It was during their first year at Big Creek that Lila became the Camp 62 Librarian—the only woman in a camp of 300 men. It was here that she earned the love and respect of those men, as she never knew a stranger. Meeting someone for the second time, she was apt to greet him with a big hug if he had met with her approval. And most did, as she looked for good in everyone. She and Ted had a host of friends among Edison and Forest Service employees who stopped by the intake to see them, and later to see Lila after Ted had passed away. She would counteract a bit of idle gossip concerning someone with something nice about that person. Erina Hackley once asked Lila how old she would have to be before she would be able to kiss the men the way Lila did.

Ted Lofberg was himself an unusual person, although he was almost overshadowed by his wife. Christened Algot Theordore Lofberg, he was raised in Sweden. His family was of the ruling class in that country and he received a superior education, which included learning to speak and write seven languages—Swedish, Spanish, French, Italian, Portuguese, German, and English.

Edison Intake during construction, 1918, looking downriver. Large rocks in the middle of river are now right below intake dam and fish ladder. Small shed, *far left*, was still there in 1973.
Southern California Edison Company Photo.

Ted, who many people called the Count, not quite fitting into the mold of Swedish aristocracy, was more or less the black sheep in the family. As a boy, he sailed away from Sweden on a small fishing boat bound for the North Sea, then on around the world. Only at the insistence of his parents did he enter as a cadet into the Swedish "West Point." He graduated, but overstayed his leave of absence in South Africa when he decided to fight with the Boers against England. He fought in the Mexican Revolution, becoming a lieutenant colonel in the Mexican army, and had many stories to tell about Pancho Villa. He was present with Diaz, long-time Mexican president, when he gave his farewell message and could quote it word for word in Spanish. It was said to be most touching.

Ted's sterling character, coupled with his great love for nature and wild creatures, served to nurture the very best in his mate. The most exciting period of Lila's life began when she and Ted spent the winters of 1926-28 at the intake of Florence Lake. It was here that Lila first had the opportunity to get close to nature and start her studies that continued for the next forty years. Her knowledge of wild animals and birds was respected by naturalists and researchers. Walt Disney studio experts consulted her about material to be included in several Disney nature pictures.

The eleven years spent at Florence Lake enabled Lila to collect material used in her book, Sierra Outpost, a truly outstanding work. One of the stories she relates is about two coyotes, Tom and Jerry, who became pets, though they were never caught or caged.

While at Florence Lake in 1928, Lila gave a report on bird banding for the Condor, a bi-monthly magazine of western ornithology, which was carried in the September-October issue. Although the report is too long to cover in its entirety, this excerpt will give an insight into Lila's patient study of birds that came to visit her home.

One of the birds she reported on was the Blue-fronted Steller Jay. The Lofbergs had a jay named J. J. that they had raised and which stayed with them as a domestic pet. Therefore, Lila had an excellent chance to learn the habits of this species. It was well-known that jays hid their food, and the Lofberg's experiments with J. J. proved that they remembered where they hid it by later returning. Their records also show that they were decidedly clever about a trap. If the doors are fastened open

with the treadle in place, they go in and out quite unconcernedly. But when one set the trap, the jays would stand just outside, reach over the treadle, and get the bait without springing the trap. They found that during the nesting season the jays seem to get careless and get caught. But even then, "once but not twice" seemed to be the motto of the adults, for they were never caught the second time.

Lila found that a jay will handle scraps of food many times—they would carry the smaller pieces next to their throat and the largest on the very end of their bill. Lila told of J. J. once taking 78 grains of her scratch feed, including some sunflower seeds, which he always selected first, into his mouth. When he was loaded up he proceeded to hide a few here and there all over the yard. She could never determine how he was able to hold so many. If she held sunflower seeds in her hand, he would take them one at a time. After he cracked them he would drop them back into her hand, eat the kernel, then flip the hull out of her hand before doing the same to the next seed.

She also noted many interesting habits of the birds they fed, such as the way the Cabanis Hairy Woodpeckers would maneuver. If other birds were on the table, they would seem to be intent on examining every inch of the bark on the fence, when in reality they were only biding their turn at the table. She told of how the Brewer Blackbirds would dip a large, hard crust of bread in water, then after eating the softened portion, they would douse it again and again until they had eaten the last crumb.

These birds were fed each winter by the Lofbergs, who stocked provisions before they were snowbound. They purchased at least 700 pounds of stale bread at two cents per pound from a Fresno bakery, as well as laying in gunny sacks full of peanuts and suet. Their supplies had to last at least eight months.

While Ted and Lila were at Florence Lake they discovered many of nature's secrets. This was not only because they had taken the time to observe the countless happenings around them day and night, but was also due to extreme patience in gaining the trust and confidence of their furred and feathered friends.

They had been told that the common housefly would be a real problem at certain times of the year. Then they found the answer when Lila discovered that hornets destroyed the larvae that hatched from the fly eggs. The same proved true in controlling the ants that swarmed in the house at times. Lila observed that a lizard, who had taken up a homestead in their yard, relished the very ants they were trying to control. A study brought to light that lizards love milk, so the Lofbergs set tins of diluted condensed milk around the yard. Soon a whole colony of lizards were controlling the ant problem.

Both at Florence Lake and the intake on the Kern River, the Lofbergs were never without their "house skunks." While never de-scented, they were well-mannered and not once forgot they were among friends and let fly with their objectionable spray. They were kept for company, and because they were such terrific mousers. When a skunk killed a mother mouse, Lila raised her baby. She said the little one had run from the cold ground to her open palm for warmth, and she could do no less than raise it. She likened this little white-footed mouse to a fairy, and it learned to come running up her dress and perch on her hand to sleep.

While at Florence Lake their pets included Charlie, the woodchuck. Ted had killed his mate thinking she was attacking the chickens. Ground squirrels had to be controlled or they would have taken over the place. But, Ted spared one who gained the name of "Pop" and soon became a part of the family.

In 1936, after nine years at Florence Lake, the Lofbergs transferred back to the Kern River. They had their home at the intake, a mile above Pascoe's Lodge. When the government decided to give this little settlement a post office, Washington chose Lila's suggestion of the three or four sent in. It became Road's End, California.

They found life at Road's End to be easy and without hazard. In the morning they did not have to shovel the snow from the door, and they soon found that the jumble of rocks and digger pines that seemed so scraggly at first can be lovely in the rain.

On her drives to Kernville the first spring, Lila was able to identify one hundred and eight varieties of blooming wildflowers.

The altitude was lower and the natural food for birds was plentiful. Lila's first year's migration reports listed twice as many varieties as for all the years at Florence Lake. They also found the birds on the Kern River to be brighter, more gaily colored, and that they had sweeter songs.

Lila and Ted Lofberg in front of their home on the Kern River that was formerly the Hazel Dean cabin.

After Ted's retirement, for some years the Lofberg's home was a cabin by the river, some eight miles below Old Kernville. This cabin was built in the late 1920s by Hazel Dean, queen of western movies. While Miss Dean was on location in the Kern River Valley she found a spot with a white, sandy beach along the river. It was completely surrounded by bull pines and was the type of secluded location she was looking for to build a retreat. She purchased the property from Irven Wofford and had a house built on it with a wide veranda spanning the entire front. On this porch many a summer evening was enjoyed as cowboys, real and make-believe, strummed on guitars and danced or swam with cowgirls and extras. When the weather was cooler, they gathered around a roaring fire in the big fireplace.

Before long the attractive owner married and moved away, leaving the house deserted during the depression years. Finally, during World War II, the Lofbergs found it and decided it would be just the right place for Lila's uninterrupted writing.

Movie companies soon discovered the photographic value of the house and, with the Lofberg's permission, constructed a wishing well near the house and a rail fence around it. A hitching post was also added. For some time the cabin was used by several motion picture companies. It was here that screen cowboys rode up in a cloud of dust, while fugitives hid in nearby ambush. Such famous horses as Silver and Trigger were tied to the hitching rail.

When word came that this property, along with the towns of Old Kernville and Isabella, must be vacated due to inundation following the construction of Lake Isabella Dam, the Lofbergs reluctantly sold to the government and moved away. The house was then occupied by one of the U. S. Army engineers and his family. In the fall of 1950, the Kern River in flood stage all but washed the house away. But as houses were scarce it was repaired and again occupied.

After the dam was completed the old house was put up for sale by bid and sold to John Stine. With a great deal of trouble, Mr. Stine moved it the ten miles to what was then called New Kernville. It was given an exterior coat of stucco, a new fireplace was built, and the front porch was replaced with a smaller rock faced one. With all this and a new roof, one could hardly recognize the old cabin. This home was still occupied by John Stine at 318 Sirretta Street in 1972.

It was at their Road's End home that so many friends came to visit, and it was especially interesting in the evening when the patio lights went on and the wild creatures came to feed. The animals accepted any visitor as a mutual friend and anyone could hand feed dried dates to Helen, the ring-tailed cat. Lila had two raccoons brought to her as babies by two boys from the South Fork. These raccoons were her house guest for years, and would amuse visitors for hours.

Of equal interest is the story of a baby humming bird that Lila raised that would at times ride downriver to Kernville perched on her shoulder. Mrs. Parr, mother of Florence Pascoe, gave her the little bird, and the following is the account from the *Sierra Outpost*:

Mrs. Parr found the featherless mite sprawled on the porch, in July, seven days after the two pearl humming-bird eggs had hatched in a nest of plant fibers and spider web. One side of the nest had broken away from the supporting vine. The stronger twin crowded the weaker brother out of the tipsy cradle.

Mrs. Parr climbed on a chair and put him back in the nest. The next morning down he came tumbling again. She put him in an empty nest in a rose bush. The parents did not respond to the baby's feeble calls. She did not know what to do. Our reputation with the animals had preceded us into Kernville, so she came to me.

Six hours had elapsed since the parents had last fed the baby. His nude body was cold. I tapped his bill and it opened slightly. We clipped the three-pronged rose twig and carried the cradle into her house.

It took but a moment to mix a solution that my outdoor hummers like in their feeders: a teaspoonful of honey in a cup of water. Carefully the baby's soft needle bill was opened and with a medicine dropper I put a drop into his throat. His head slipped and

hung limply at the nest's rim. He tried feebly to jerk it back. I rested his head against the slanting twig and gave him another drop. In a few minutes Parrbaby opened his bill and eyes.

For a quarter of an hour we hovered over him, giving him a drop at a time until his transparent crop stood out on his neck like a bead on a bit of twine.

We fastened the nest twig with a safety pin to the car seat. The bumpy eighteen miles home were endless. Every five miles I used the medicine dropper and the jelly-glass supply wedged in my lap.

"Only parent hummers can raise their young," said Ted. I had read it, too, and feared that he was right. But I kept up the five-minute feedings all evening and Parrbaby gained in alertness. I let myself hope.

Ted and I had raised other fledglings and felt no need to feed them during the night, but Parrbaby was weakened from his fast. Every half hour that first night I got up and fed him and made sure his flannel blanket was tucked about him. Next morning Ted, too, felt there was hope.

His bill opened wide when I reached for the dropper. He took what he wanted, and when he grew hungry again he squeaked. These squeaks showed that ten-minute feedings were proper. Already Parrbaby knew that this huge gray-haired thing had taken the place of his exquisite mother. From his first day of adoption Parrbaby began teaching us the way of his kind. We were willing pupils who learned more from him about humming birds than it is possible to observe from those outdoors.

We needed a feeding formula close to the diet the parents would have supplied. We had watched them snatching gnats out of the air. If hummers feed their young by regurgitation, the youngsters no doubt get gnats with their nectar. That evening I put a light globe outside the screen of the sleeping porch and caught gnats to put into a small bottle holding a day's supply of nectar.

On the third day insect fare was drawn into the dropper and put into Parrbaby's mouth. All that day he did nothing but eat, sleep, and grow wings. When he had fallen on Mrs. Parr's porch his only covering was wisps of fuzz. Now this was turning into wing feathers.

The small bottle held a little more nectar than Parrbaby could take in one day. What was left over fermented in the sun, and from this sour bottle Parrbaby received one breakfast and one supper every day, on the theory that food from the mother's stomach must become a little fermented. He refused solid foods on which other foundlings had thrived. Only by mixing a few drops of raw egg yolk or raw liver juice in his sweet nectar could I give him these added vitamins.

To make sure that infant birds have a proper diet, the foster parent must watch the telltale droppings.

*Reprinted from the author's *Sierra Outpost*, © 1941 by Lila Lofberg and David Malcomson.

For this purpose and to keep his nest clean, I lined the downy cradle with cleaning tissue. His sheets remained spotless. Some young birds are able to keep their own nests clean by expelling their droppings over the rim. All through Parrbaby's second and third day with us, that table top remained immaculate.

On the fourth day I wondered if a drop of castor oil added to his nectar bottle would kill him. The dust mop pushing on the floor boards beyond the rug, struck a gummy spot. This might be the answer. I sat down to watch the sleeping infant.

In perhaps five minutes his head lolled and was jerked backward until the tip of his bill jabbed against the bottom of the nest. Then he managed to rear up and expel a drop with such force that it fell in a wide arc, clearing nest and table and the rug under the table. At last I could be sure that Parrbaby was getting proper food.

That afternoon he turned part way in his nest and wriggled forward as though trying to perch on the rim. His head, as big as a hazelnut kernel, was too heavy for his inch-long string neck. He fell back and napped and tried again. By evening he drew up his heavy head and rested it between his shoulders and he got up and balanced himself on the nest rim.

Fuzz was making a tail. Each wing was half an inch long. His body was still bare. Shakily he moved his wings up and down. Then he squeaked for the medicine dropper, a squeak that could be heard all over the house.

All that fourth day we no longer expected to find Parrbaby dead at any moment. He had doubled in size. His wings seemed to lengthen before our eyes. The fifth day there was fuzz on his head and upper body, and his rubber bill and legs hardened. He climbed to the rim of his nest and moved his wings up and down for five minutes at a time.

I could turn the nest upside down without dislodging him. When I wanted to change the tissue, I had to loosen needle claws one at a time. We learned from Parrbaby that humming birds' feet are not made to walk on. Tiny curved clams cling tightly to perches but forever prevent humming birds from standing flatfooted.

A week after we brought Parrbaby home, when he was two weeks old, he was far from beautiful but looking more like a bird than a beetle. His wings, practically full-grown, and his three-quarters tail, were greenish black. The top of his head and his upper body were covered with metallic green down, with a bronze overlay.

Parrbaby experimented with the beat of his wings, moving them rapidly in the way that enables hummers to suspend themselves in air or to fly backwards. He learned to control his heavy head. The inner nest wall interfered with his wing tips. He taxied along the rim to a horizontal twig which extended well beyond the nest. Perched on that twig he whirred without losing balance, without tiring.

I watched his wings pull him from his perch and let him down to the table top. On the flat surface he could not keep himself right side up. Soon he was helpless on his back, until I lifted him to his perch.

If he had flown from an outside nest, he would have dropped from that twig to a lower twig, not to a flat surface, and carried on his exercises until he could fly up as well as down.

Parrbaby was again vibrating his wings. They pulled him off the twig and gently he settled to the table top. I lifted him to my left palm. When he was ready I tilted my hand. He slid down the palm, his wings whirred, and he flew safely to my right palm, two inches below. A moment later I poured him from my right palm to the landing field of my left. Parrbaby thoroughly enjoyed this game. After a feeding he was fluttering downward with confidence when my hands were two feet apart. That evening he shot forward several feet before gliding to the floor.

The next morning, July sixteenth, I came in from the garden at five-thirty to give Parrbaby his first breakfast. He was not under his blanket.

"Where is my Parrbaby?"

His answering squeaks seemed to come from above. Not believing my ears I vainly searched on hands and knees.

He was clinging to the top of a window drape. From his nest he had covered a distance of twenty-five feet. He buzzed down from the drape to light on an outstretched finger. After his feeding his flights became a new worry. Other adopted birds had banged against windowpanes, furniture, and were not injured only because they flew falteringly. Even Parrbaby's early flights were bullet-like.

I put him in the nest and pinned the blanket down, with an opening for air. Half an hour later Parrbaby was out of his cradle and perched on an inverted light fixture. I could not stay in the house to protect him, so I put him in a small cardboard box with air holes pricked in it. He liked the prison and snuggled into its soft cloth nest during his feeding.

"Let him practice flying on the sleeping porch," Ted suggested after breakfast. "He can hook his claws into the screens, and beds are there to fall on."

Soon we realized that all our house was ideal for the young bird. He knew his way. For two days he made circle flights. He practiced dropping straight down, shooting up, or suspending his body in air. By July eighteenth his flying technique was perfected. From room to room he kept close to the ceiling, dropping only at the last instant before dashing through doorways. When he had the entire house to fly over he could build up the speed that sounded like an airplane.

He tried to reach perches around which his toes could curl. A slight push launched him into the air. If he lighted on a windowsill or a table top he taxied with whirring wings to the edge and dropped a dozen inches before his wings gained speed to support his weight. Sometimes he was forced down on the floor. Then only with great exertion could he taxi and raise himself the few inches necessary to reach the lowest rung of a chair.

He was perpetual motion. When not flying he preened his feathers or pecked at his perch or bobbed his head to see the new world. It was hard to realize that such a lovely animated jewel ten days before had been an inert blob we feared to touch lest his yolk-like body would burst. His head and upper body were covered with metallic green, bronze-meshed. A pink band made a neckless below his yellow chin. His lower parts were dirty white, with a fluff of snow-white below the base of his tail. Only when he extended his head to sip nectar did his bare neck distress us.

The long frail neck which enables hummers to sip from deep-throated flowers apparently cannot support the extended head. I notice birds in our garden using the blossoms to help bear the head burden. Perched or in flight, Parrbaby made a loop of his neck and rested his head between his shoulders.

His daily ration bottle now held four tablespoonfuls of nectar and often that was not enough. I still fed him with a dropper and after he became active, sticky nectar spilled on his feathers. I removed what I could each morning with a bit of wet cotton, but these sponge baths made the little mite look so forlorn that Ted was sure that they would kill him. He soon dried, and the next day his futile attempts to preen gummed feathers made me try again.

Until July twentieth Parrbaby snuggled in his babyhood nest each night to be covered with his woolen blanket. That evening he chose to sleep on an extension cord stretched a few inches below the ceiling. The high perch was partially protected from chilling breezes. For a few nights Parrbaby did not object when I placed a teepee of flannel over him; then he refused my covering.

He still coaxed hand-squeezed feedings and I still caught him his gnats. I suspended half a dozen small flower vases about his sleeping porch, with petunias and nasturtiums that held added drops of nectar. Parrbaby ignored the reinforced posies. When he was hungry he perched on the finger of my left hand and squeaked. Instead of getting his dropper I carried him to the flowers. Instantly his long double-straw tongue dipped into a petunia. He refused to sip from the flowers, however, unless carried to them on a finger, or when I was strong enough to ignore his squeaks for an hour at a time.

Perhaps this was because a dropper held more sweetness than a flower. I prepared him a vial like those hanging outdoors for the wild hummers, a two-inch perfume bottle wrapped in a four-inch square of blue cellophane. I tied the cellophane snugly just below the open mouth and pulled out the blue edges to make it look like a flower. He sipped its plentiful nectar only when I carried him to it on a finger. I changed the cellophane to red with no better results.

In the latter part of July on oriole with a broken wing shared Parrbaby's sleeping porch. Her saucer of fruit attracted flies. My gnat-catching nights were over; Parrbaby whisked tiny insects out of the air. I put a grapefruit shell in front of the west window,

Parrbaby's favorite afternoon spot, and that brought him more flies. Oriole's drinking dish caused Parrbaby's first almost fatal mishap. On the evening of July twenty-seventh I went to the porch to give him his final long sip for the day. He was not on any of his perches.

"Where's my Parrbaby?"

A feeble squeak came from the dish on the floor. Parrbaby was in that half-filled soup plate, his bill and head reaching above the water's surface up the dish's slanting sides. I picked up his cold wet body and wrapped it in my handkerchief. His head hung limply.

"Now he's dead!" Ted exploded. "You shouldn't have had that water bowl on his porch."

How might I warm Parrbaby back to life? My hands were like ice. I slipped him inside my blouse.

After five minutes, tiny claws hooked into my skin as Parrbaby struggled to right himself. A few minutes later he was climbing with scrambling toes and fluttering wings toward my neck, dry and warm. When I perched him on a finger he squeaked for his medicine dropper.

Three days later while I still quaked at the thought of his close call, I went out to mop his porch. I had hardly put down the half-filled pail when he hummed down and skittered across the water like a tiny motor boat. He shot up, grazing the opposite steep barrier and lit on the extension cord. Spray had wet his body, leaving his head and wings dry. He shook off drops, flew to a sunny perch and began preening and fluffing his feathers. Back he dove for another spin across the scrub water, managing to dip his head twice before rising over the bucket wall. A third time he repeated the whole performance.

Next morning I lined up vessels of various sized and depths on the porch floor for him to choose. While I stood guard he paused in mid-air over each. Then he flew up and dropped down to a pottery dish to skim across its two inches of water. Three dips again made his bath routine.

Every hour or so, beginning about 8:30 a.m., Parrbaby had his three-dip bath. After feeding he hovered over the water and washed his bill by jabbing it in. He wiped it dry on the extension cord. Soon he was insisting that his bath dish be placed where the sun would shine on it. When the patch of sunshine had left the dish, the strong-minded imp squeaked and suspended himself over the sunny spot where he had determined his bath should have been. I hurried to move the water to the place he wanted and he dipped into it. And why not? Outdoor hummers have a succession of sun-kissed pools to visit in sequence throughout the day.

Out in the garden other young humming birds would see Parrbaby and hover just outside a screen panel to call him out to play. But Parrbaby cared only for us. When Ted and I approached his porch he was beside himself for joy. He flew madly about until we opened the door and then like a bullet he shot to finger or shoulder, snuggling close to caress us with his bill. He was elated when I left the porch door

107

Lila Lofberg sits at her typewriter. Her unusual book, *Sierra Outpost*, can be seen on her desk.

open and let him fly about the living room with us. Every few muintes he came to perch on Ted or me.

Parrbaby adored riding in the automobile. When I took his deserted nest from its hook, he knew it meant a trip. He snuggled down in its cobwebbed softness and we carried him to the car. No restraining hand need be cupped over him. The last thing he wanted was to fly away. In the car he stayed in his nest and his bright eyes darted this way and that as he took in the sights along the highway.

When he was left at home alone and heard our returning car stop below his porch, he squeaked loudly and flew about anxiously. He never did this for any except the Lofberg motor. However, he was always interested in our guests. Like a pendulum he swung in front of them, inspecting eyeglasses or gaily-flowered gowns, waiting for a finger.

In August the Schellings came to spend ten days, and Parrbaby was spoiled worse than ever. At his first squeak, Mary, Lucille, or Jack would rush up to feed him.

After they had been bullied all week, on a sleepy Sunday morning Parrbaby determined someone must play with him. He woke me at dawn for nectar, buzzing about my face and tapping my eyelids with his bill. After his first feeding he flew to Lucille and tapped her eyelids, buzzing back and forth over her nose. She pretended not to notice. Through the open door he zoomed to disturb Mary and Jack in the same way. With dropper in hand I was trying to coax him to my finger, for it was only a little after five o'clock in the morning. Not until he was hungry again did he light on my finger to have a hand cupped over him and to be carried out to his porch.

I closed the door on him and went back to bed. Parrbaby yelled like a high-pitched banshee. I had to keep him company.

A day or two later, on the August morning picked for the Schelling's departure, a chilling wind was blowing. At dawn Parrbaby did not fly to meet me at the porch door. He was not on his perch. I found him clinging to the top of a screen, sheltered by a two-by-four. The only evidence that the bird was still alive was his tightly hooked claws in the wire. I pried him loose. He was icy cold. I crawled back under warm blankets and held Parrbaby on my chest. For ten minutes he did not stir. The others were moving about in the house. Our guests were to leave immediately after an early breakfast.

It probably would be years before we saw them again. If Parrbaby should die before they left, it would make the parting harder than ever. I tucked his body under my blankets until I could warm some nectar for him and heat small flannel blankets. The others were too busy to notice my quick trips.

"I want to say good-by to Parrbaby," Mary said at breakfast.

"It's chilly today. I think it's best to keep him wrapped up."

Only Ted sensed that something was wrong. He said nothing until the car pulled away. Then he said, "Parrbaby is dying, isn't he?"

"I don't know." We went to the bed. The little fellow had not been thoroughly warmed by changing those blankets. He squeaked faintly for us to feed him. He seemed reluctant to come back to life. With the switch on low, we placed him in the electric oven and stood in front of the open door, watching for the first movement in that small roll of blankets. In about fifteen minutes Parrbaby wriggled out of his cocoon, taxied out of the open oven and was flying all over the house.

"Why should he freeze?" said Ted. "The outdoor hummers don't, and it was colder for them than for him."

What do the outdoor hummers do? Because of Parrbaby we were able to find the answer, though not until the following spring. The hummers returned to our garden on April tenth and found their feeders brimful. Late one evening in mid-April cold rain turned to mushy snowflakes. At dusk a male hummer swung back and forth in front of the living-room window, tapping the pane with his bill. He seemed to want to come inside. I lowered that upper sash but it frightened him. He dashed sharply to the right, close to the wall. I went out hoping to pick him off his cold perch and bring him in the house for the night. The flashlight did not reveal him in the vines. If Parrbaby had never clung to the screen, I would never have thought of examining the object wedged between window frame and a thick branch of Virginia creeper. When I looked closely, the hummer stirred. Should he evade my grasping hand and leave that niche, he might not find another sheltered spot in that dark snowy world to wait for the rising sun to thaw him out.

At dawn the next morning I went out to see if the stranger needed help. His claws held tight when I tried, gently, to lift him from the wall. He was still alive. I had to overcome a temptation to take him back to bed with me to warm him back to consciousness.

It was a brilliant morning and the sun's rays reached him. After a fifteen-minute sunbath he still clung motionless, though he moved slightly when my fingers stroked his back. I made two more trips in quick succession and there was no change. The next time I found him out of the niche, perched on a vine twig where the sun shone without a shadow. Ten minutes later he was hovering over a feeder close by, filled with sun-warmed nectar. It had taken the morning sun slightly over forty-five minutes to bring that body to normal bird activity.

In August there were other cold mornings though not so cold as on the tenth. When the wind was chilly Parrbaby would leave his horizontal perch to cling vertically to the screen with the best east exposure. In the morning I would find him cold but conscious. If I placed a finger under him, he would flutter to it and be fed, but he would not want to play about as on warmer mornings. Instead he returned to cling to the same spot on the wire screen, to remain motionless until well after the sun was up.

The sun would shine directly upon him. It warmed his lethargic body and brought back his vitality. Instinct guided him to this place where the sun would shine in the morning, so that his chill would not last forever.

A month and a half remained until the time when Parrbaby's fellows would fly to Mexico. Should we let him go? He was not one of them! Not after what we had done to him. Or was I being honest? Was I arguing against his release because I did not know what I would do without him?

Parrbaby would need the six or seven weeks to strengthen his wings for the long flight. He had to learn that ordinary flowers do not hold so much nectar as the blossoms on his sleeping porch. We had to take the chance of his forgetting us the moment he found how much fun a humming bird could have outdoors. If all went well he'd come back to our house in spring and still be our friend.

On August eleventh the medicine dropper was put away. We left him alone most of the time, though I spied on him as he took his nectar from the porch flowers. Our absence only made him love us more. When we did go to see him, he hurtled toward us to snuggle against a neck. When we left the porch we had to pry his claws from our skin.

At dusk I would take his feeder vial in my hand and call him from room to room. "Come on, Parrbaby." If he learned his call now and came to me for food, then on lonely evenings when I missed him too much I might call him back from his freedom.

On the morning of August sixteenth, I carried Parrbaby outside, not in the baby nest but perched uncovered on a finger. I sat down at eleven-thirty in the morning on a shaded doorstep knowing that his love for sunshine would force him to desert me. Not for a

quarter of an hour did he launch out into the world for a circle flight of about fifty feet, his first flight out of the house. When he returned I was not in sight. He perched on a sunny twig above the doorstep and squeaked.

His bright eyes found Ted and me watching him through the curtains. He swung back and forth in front of us, squeaking for us to let him in. We ignored him and he returned to his twig. He did not go to the petunia bed across the walk. He was crying, he was hungry, and at twelve-fifteen I had to let him in. He zoomed through the open door and after a long sip washed his bill and went to his window perch. All afternoon Parrbaby was happily forgetting his first chance to go free.

The next morning the door was left open. He played in the streaming sunshine but he did not pass through the doorway. Again I carried him out and he was off for more and greater circle flights. He complained less than on the day before, and found that gnats were to be caught from that twig. Eventually he dropped down to sip from those near-by petunia cups.

Wham! An adult male humming bird who had considered that flower bed his private preserve, shot from the rear of the house and knocked Parrbaby almost to the ground. Before I could save him, Parrbaby regained his balance and was speeding across the road below, a few inches ahead of the indignant pursuer. Both disappeared beyond the Kern River a hundred yards north. I rushed to the river bank, feeder in hand.

"Come on, Parrbaby!" No Parrbaby came. Back at the house the old fellow who had been offended was dipping into his petunias. There seemed to be no question but that he had murdered my Parrbaby.

In half an hour I heard the familiar "Squeak, squeak, let me in!" Parrbaby whizzed triumphantly through the open door to alight on my finger. He had not so much as a broken feather. He had had three hours of exercise and he did not have to stay outside any more that day.

From then on, when I went to the garden at dawn the door was left open. Parrbaby followed me while I moved the sprinklers and pulled weeds. He came and went as he chose. Rarely did he willingly stay outside more than fifteen minutes at a time. He found petunias and nasturtiums not claimed by outdoor hummers. Best of all, he would come speeding from nowhere when I called, "Come on, Parrbaby!"

The young garden hummers, who could not yet claim preserves of their own, tried to make friends with him. He would have nothing to do with them, and I had to admit to a flush of satisfaction. Two of these followed him onto his screened porch. He ignored them when they perched beside him and rubbed their bills against his cheek.

When these two wanted to go out again, they became confused and missed the open door. They rammed against the screen, their bills passing through the mesh and holding them long enough for me to take them in my hands. The first was a male. His

Lila feeds Helen, the ringed-tail cat.

gradually changing coloring was identical with Parr-baby's. The young female was lighter, and her wings and tail, tipped with tiny white dots, were darker than her body. Both of them had necks as bare as Parrbaby's. We can always distinguish the young from the adults now by the bare necks.

On the evening of August twenty-sixth, I left Parr-baby whizzing about his porch while I went the mile down the road to the post office. The sun had set and he was left closed in the house. Ted had gone for a long walk.

When I climbed the steps Parrbaby squeaked his usual "Welcome home!" Before going to his porch I sat down to read a letter.

About fifteen minutes later it was dark. I switched on the light. Parrbaby was not on the twig under his small flannel teepee. He was not on any of his perches.

"Where is my Parrbaby?"

There was no answering squeak. Parrbaby lay submerged in his bathtub.

Had I not stopped to read that letter, this would never have happened. Parrbaby had expected me to come through the door and had flown wildly about, waiting to perch on my shoulders. The activity had made him thirsty, so when I did not come he dropped down nervously for a sip of water. It was dusk. He misjudged in his excitement the hovering distance above the water. His soaked wings stopped whirring.

And all the time I was in the next room, unaware, reading my letter. He had no strong legs to carry him out, head high. He did not even reach the edge of that bathtub he had used so often before.

This time there was no warming back a spark of life. For an hour he lay close to my heart before I abandoned hope.

Such a wee thing to leave behind such a void!

One evening a friend named Warren Wood brought a pet that was by far the most unusual one the Lofbergs were to ever own. This was Ansel, a month-old horned owl, named for Ansel Dotters, a logger who rescued him. He was described by Lila as being a football of yellowish fluff with huge, miraculous blue eyes. His first meal was about a half-pound of hamburger. Although Ansel, like all wild birds, disapproved of any human hands closing around his body, within three or four days he had accepted the Lofbergs wholeheartedly and proved to be the most adorable baby they had ever raised.

Lila bought half pound samples of everything in the butcher shop and Ansel soon showed his preference for liver or kidney. At the same time, they purchased several mouse traps and when Ted brought him his first mouse it was a sight to behold. He tried to stand on his wobbly legs, chattering "gimmee, gimmee, gimmee," his elations being that of a child over a new toy.

In five weeks, Ansel went from a roly-poly, three-inch ball of fluff to a bird with bones as big as a grown Plymouth Rock chicken, but he was very thin, and his legs were still useless. Ted insisted that Ansel was on the wrong diet and Lila decided that he might need sunlight. This started the owl's daily sunbath which he seemed to enjoy immensely. He would sprawl on the ground with wings wide spread, exposing first one side, then the other, until his white skin turned pink. He would then sit up to preen for awhile before shuffling to a shaded spot, picking up bugs and gravel enroute. However, neither the sun's rays nor the bugs stiffened his legs.

Ansel started moving his wings before he could handle his feet. Sitting on the arm of Lila's sea-grass chair, the young owl first started to flap his long wings, making the Lofbergs realize why he started with his wings first. He braced himself upright with the tips of his wings when he tried to walk. The Lofbergs used these weeks to their best advantage, knowing that this was the time to gain his complete trust before the young bird would use his wings to carry him out of reach. Wild birds, even when young and helpless, resent being held; however, they will voluntarily perch on a finger and enjoy riding from one place to another even after they become free adults. Fingers being too small a perch for a horned owl, the Lofbergs offered their wrists and this style of riding soon completely intrigued Ansel.

A few yards east of the Lofberg's house was Packsaddle Canyon, its rim topped by a succession of narrow stairstepped flower beds. These proved just right for Ansel's first flying lesson. When Lila went at dawn to water their garden, Ansel rode on her wrist to the lowest flower bed. With head weaving and ducking he waddled back and forth until he found the proper takeoff for insufficient winds to take him to the next higher goal. Arriving at the other end of their outdoor nook, he would turn and practice flying downstairs, a step at a time. It would take about an hour for him to make this 120 foot round-trip, but he practiced until he knew the exact spot from which to take off from the curved path to reach goals of one to eight feet above the ground.

At dusk Ansel waddled around to the front doorstep where he mutely waited to be invited inside. Even after his wings could carry him across the canyon or lift him to the housetop, he never failed to join them at dusk.

Lila and Ted often thought Ansel's I.Q. was almost zero, but they later came to the conclusion that every seemingly moronic action had reason behind it. Watching Ansel go about life in his calm, unhurried way made the Lofbergs wonder if this fact might attribute to horned owls being exceptionally long-lived for birds. He wasted neither time nor energy on a single useless activity and, as soon as he could confidently take off and be able to reach a goal, he did not care whether he could fly across the canyon or not.

At first the Lofbergs were a little concerned that Ansel's predatory instincts might prove harmful to their voluntary house guests such as the ring-tailed cats. But as none of their furred guests had disappeared since he became completely free, they soon realized they had nothing to fear.

Another brief guest was Silky — an inch-long baby bat which was as lively as a cricket. The first morning Lila had her, she spiraled around her arm—the tiny claws and hooks on the tips of her wings feeling like pin pricks. Ansel flew to the arm of Lila's chair, his erect shoulder feathers and tensed muscles omens of his killing intent. Lila

said "no, no, Ansel—bad"; then stroking Silky, she said gently, "isn't she a cunning wee thing?"

For three days and evenings, every time she said, "Silky want milk?", Ansel came flying to the arm of her chair, even if he had been sound asleep. From his perch he would watch intently while Silky hung from Lila's little finger, neck curved upward, nursing from a tiny medicine dropper. After her stomach was full her wings unfolded and hooks caught the next finger to her so she could play merry-go-round on Lila's hand and arm. Ansel's head was kept weaving and stretching so his eyes might not lose her, but not once did he try to snatch this soft morsel.

The fourth morning Silky was dead and Lila thought it probably was her formula, which was equal parts of canned milk and water. Lila decided that Ansel might as well have her now, but as Ansel took the baby bat into his beak Lila hurried from the room, not wanting to watch. She was startled to hear Ansel call out, "Gimmee, gimmee, gimmee," and returned to the room as it was strange that Ansel would ask for breakfast. But Ansel was not asking for his mouse. Lying on the chair arm before him was Silky. Just as Lila had done, he was talking to her and stroking her with his beak. He carried her along to his ten o'clock nap, and again in the afternoon he slept with his beak resting against Silky's cold body.

By autumn Ansel no longer needed the care or protection of the Lofbergs in the daytime and slept on secluded perches around the bend of Packsaddle Canyon. But each day when the setting sun touched only the highest peaks, Ansel would perch on a wooden upright atop the opposite wall of the canyon. From this point he could see Lila or Ted emerge from the door and hear them call him. With the deliberation that was so typical of him he would wait a few moments before flapping his wings (which then reached a four foot spread) five or six times to gain enough momentum to come like a streamlined glider the 200 feet to the doorstep. When he got to within a yard of the nook and the flat stone that lay at their feet, his legs retracted, his body swung down and forward, and with his wings closed, his tail became a vertical fin. Lila described his landing as being as noiseless as a falling leaf.

The evening visits seemed solely a result of the owl wanting to be with his foster parents. They no longer had to call him since he came without prompting. The thud of his landing on the window sill and the rapping of his beak advised them that he had not forgotten the old folks.

Throughout that summer Ansel turned their living room into the likeness of a gay and popular night club. Successive waves of friends knocked at the door, stating that they had come to see Ansel. Many thought he could not be a horned owl, as they were supposed to be ferocious and untamable. Beautiful Ansel, gazing at the staring strangers, quickly changed their skepticism and idle curiosity into awed adoration.

Finally Ansel found a companion and although he did not desert them, he divided his time between them and his new friend. Before facing their way and leaving the canyon rim railing, his eyes searched up and down the canyon. He would question quaveringly, "Whooo, whooo, whooo?", and his waiting mate would call back, "Whooo, whooo, whooo!" He would then go through the established ritual of gently closing his feet over their hands and chattering, "gimmee, gimmee, gimmee," while caressing their cheeks with his beak.

Although Ansel deserted the Lofbergs for a while during the nesting season, in November of that year he started coming back. Their evening call of "Come on, Ansel" brought him. He remained a few moments, taking food from their hands and accepting a little stroking as fearlessly as ever. If company was present, he would hesitate on the railing for a time before coming through the window and stay only long enough to exchange stares with each person as they, in turn, bid him hello.

Among the many children who became Lila's close friends were Raymond and Carolyn Pascoe, children of Earl and Lucille Pascoe who owned the lodge and pack station at Road's End. Each summer when the reading club at Kernville library was almost to a close, the young folks would look forward to Lila's "Story Hour." She always had time to answer questions, and this traditionally climaxed the vacation time program.

She continued to entertain friends at her Road's End home. The last group to visit there was a group of ladies whose husbands worked for the Forest Service in Kernville. Lila had asked them up to spend the evening, but this time was one time the show did not begin. When Lila failed to answer her door, they found she had died in her sleep the night before.

Fairview on the Kern

"FAIRVIEW-ON-THE-KERN." Nobody seems to know who gave this picturesque spot its name. But as far back as anyone in the Valley can remember, it was called just that. In the early days the name, "Fairview," applied to a two-mile section along the river from the cow camp that Stony Rhymes and Lucien Barbeau had on the bend of the river below McNallys up to and including what was later Road's End.

Then in 1910 a couple moved to the upper Kern that started the name Fairview on its road to fame. This was Matt and Lupie Burlando. Matt was born in Turin, Italy, in 1886. After coming to the Valley as a young man, he went to work for the Edison Company. In November of 1910, he married Lupie Apalatea, whose father, Francisco, lived where the town of Kernville now stands. Soon after Matt and Lupie were married, they moved upriver to the Edison camp at the end of the wagon road. Matt packed and did blacksmith work for the Edison Company. Then called Fairview, the Edison Company later changed the name to Camp 8.

In December of 1911, Betsy, the Burlando's first child, was born. Soon afterwards Matt decided he wanted to go into business for himself. Moving his wife and young daughter downstream half a mile, he started what was later known as Fairview Lodge. The spot was nothing but a big brush patch with a wagon road through it when they first started. Lupie had her sister, Marie, come up to take care of the baby. She helped her husband hand-clear and pile the tons of brush.

Matt also built a swinging bridge across the river so he could utilize the natural hot springs that came up on the west side of the river. The

Fairview-on-the-Kern River—taken in 1915. Small girl on burro, *second from right*, is Betsy Burlando.

Burlandos, after living in a tent almost a year, built their first home. This home also served as a cookhouse where Lupie served meals not only to Edison employees but also tourists that by this time were beginning to discover the outstanding hunting and fishing of the area. This same building that was used as a dwelling, dining hall, and

also a store was later used as part of McNally's Steak House.

Matt acquired a string of burros and started packing people into the back country. One of the shortest trips he made was a five-mile round trip to Packsaddle Caves. In those days, these natural limestone caves were quite an attraction. But in

Matt Burlando, pioneer Kern River rancher.

Two of Matt Burlando's riding burros ready for a day's ride out of Fairview.

Left to right, **Lupie Apalatea Burlando and Ellen Apalatea Cisternas—early 1900s.**

years since they have been vandalized to the point where much of their natural beauty has been destroyed.

Flows of Tobias Creek enter the river to the south. Matt was quick to see that a ditch started far enough upstream would not only supply water for a garden on the west side of the river, but could also be used to power his own little electrical power plant. He dug the ditch, and where it dropped 50 feet at the south end of the flat, he installed a Pelton waterwheel to power the generator.

In the meantime another child, John, was added to the Burlando family. This time, though, Matt took Lupie downriver to the Edison Company Hospital at Hospital Flat instead of delivering at Fairview. In 1916, Matt had a chance to buy his father-in-law's ranch at what is now Kernville.

Left to right, **Johnny and Betsy Burlando at Fairview.**

As they had two children who would soon be of school age, they moved downriver.

Matt ran a small herd of cattle, and butchered and sold meat to the Edison Company for their construction camps. Two more boys were born to the Burlandos, Billie in 1917, and Claud, known as Skeeziks, in 1920. Matt Burlando passed away in 1930; Lupie in 1955; and their youngest son, Skeeziks, died in 1938. In 1973, Betsy and Johnnie still lived in Kernville, where Johnnie owned and operated the Burlando Nursery. Billie Burlando lived at Camp Owen, where he worked for Kern County as a group supervisor.

When Burlandos left Fairview in 1916, they sold their resort to a family by the names of Symes. Frank A. Garbut, founder of the Los Angeles Athletic Club, lent money to Symes and, after his death, took over the property. A number of individuals leased Fairview from the Garbuts during the years they owned it. One of these was Tom Allred, and in 1928, the Wortley Brothers. Ken and Chet Wortley moved their base of operation for their summer camp from Coogan's Cabin on the South Fork to Fairview. The Car.

Burlando children, *left to right,* **Billy, Claud, Johnny, and** *in front,* **Betsy.**

Carl Curtis Boys' School Camp at Fairview, 1928. Some of the staff are, *left to right*, Chet Wortley, *top right*. *Top center*—Dr. C. H. Wood, camp doctor and nature studies director; *top left*—Noah Beery, Jr., nephew of Wallace Beery; Carl Curtis, head of Carl Curtis School; Doane M. Lowery, first assistant to Carl Curtis; Frank O. Maxwell, head of the junior camp. Most of the boys are unidentified.

Curtis Boys' School, whom Wortleys had been previously packing for, also moved their summer camp to the Kern and set up where Soda Springs Trailer Park was later located. Curtis brought with him a full complement of counselors and activity directors. The program included hiking, horseback riding, swimming, fishing, and a multitude of nature and craft classes.

McNALLY'S

One of the locals to pack for Tom Allred in 1935 was Clifford Cross. Clifford and his wife, Trudy, leased Fairview in 1937 and for five years operated the dining hall, rental cabins, and pack outfit. Then in the early 1940s, Johnny McNally's parents, John Edward, Sr., and his wife Rose, operated Fairview, with Johnny and his wife, Pauline, helping in the fall. During this period they were also farming the Hot Springs Ranch and the former Palmer Ranch, now recognized as Kernvale.

Johnny and Pauline, who had both lived in the Kern River Valley since the early 1930s, were married in 1936. During the 1940s, Johnny produced the Sierra Roundup Rodeo at Scovern Hot Springs and for years had his own rodeo stock.

When Johnny put together this first string of rodeo stock for the 1945 Sierra Roundup Rodeo at Isabella, two young Valley men named Dick

115

McNallys on a pack trip to the high country, camping overnight at Cannell Meadows. *Left to right*, Red and Helen Bray, Helen Reineking, Pauline McNally, John McNally, Dick Pascoe, and Fuzzy and Kay Fuhrman.

The Coles, *left to right*, Billy, Bill Jr., Mary Anne, John.

Butch McNally grew up on a horse.

Pascoe and Bob Powers went around to the ranchers with a stock truck and gathered up all the suitable stock. This included horses that were known to be hard buckers or work horses that had never been ridden and acted as if they might be pretty salty. They also collected ten head of white-faced Hereford bulls from the Rudnick ranch which were as wild as March hares, and proved a real challenge to the cowboys' ability to stay up on top.

Pascoe and Powers felt that each head of stock should be turned out of the chute before the rodeo so they would know which way to go, and they were also anxious to know what these ponies and bulls could do in the arena. Ten head of bulls were tried out, five bulls for each man. Powers suffered a broken arm on his last try, so had to be scratched from the bull riding competition. He decided to seek fame in some other line for, while he could stay on some pretty rough horses, he did not ride with the natural ease and grace that Dick Pascoe did. Johnny McNally went on to be a rodeo stock contractor until the mid-1950s, producing shows not only in California but Nevada as well.

Then in the late 1940s, Johnny and Pauline started the steakhouse that in ensuing years attained a reputation for fine steaks and western hospitality that spread for thousands of miles. Yet if it were not for a large neon sign that proclaims "McNally's," you might drive right on by, for on the narrow mountain road the buildings seem to blend right into the scenery. Maybe that is because some of them have been there for over 60 years.

As you turn into the driveway, you start to flavor the western setting. Wagon wheels line the walk and oak trees spread over the buildings that house the steakhouse. Entering the front door, you return in time to when the West was young by means of wood carvings of Gene Hoeback that line the walls of the western bar. A fire crackles in the fireplace of native rock almost every night after early fall. Johnny and Pauline had seating for 40 people and were going strong when in 1961, without breaking stride in its fast growing reputation, the McNally's daughter and son-in-law, Mary Anne and Billy Cole, took over the business. The Coles continued to add more dining area, which also included a banquet room until, in 1973, they had a seating capacity of 150. Even with this much room, many summer evenings still result in a waiting list. In 1973, a gift shop was also added where browsing is welcome and which, among other items carried, are beautiful handcrafted Indian jewelry. All these things combined makes Fairview-on-the-Kern a spot one should be sure not to miss when in the Kern River Valley.

Pauline was, herself, an exceptional person and a great help to her husband in his years as deputy. She was completely at home in the outdoors and could handle a string of pack mules with the ease of a veteran packer. A crack shot with a rifle, she

John McNally, typical cowboy-type Deputy Sheriff who relied on his quick thinking and knowledge of human nature to stay alive and healthy.

many times killed a running buck from the back of her saddle horse. It was this type of talent that prompted the City of Bakersfield and County of Kern to choose her to represent them in separate years at the "Miss Outdoor Girl" contest at Salinas during the 1930s. She later served for two years as president of the Kern River Valley Chamber of Commerce and as secretary for the Kern Plateau Association on conservation projects related to the interests of the area. She also worked at furthering youth interests in animals at the fairs and horse shows.

Regardless of all her accomplishments and civic duties, she counted the raising of her children to be of prime importance in her life. A devoted wife and mother, she dedicated her life to her family.

Besides Mary Anne, who cooked those delicious steaks, there was a younger daughter, Joan (Bailey), who operated the High Sierra School of Western Horsemanship in Lake Isabella, and a son, "Butch," who in 1973 was following in his Dad's footsteps as a logging truck driver.

When Johnny McNally retired from the resort business, he stepped into another occupation which spread his fame even farther—that of being the only deputy sheriff for Tulare County in the remote 1,000 square mile section in the southeast corner of Tulare County. Johnny's life had been varied, colorful, and interesting since coming to the Kern River Valley. Besides farming in the Hot Springs Valley, he had worked five years for the Southern California Edison Company as a hydro mechanic. He also did a stretch as a logging truck driver for Mt. Whitney Lumber Company and drove a DW-20 on the Isabella Dam job, where he worked until its completion.

Each of his former jobs, plus the fact that he knew every foot of the country, made him a natural for the job of resident deputy sheriff in this remote area. His work was a highly personalized kind of law enforcement. In policing the mill town of Johnsondale, comprised of 300 loggers and millhands, he explained, "I get along well with the loggers and the men at the mill because they know me, and they know there isn't anything they do that I haven't done."

Johnny had no office or staff. The closest Tulare County jail facility was in Porterville, two hours away by mountain roads that were closed much of the time by snow during the winter months. The alternate route was by way of Bakersfield, which meant a three-hour trip. His wife, Pauline, donated many hours to writing the crime reports and case files. Hundreds of times he went out on night calls with only sketchy details and only one thing to depend on — that he would have to handle whatever problem came up by himself. His wife would not know (until she heard his car in the driveway) whether or not he had come out of the incident alive or unhurt.

On major summer weekends, the Tulare County Sheriff's Office in Visalia (three hours away via the Greenhorn Summit) would send an extra deputy or two. When McNally took on the lawman's job, he was furnished with a two-way radio, which proved useless due to the height of the mountains and the great distance to Visalia. Therefore, he communicated with the outside world by telephone, or he could radio the Kern County Sheriff's Department fifteen miles away if he happened to be in the right location. In some sections of the Kern River Canyon it was virtually impossible to transmit or receive radio messages. In Johnny's territory in any month there could be five to ten burglaries and as many grand thefts, twenty to thirty petty thefts or forced entries into parked cars, and perhaps two or three homicides a year. Johnny also served as coroner. He many times used Jack Moore's garage at Road's End as a temporary morgue.

Much of his work involved searching for lost hunters and hikers, and each year led trackers and search parties to comb the rugged mountains and desert east of his headquarters. He traveled by patrol car or jeep to the end of the road, then continued by foot and horseback or snowmobile. Occasionally there would be a helicopter available for searching, and many times local pilots flew him over the search area. His prime asset, though, was the ability to track the lost person. His only sign in the timber country might be freshly crushed pine needles or a recently broken twig. Although he worked for Tulare County, he received much help in rescue work from the Kern County Rescue Posse, of which he had been an active member since 1959.

He worked with friends who, like himself, had been raised in the mountains and tracked cattle and deer all their life. They could almost guarantee finding a lost person unless a storm wiped out the tracks. Some of the best trackers Johnny worked with were John Nicoll, Sunday Andreas, and Bobby Robinson, all of whom lived on the South Fork of the Kern River. What makes this

Bob Welch, 1930s.

tracking service so outstanding is that most of these men worked hundreds of hours without pay.

Endless stories could be told of the difficult circumstances in which Johnny found himself. But, in a way, this is typical of all law enforcement officers. They put their lives on the line every day, and if they received ten times the pay it possibly would not be enough.

From 1957 until he retired in 1973, Johnny McNally served Tulare County in a job reminiscent of the frontier days when a cowboy-type sheriff worked a small town with dirt streets and a vast, roadless area beyond. Only once in those many years did he draw his gun, and that was to take into custody a murder suspect.

So our hats are off to Johnny McNally and all like him who are rugged enough and care enough to take a job such as he held. They must get tough once in a while to survive, and do make mistakes because they are human, but I would hate to live in this country without them.

BOB WELCH

Up the road to the north of Fairview and only separated by a small border of brush was a spot marked for many years by the highway department as "Welch." This was the home and pack station of Bob Welch. Bob was the kind of man who never met a stranger, and although he had a heart as big as all outdoors, he was also as wild and woolly as they come.

Bob was born in New Hampshire, and by the time he was seven years old he was driving oxen on the farm. The oxen performed many chores, but the job they did best was to pull stumps when there was new land to clear. Where a span of horses jerked and lunged, hitting their collars and generally causing a stir without moving the stump, the oxen would lean into their yokes, slowly pouring on the power with first a "gee," then a "haw." They pulled one way and then the other with such brute strength that something had to give—and usually it was the stump.

By the time Bob was 21 he had become a serviceman for the Dort Motor Car Company. He was sent from New Hampshire to Florida for a year and a half, then was reassigned to the home office. As Bob put it, "by that time my blood had thinned down so much I just sat around shivering all the time, and all I could think about was getting back to a warmer climate." When the company needed a serviceman to go to California, he was packed and on his way before they could bat an eye.

In the early 1920s Bob Welch began packing into Fairview. He would get together a party of friends, rent the pack stock and saddle horses from J. C. Howe and his partner, Monroe George, and guide the party into the back country. Howe and George were more interested in trapping and lion hunting than packing and were glad to have Bob take in his own parties. Each year Bob bought more saddles, saddle blankets and other related pack gear until the only way he could come out ahead was to buy out Howe and George's business. This he did in 1929 when he started packing in full time, except for the snowy winter months. From that time until he went out of business in 1959, he built up a horse and mule string that at times numbered 75 head.

Bob packed parties into five main camps in the high country. One was on the east side of the Kern River, about 100 yards above where Needlerock Creek comes into the river, and another was on the upper end of Durrwood Creek. These two were used mainly as fishing camps, but each fall he also packed quite a few bucks out of these locations for his parties. The other camps were on the upper end of Trout Creek, on Smith Creek, and

Bob Welch's camp on Trout Creek was typical of his back country camps.

also a good camp on Rattlesnake Creek. These camps all had excellent fishing, and every fall the pack strings would come out loaded with bucks. In 1930 one party took 18 bucks from Upper Trout Creek, many of which had record heads.

Bob said that he started in the business at the wrong time financially as his pack station was located about halfway between the Wortley Brothers' pack station and Earl Pascoe's, and those two had a continuing price war. At one time their prices came down to $1.50 per day for pack stock. Because of this, Bob started to charge a flat price of $25.00 per person, which included the packer's wages, an animal to ride, and up to one mule load of supplies for each person. The trip out was also included. The pack animals had to be limited to one per person because some people thought they had to take all their worldly possessions with them. One party of two men going into his Trout Creek Camp ended up with nine mule loads of supplies and gear; however, when Welch threatened to charge for the extra mules, the amount of gear was cut down considerably.

Some parties wanted a cook to go along and also wanted to keep stock in the back country. In this case Bob would send Bill Peyton. Bill was one of the first people to pack people into the mountains from the Kern River Valley. He first ran his business from a pasture near where the golf course is now located and above what was then the Big Blue Mill. Peyton took his parties up through Bath House Canyon which lies east of the Kern County Airport. Besides being a top flight camp cook and

A string of trout caught out of Bob Welch's camp on the Kern River by the Needles in 1926.

an expert stock handler, Bill was an expert with an ax. If he had been dropped into a spot in the wilds, in just a few hours he would have had a first class camp set up, complete with table, log seats, and all the comforts of the best backwoods camp.

Bob Welch's packing career started during the prohibition era and he told of taking straight alcohol to the mountains to mix with fruit juice. One event that happened as a result of this practice was when the James brothers, Bill and George, were camped on Smith Creek gathering cattle. Bill was sick in camp and George had gone down Rattlesnake Creek to look for stock. When he arrived at the cabin beside Rattlesnake pasture, Bob Welch and some of the boys decided to help him gather cattle.

Everything went well and by evening they had 60 head gathered. George said he would go on ahead and get supper ready if they would take the cattle back up the creek to the holding pasture. By this time the boys had hit the bootleg whiskey and started out from camp singing to the cattle. A few hours and four miles later they ended up with one cow and found a very angry cook in camp.

Bob Welch was originally in partnership with J. C. Howe, but before long he bought Howe's interest and continued on his own. Along with the packing permit, he acquired the small shack Howe had built out of material left over from the Edison construction some eight or nine years previously. Over the years Bob added more rooms and built an excellent fireplace out of native rock. He worked his stock hard, but also fed them well and took the best care of them in every way. He

had so much business in the fall that he usually doubled back, or took in a party and then came right back because he had another party going in the next day. The trip to the Needles Camp was 18 miles away and this round trip taxed the stamina of even these salty old packers.

Bob said he had been in towns all over the United States, but Old Kernville was hard to beat. Some of Bob's most fondly remembered good times occurred when one of the many movie companies arrived in town for location filming. Bob was considered a permanent fixture in their nightly poker games, as was another local fellow, Irven Wofford. Someone would ride up to Fairview to tell Bob that the movie people had arrived. After an all-night poker game, Bob would usually work on one of the sets.

A wild time was had by all one night when Bob had spent the whole evening in Don's Bar in Old Kernville. In those days the boys lined the bar with drinks at 2 A.M. and the bartender had to stay until everyone had finished. About 3 A.M. Bob and Carl Larson got into a discussion about Bob's pinto horse, Buttons, who was in a horse trailer

Bob's favorite horse, Buttons, that he rode into Don Hannings' Bar in Kernville.

in front of the saloon. Bob said he could ride Buttons anywhere a man could take a horse, to which Carl replied, "If that's so, bring him in here." The bartender for Don Hanning agreed to let the horse come in, knowing it would do no good to refuse. Proceeding to bring the horse through the door, Bob had to hang way off the side to clear the top of the door, when Buttons suddenly lunged inside and slid to a stop. He slipped on the slick floor of the bar and went down. Buttons and Bob got right back up. In doing so, tore up three or four tiles. Bob told the bartender he would pay for damages, finished his drink, loaded his horse and headed back to Fairview.

When prohibition ended, one of Bob's friends offered him a drink of legal whiskey. Bob took a big slug and nearly spit it out, remarking, "If that's legal whiskey, I'm sticking to Don's moonshine variety, as there is no comparison." He later explained that Hanning also had a poorer brand called Indian Whiskey, but the better grade was hard to beat.

In 1972 Bob was enjoying his retirement in Kernville, where he would frequently get together with his old friends to talk of old times. In reminiscing, Bob said, "If you had all the money in the world you couldn't bring back Kernville or Fairview the way it used to be in the '30s; that's gone forever."

DICK WEED

The story of Fairview would not be complete without mention of Richard "Dick" Weed. Dick had lived in the Kern River Valley since 1921 following his discharge from the Navy. He was most in evidence every Memorial Day, Fourth of July, and Veterans Day when he dressed in his 1917 vintage seaman's uniform to take part in the patriotic ceremonies.

Dick joined the Cavalry in 1912 to serve under General John J. Pershing in the border fighting between the United States and Mexico. In those days the Cavalry used horses, Dick often repeated the old saying, "Cavalry men didn't have to know much—but the horses did." He served for one year during that hitch.

In 1917, when the United States entered World War I, Dick enlisted in the Navy at Bakersfield, taking his boot training in San Pedro. Signing up for submarine service, he was sent to Mare Island as a fireman third class. After a siege with the flu,

Dick Weed celebrates the 4th of July by wearing his World War I Navy uniform and strumming out a few patriotic tunes at McNally's Bar.

he went on the submarine *Collier Mars*, traveling from the west to the east coast via the Panama Canal. The sub made many trips across the Atlantic carrying fuel to ships in the Azore Islands, England, France, Spain, Ireland, and Scotland.

After being discharged in 1921, he first visited his birthplace of Riverside County, California, then decided to try mining in the upper Kern River Valley. In 1924, Dick and J. C. Howe filed on the Thousand Stamp claim where he later built a cabin and mill. There was no road to his claim and the closest bridge was three-fourths mile below at Fairview, so Dick constructed a cable car. He hand hewed the logs for his cabin and split the shakes for the roof.

When the United States entered World War II, Dick again went to Bakersfield to rejoin the Navy, but found he was two months too old to return to active duty. He then spent six months in the California State Guard.

Dick liked the solitude of his claim on the Kern River, and, as the years passed by, the flatlanders became more plentiful, causing him to put a sign on his cabin (pictured below). Although many of Dick's friends said he would not hurt a flea, all of them called out and identified themselves before they crossed the river to visit. They knew he was a dead shot with the .44 pistol he always carried, as he had killed more than one deer with it. So instead of taking foolish chances, they waited until Dick called for them to "come on over."

Friendly welcome sign on Dick's cabin, 1930s.

Bert James was one that told of Dick's prowess with his .44. It seemed Bert had been up to the intake visiting his father, Billy James, and as it was nearing the noon hour the old miner asked if Bert would eat with him. As he never turned down the offer of a free meal in those days, Bert accepted. Dick took his pistol from where it hung on his wall and stepped into the yard to shoot one of his chickens for the meal. As luck would have it, the rooster that Dick wanted to kill was perched on several cases of dynamite stacked under a tree. Bert said that as Dick leveled his gun to shoot the bird's head off, he started running and as he was pretty fast in his younger days he was in the middle of the river headed away from there before the shot rang out. He said he glanced back over his shoulder without breaking stride and saw the chicken flopping around on the ground minus his head. Dick hollered at him to come back, but he said he had lost his appetite. And with a wave to Dick, he jumped in his Ford and took off down river, driving almost to Kernville before his nerves calmed down.

In the 1940s, Dick began to receive letters from the Navy. As he could not read very well, he had his friend, Jack Moore, read them to him. They stated that he had a small pension coming, and all that was necessary to receive it was to fill out some papers. Dick told Jack that he did not want something for nothing, so it was many years before he was talked into taking what was rightfully his. By that time, he had accumulated a lump sum settlement of over $600, plus a small check

each month. Moore advised him to put it in the bank so that he could write checks on it.

Dick was very thrifty. When he stopped at Bert James' store in Old Kernville, a big purchase for him might amount to 53 cents. Whereby, he would write a check for 53 cents. Bert finally told him he would not accept a check for less than $1.00. It was the same story when he ate at local restaurants. Whether he spent 60 cents or splurged for $1.25, he would write out a check. Jack Moore had shown him how to fill out the checks, but he was not going to rush into a transaction like this without due caution. He would first read the front of the check, then turn it over to look at the back. Talking to himself, he would mutter, "It's July 28, so I put that in here." Then he would pick the check up again and read everything out loud that was printed on it, proceeding once again to fill out another line. It would take him at least half an hour to fill out the check and pay for his meal.

When he made these rare trips to town, he slept many times in the post office. It was warm on the floor, and Bill Stewart, the postmaster, felt that it did not hurt anything. It gave more than one citizen a start when they went to check their mail at night to find Dick sound asleep beneath a pile of newspapers.

The Country needs more people with the same patriotic pride displayed by Dick Weed. He marched with fire and spirit in parades, keeping cadence with the youngest Cub Scout or any of the more seasoned V.F.W. Color Guard.

Dick's cabin — The Dick Weed Conservatory of Music, taken in 1932.

Dick will be best remembered for his talent with musical instruments, and among those he started in music was Don Levy, alias Don Davis. The year was 1932 and, although Don was born in Los Angeles as was his father before him, he had spent every summer possible in the High Sierras since 1926. In 1928, he first visited Fairview while attending the boys' camp sponsored by the Carl Curtis Boys' School.

In 1932, he spent twelve weeks there with two friends, Bill Worthington and Chuck French. And it was in Dick Weed's old cabin that Don's musical career began. Dick first taught him to play the banjo and harmonica at the same time, and Don kept adding instruments until he was playing six at once (four melody and two percussion). While in the Army, he entertained extensively with these instruments in and around Fort Lewis.

After the war, he entered his father's insurance firm (Donald L. Levy), one of the oldest in Los Angeles, keeping music as a hobby. Finally, he left the firm to devote his entire time to music, touring the United States for a year and a half. He also appeared in Las Vegas and on about twenty na-

Outside his cabin on the Kern River. Dick Weed shares his love for music with Don (Levy) Davis in 1932. It was Dick's encouragement that started Don on his lifelong vocation.

tionally televised shows, some of which were: Bob Hope Special, Danny Thomas Special, Johnny Carson Show (five times), Love American Style, Merv Griffin Show, Truth or Consequences, Japa-

Ken Wortley introduced Don Davis to Dick Weed. Davis sent Ken this card in 1971.

DON DAVIS
THE ONE-MAN BAND AND TOTALMEDIA ARTIST

nese TV, the TV Special "Winchester '73", Run-around, Ralph Story's L. A., Here Come the Brides, Joey Bishop Show, Lohman-Barkley Show, and the Mickie Finn Show. He was the first entertainer ever to perform on "What's My Line?"

Known as "Totalmedia," Don's act combined Music and Drama, Art and Sculpture, Science, Technology, Athletics, audience and everything else—all at once!

The origin of Totalmedia? It all started at Fairview-on-the-Kern in Dick Weed's cabin.

Dick was missed around Roads End and Fair-view, where many times he sat under a shade tree in the cool of the evening, and after drinking a little wine, he would strum out "Little Brown Jug" and other old time favorites. He would soon have an audience of young and old alike and make the evening one to remember.

He died in 1965. He had left his cabin to cross the river, and died alone there on the river bank where he had lived most of his life. But he will always be remembered as one of the most colorful characters who made the Kern River Valley such an unusual place.

Mountain Men

For many years certain individuals living at Fairview could have returned some 150 years to the uncivilized wilds of the west and would have fallen in naturally with their predecessors. These 20th Century mountain men were a distinct breed who congregated around Fairview, just as buckskin clad trappers had done around Wind River Mountains of Wyoming during the height of the fur trade. They included such colorful characters as J. C. Howe, Kenny Keillor, Howard Bilton, and Bill Douglas—the latter, while not living at Fairview, worked the same area as the others.

Though he did not live in this area long, the first of the mountain men to trap and hunt on the upper Kern River was Tommy Fitzgerald. It is fairly certain that Fitzgerald came into California with Jedediah Smith in 1826 and, when the party returned east, he stayed. Fitzgerald had a hunting lodge constructed of tules that stood where the city of Bakersfield now is located, and supplemented his trapper income by supplying the soldiers of Fort Tejon with elk meat killed in the lower San Joaquin Valley.

Although he traveled around quite a bit, his permanent headquarters was at Glennville. It was there he built his house, later called the Glennville Adobe. All Kern County historians agree that this dwelling, built of adobe brick, is the oldest structure in Kern County. David Lavers, who settled in what is now the Glennville area, tod Guy Hughes,

a local historian, that the Glennville Adobe (which stands just east of the Kern County Fire Department) was an old building when he came there in 1854.

Trappers and hunters such as Fitzgerald were a rugged breed who were perfectly at home away from civilization. Completely on their own, they depended solely on their hunting skills and knowledge of woodcraft to sustain themselves.

The following material has been given by trappers, lion hunters, and other locals in the Kern River Valley. While it might only present one side of the issue and could be opinionated, the writer feels from personal knowledge of these people that their experience and integrity should make one concerned with conservation sit up and take notice. There has been no attempt to present both sides of the story but only to present the subject of predator control as the mountain men of the Kern River Valley saw it.

The first to make his home on the Kern River was J. C. Howe. The following account was related by Ken Wortley, a good friend of Howe's. Besides being a trapper and lion hunter, Howe was also among the old time prospectors who remembered first hand the period when Searchlight and Goldfield, Nevada, were roaring mining camps. In 1905 he took part in the celebration at Goldfield that followed the driving of the last railroad spike. This spelled doom for the freighter and linked the famous desert towns with modern transportation. He was also on hand a year later when the roar of the stamp mills at Searchlight was stilled for a day in celebration of a similar occasion.

After the Southern California Edison Company built their road up the Kern River in 1910 to construct the intake for the Kern River No. 3 power plant, Howe built a little cabin right above Fairview-on-the-Kern. From there he started his trapping and prospecting trips into the high country. His friend, Dick Weed, built his own cabin across the river. Weed and Howe filed together in 1924 on the Thousand Stamp Mine back of Weed's cabin. Besides several gold prospects in the back country, he was also part owner with Ken Keillor in the Casey Jones Mine near the fork of Machine Creek and Little Trout Creek. And, as late as 1955, he had promising tungsten property on Brush Creek which he was trying to develop.

Howe also ran a pack station at Fairview in the mid-1920s in partnership with his trapping associate, Monroe George. He and George spent the fall of 1918 trapping at Big Whitney Meadow at the head of Golden Trout Creek. The fur market was at a peak when Howe and George came out with the finest catch on record in the Southern Sierras.

Big Whitney is close to timberline and is a cold spot even in the summer. In the winter, when freezing air from Mt. Whitney sucks down through Siberian Pass from the north, temperatures drop far below zero. Because it is so cold, the furs are in prime condition by early fall. The cross fox caught by Howe and George brought $110 apiece; the red fox, $25; wolverine, $50; and marten and coyote hides, an average of $15.

The wolverine is the trappers' nemesis and a vicious animal. Sometimes these animals will follow a trapline day after day, spring traps, and destroy any animal he finds in the traps; as camp raiders they have no equal.

These two trappers caught six wolverines on that trip. On one occasion when George was running his part of the trap line, he heard a terrible commotion up ahead. There was a wolverine in a trap and its mate had come to its rescue. A life and death battle was going on between the wolverine that was loose and George's two airedale dogs. They were fighting all over the place, and when they got close to the wolverine in the trap, he got in a few licks too. In the confusion and in

Two mountain men of the Kern River in front of their cabin on Rattlesnake Creek. *Left to right*, Monroe George and J. C. Howe and some pretty big bears. Year is 1918.

his haste to save his dogs, George shot the wolverine in the trap and the dogs jumped it, letting the other get away.

Howe was one of few people who had been on the top of Mt. Whitney in the winter. In referring to the event, he remarked, "I sure found out the meaning of the saying, 'As cold as the top of Mt. Whitney.'" When they came out from this trapping trip in a snowstorm late in December, they stopped overnight at the Forest Service cabin at Beach Meadow, which they hoped would be next to the last night they would have to spend in the frozen wilderness. On their burros, along with their pelts, they had a sack with the skulls of the six wolverines. In their haste to get out of the cold, they brought their pelts inside but hung the sack of skulls on a tree limb. They were running short of supplies for their dogs as well as themselves, and during the night the dogs jumped up and pulled the sack down. The next morning they woke up to find four inches of fresh snow. Being no time to look for wolverine skulls, they packed up and struck out for the cabin at Cannell Meadow at a lower elevation, hoping with one more night to spend out that they would not get snowbound. When they returned to Beach Meadow the following spring, they found one skull. Howe brought it out with him, giving it to Bill Douglas in his later years.

Kenny Keillor with a lion his dogs treed a short distance from its last kill. Year is 1930.

During his lifetime and with the help of his hounds, Howe caught over 60 mountain lions. Between his trapping and lion hunting, many feel that he helped control the predators to such a degree that the 1920s and 1930s yielded the largest number of bucks killed per year than any time since. This of course was tied in with other prevailing conditions such as excellent habitat on winter ranges due to large burns such as Brush Creek and Bull Run and the fact that there were very few hunters in the area in comparison to the 1960s and 1970s.

Howard Bilton was another mountain man who did a lot for the Kern Plateau. Bilton was a lion hunter for the State Department of Fish and Game, and in his lifetime killed over 600 mountain lions. He moved to the Kern River from the California Hot Springs area just across the Greenhorn Mountains. When he was not hunting lions at Hot Springs, he worked in Ralph Gurnsey's sawmill. For pay he took lumber with which he built the Sugarloaf Lodge. Although Bilton was more at home in the wilds than in civilization, he was a well-educated man. His neighbor at Fairview, Dr. Dickins, said that he had never observed Bilton to use any but the best English as long as he had known him.

THE MOUNTAIN LION

In the 1950s the State of California had four lion hunters in its employ: Howard Bilton, Steve Matthes, Bill Dye, and Lyle Simpson. The sad part is that none of these men left any written account of their experience and knowledge of that elusive cat, the mountain lion, except for an unpublished and incomplete manuscript left by Bilton before his untimely death. The total experience of these four men amounted to over 120 man years; and while a lot of their findings were passed on by word of mouth, much of this knowledge has been lost for good.

One thing they pretty well agreed on though was that a full-grown mountain lion killed a deer at least every three days to fill his basic food needs. Linsdale and Dixon, in their book, *Fur Bearing Animals of California*, report that stomach analyses indicated deer meat to make up 75 percent of a mountain lion's diet. Most of the old lion hunters felt that if more stomachs had been analyzed, the percentage would have been even higher.

The mountain lion is a predatory animal, evolved through eons of time to keep nature in balance. When man, no matter how well meaning he may be, upsets that delicate balance and controls one factor, such as fire, he must control others too. An overabundance of predatory animals is not all that influences the game population. Most experts would agree that survival of the deer herds, for instance, is primarily affected by the condition of their winter range. Summer food is usually unlimited. But if their winter range, which in most instances is fairly small, gets in poor shape there is a very definite effect on the condition of the herd. If left in poor condition long enough, a

Howard Bilton, "A Modern John Muir of the Sierra Nevada Mountains."

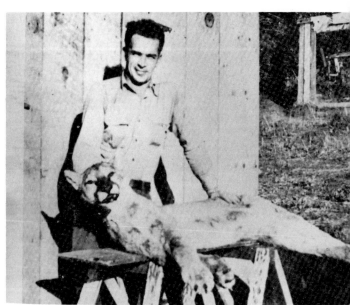

126

sharp decline in number and health of these animals will result.

Deer are strange creatures. A herd's winter range might consist of only two small canyons. If it becomes overgrazed or the brush, which is their principal winter diet, is allowed to grow too thick or high, the deer will not go further afield to feed or cross over into another canyon as cattle would do. They will simply stay while their health and range condition continues to worsen. Cattle can be lured to better feed by placing salt in a choicer location, or they can simply be driven there. Not so with deer—they cannot be lured or even driven off a range in poor condition.

The Department of Fish and Game experimented with this fact in the Kaibab National Forest, Arizona. Quite a number of horsemen were able to start a large bunch of deer, and it looked as though the plan would work until the deer realized they were being driven from their range. They started breaking back, showing almost no fear for the men on horseback while nearly running under the horses in some cases, to return home.

So this winter browse or feed is most often the critical factor with each deer herd. Years ago, before white men came, fire that started by lightning burned uncontrolled over these brush fields. In most cases, the fire does not kill the brush roots, but only burns it off to a degree where the deer have plenty of fresh sprouts that they can reach. But in the Brush Creek area, for instance, where there has not been a wild fire since 1941, the deer herd is trying to graze on brush that is either too thick or too old to be anything but poor. Even the Indians set fires when they came out of the mountains in the fall. In 1902, James Powers, who was a ranger for the Sierra Forest Reserve, mentioned in his diary that he had "talked to the Indians about setting fires when they were hunting deer and gathering piñons." The early sheepmen also set fires in the fall as they brought out their herds.

For years forest fires or wild fires were confronted as an enemy, but in more recent times it has been realized that fire is a very significant factor in the forest and brushland environment. Taking into account the many environmental variables, fire can sometimes be an enemy; at times a friend; its effects will sometimes be a mix between the two extremes. Fire can be used to enhance productivity of the earth's eco-systems in all their infinite variety, and may be the ultimate tool in

Bill Douglas takes a busman's holiday to hunt deer while he was working for the State Fish and Game Department of California. Year is 1945.

maintaining the balance between food production and herbivore usage in specific areas.

In the Rocky Mountain region, scientists who study the inter-relationship of plants, animals and their habitat, say that the forests in these areas owe their existence and continued presence to a long history of periodic fire. In the past, forest fires were beneficial to the whole forest system because their frequency was determined by the system's natural readiness to burn. When there is a departure from the accustomed fire cycle and fuels accumulate beyond the readiness point, the ultimate, inevitable fire will be more severe. Fire is neither all good or all bad, but it is natural and powerful. In the proper places, in the right hands, at the right times, and under adequate surveillance, fire can be an asset and an ally. The effect of smoke from a burning brush field being injected into the environment has to be balanced out with the increased productivity of that brush field. Although we very definitely need the efforts of the environmentalists, each individual case has to be judged on its own merits. Too many armchair experts have made flat statements advocating no more burning, agriculturally or otherwise. Those who stick to their guns on such issues, even though they may know little about the overall problem, make the job of people entrusted with proper game management and overall forest management even harder.

Bill Douglas was the last of the mountain men to work the area in and around Fairview, and from him has been gleaned much of the information about the hundreds of man years' experienced by

Frances Douglas and "Trapline Running Red" pose for a photo during a move from Sonora to Lompoc, California in February of 1945.

old-timers who spent their lives in predatory animal control. Bill Douglas was born in 1911 near Crane, Missouri. Here, in the Ozark Mountains, he started trapping wild animals as a boy to make money for his clothes. He came to California in 1937 and started trapping for the old U. S. Biological Survey.

Trapping in the West was a lot different than the trapping he had done in the Ozarks, but it gave him a good background. After a week with his field supervisor, he worked mainly alone. This field supervisor was Bill Mouser, who already had 25 years of experience in trapping predatory animals before Douglas went to work. As Douglas explained it, Mouser showed him where and how to set his traps, saving him a lot of work in future years with the short-cuts learned.

About six months after World War II broke out, Douglas joined the Navy and, a little more than two years later, was given a medical discharge after being bounced around by a torpedo. He went to work for the State Fish and Game Department in Sacramento. During those early years he worked with such experts as Charlie Jones of Merced County, Nick Cosovich, and Noe Chalfant. In 1973, Bill Douglas had more years in service than any other trapper in the State. He stated that even though he had learned a lot in the past 36 years about predatory animals, he felt if he worked another 36 years he would learn just as much more.

It was while trapping for the State Fish and Game Department in the area around Fairview that Douglas met Howard Bilton. For the next sixteen or seventeen years, Bill Douglas' wife, Frances (who was a teacher for the Kernville Union School District), said she was a lion hunter's widow. Not only did he spend many of his weekends with Bilton hunting the big, elusive cat, but even took a busman's holiday to hunt lions. Bilton and Douglas were working the same country in those days. And when in the rounds of running his traps, Douglas came across a fresh lion track, that evening he would tell Bilton. The next day when Bilton started on the lion's track with his dogs, Douglas was right along with him.

Douglas loved to tell of these hunting excursions. His account of a lion killed in the Nine Mile area follows, word for word, the way he told it:

One of the most confusing and frustrating lion hunts we ever got into started at Big Pine Pass, four miles up the road from the old Bales Place in the Nine Mile country.

Two separate tom lions had gone through the Pass early the night before, angling south towards Chimney Mountain. We knew this could end up in a lot of trouble and confusion, but we turned the dogs loose anyway. The dogs soon lined out pretty fast up the ridge and started to pull away from us.

Hardly more than half a mile from the Pass, we heard two big pups take off to the north on a hot deer track. Bilton told us to follow the old dogs and he took off towards the pups, using some pretty loud and colorful language concerning their ancestry.

I was with Mr. and Mrs. Bill Batley of Julian, California, and we pushed on up the mountainside as fast

Howard Bilton with a female lion he caught on Brush Creek below Embree's Mine. Dogs, *left to right*, are Rock, Baldy, and Rusty.

as our lungs would let us. Long before we puffed out on top of the plateau, we heard the last, faint murmur of the pack ahead of us.

On reaching the top we stopped to get our breath. A little cold, raw wind had sprung up, making it awfully hard to hear. We sat down and listened until we cooled down from our exertion. Still hearing nothing, we started for a long spur point to the west that would give us a good vantage point to listen down into the canyons.

We stopped right on the end of the point and listened intently for about five minutes. Nobody spoke. Then, suddenly came the sound of a panting dog, we thought, coming up behind us. We all turned around at the same time and, there as very close range, was the biggest looking cat I ever saw. When we turned, he saw us instantly and stopped and froze ten feet from me. I was on one side of a bush about six feet high, and he was on the other side of it.

We all froze, but I still had enough presence of mind to slowly raise my rifle with a six-power scope on it. (Did you ever try to shoot at ten feet with a six-power scope?) I think the field of view is about nine inches. Through an open spot in the bush I finally found two big blurred, yellow orbs, but I was afraid to shoot. The muzzle of the rifle was in the bush and that small, high velocity bullet could blow up on a twig and throw fragments all over.

After probably ten seconds of this frozen tableau, the lion turned and started away at a fast trot, angling a little to my left. I took two quick steps to the left, balanced myself and caught him in the scope. But before I could get the crosshair on him and pull the trigger, he just faded out of sight behind a fallen tree.

So far, not a word had been spoken; then we all looked at one another with shocked faces and chorused in unison, "Did you see that?" This could have been the silliest question of the day!

While we were still jittering and trying to decide what to do next, we heard Bilton yell to locate us. Here he came a few minutes later, leading the two errant pups. Of course, we had to give him our excited story of what happened. But before we finished, we heard the distant, muffled baying of the hounds. Soon we could see them through openings of the trees, off the ridge to the southeast, closely bunched and running hard in full voice.

When they came up to us, we helped them get straightened out on the lion's track, and from then on things got pretty hot and fast. The dogs got ahead of us again and back up over the ridge, out of hearing.

After about twenty minutes of pushing ourselves hard, we came out on the ridge. The dogs were barking treed about a quarter-mile south of us. It didn't take long to make that distance downgrade, but we were in for another surprise. Instead of being up a nice, handy tree, we found the dogs at the bottom of a great face of broken rocks, with huge slabs piled helter-skelter in all dirctions. Bilton and I picked our way down through the jumbled mass and began to

Bill Douglas with two of Bilton's dogs and a lion they killed on Lamont Pass, April Fool's Day, 1953. *In the right foreground* is the doe that was the lion's victim. Dogs are, *left to right*, Sparkle Plenty and Rock.

stick our heads into holes and passages. The only way we had to locate the lion was to hear him growl.

It was bitter cold under those rocks, out of the sun, and after about twenty minutes I felt like I was turning blue. When I heard a faint growl, I excitedly hurried across to Howard and he handed me the 32-20 Winchester carbine.

I went back and started crawling into a passage that I felt led toward the growl. A few feet in, the growl was repeated—this time a little louder. I continued to inch along, listening and trying to get my eyes accustomed to the dim light. The passage kept getting narrower as I moved ahead and now I was on my elbows, pushing the muzzle of the rifle ahead of me. Finally the passage got so narrow that I could just squeeze my shoulders through, which blocked nearly all of my light. By this time I was pretty sure I couldn't be more than fifteen feet from the cat, and I began to have doubts about the wisdom of my course. Just then came a thunderous, deep-throated growl from very close, and then my precarious position really hit me. What if the passageway I was in was the only way out for the lion! I could not have seen him more than six feet in front of my rifle muzzle, where the passage made a bend. Right then I quietly panicked and moved backwards, out into the beautiful light of day a lot faster than I went in.

As soon as I got out, Bilton, who was peering around and listening some forty feet away, saw me and called out, "Did you see him? Have you got him located?" I answered, "Right now, no; I'm shaking a little." Then I added, "I have him pinpointed, but I'm going to try from another angle."

I slid under a huge, flat, slab of rock which was at a 90 degree angle from the passage I had just come out of. About twenty feet back, the rock floor and the overhead rock slanted together and there was no other space. However, there was a crack about eight inches wide that I could see through, and I felt sure the dark hole beyond was where the lion was hidden.

I reached it, all hunched up and squeezed together, and cautiously pushed the rifle muzzle through. Then I sat very quietly, straining my eyes to try to see into the dark hole. All I could see was the dim side of another boulder. I didn't know it at the time, but the lion was almost under the rifle muzzle.

There I sat, immovable for about three minutes, when suddenly in the gloom a big cat's face, with its mouth open in an explosive hiss, popped up in front of the rifle muzzle. I was so startled that I flinched off a shot. It was deafening in that confined space and dust was blown around by the concussion. There was a lot of thumping and scrambling around in there in the gloom, and I could get glimpses of the lion turning and thrashing. Every time I got a look at him I got off another shot. I think I fired four very rapid shots before things got quiet and the dust settled.

Soon I dropped a few small rocks in the hole and got no reaction. Then we were faced with the problem of getting the dead lion out of the cave. We studied both of our approaches, but there was no way to even see him, and no hope of reaching him. We must have spent half an hour puzzling and crawling into dead ends. Occasionally Bill Batley would call down to ask us what we were doing, and Bilton would yell back, "We're cogitating." In the future, this lion, with a lot of chuckles, came to be known as the "cogitating lion."

Bilton explored both of our routes out and decided that we could never get the lion out either of them, so he got below and started crawling up. Finally he could barely see one foot. Bill Batley fixed up a long pole with a loop on the end of it and Bilton worked this pole into the passage, hooking the foot. But Howard was in a dangerous spot, barely hanging on. Also, we figured the dead weight of the lion would come right down on top of him if Howard started it moving. So we tied all of the dog ropes together with Bilton on one end and me on the other, bracing my feet. Bilton gave a hard pull on the pole, the lion slid down on him, and all of us darn near went over the edge.

But we didn't, and we spent the next thirty-five minutes or so heaving that lion out to a flat spot where we could skin him. By the time we got him skinned out, with Bill Batley giving us lots of good ringside advice and commentaries, we didn't care where the second tom had gone. We only cared that we had finally bagged one lion.

Now all we cared about was getting back to the car and heading for the barn. There was coffee there! We'd had enough lion hunting for one day.

The lion meat was not wasted as Bilton fed much of it to his dogs. Quite a few old-timers who had eaten lion meat said that, outside of tasting a little wild, it was not too bad—that is, if you were hungry.

Bilton thought the world of his dogs, and Old Red, a large, light-red bloodhound, was a special favorite. One time they thought they had lost Old Red for good. They had started a lion up in the area where the Rincon Trail leaves the Cherry Hill Road. The track was not too fresh and wandered around a lot. The dogs got split up, and all came wandering back to the road except Old Red. They waited a long time, then finally went home. Bilton came back the next day and looked again, and for several days afterward.

Finally, four days after they had lost him, a couple of miners coming out the Rincon Trail heard a hound baying treed way down the canyon towards the Kern River. They got a pretty good fix on it and told Bilton, as they knew he had been running lions in there. The next morning Howard took Jim Riley, a friend who sometimes hunted with him, and they went in to try and find the dog. Sure enough, there was Old Red sitting at the bottom of a big canyon oak, still barking treed. The branches were thick, but look as they might, they could not find a lion up that tree.

They found out later what had happened. After waiting there several days, Old Red got thirsty and went down to a little stream close by to get a drink. He came back and checked the tree; and according to the tracks, the lion was still up there. So he settled back to wait for his owner, sounding off every now and then. But while Old Red was watering down, the lion had climbed out on a big limb and jumped to a rock ledge above. They did not know how long he had been barking up an empty tree. It was a little funny at first, but Old Red had the last laugh. His feet were so sore that they had to carry him out, which was no easy chore with a sixty pound bloodhound.

Bilton also had an Australian shepherd who ran with his pack of hounds. This dog was quite a character. He soon learned that he did not have the nose of the hounds. When the track was fairly cold he just wandered along with the rest, seeming to show no interest at all. Then when the track got hot and he could see the general direction the chase was taking, he skirted way around with a burst of speed, picking up the trail which was so hot by this time that even he could follow. Hounds sound off all the time they are running a track, and the hunters could tell each dog by his bark. But this shepherd did not make a sound until he had treed the lion, maybe a mile ahead—then he barked for the first time. The dogs seemed to understand each other because as soon as he barked, they dropped the track and went straight to the tree. That is really using someone else's talents.

Besides Howard Bilton, Douglas was privileged to hunt with two other lion hunters who worked for the state. He spent one vacation hunting with Bill Dye and Howard Bilton out of Benton Station. During the same period, he had a memorable hunt with Steve Matthes. Douglas classed Matthes as one of the greatest lion hunters in the West, having killed hundreds of lions in the Western United States, Mexico, and Central and South America, as well as jaguar down south. Douglas asked a lot of questions and learned a little from each answer, later stating that, "If you want to find out something, go to the man that has the experience."

Through his own years of experience with lions and other predators, and from what he had learned from the older experts, his opinions regarding wildlife are not to be taken lightly, as Bill Douglas is a pretty knowledgeable man in anyone's league. There are people from many walks of life who spend most of their lives working and living in the outdoors, including people in such professions as packing, cattle and lumber. Each of these individuals will acquire a certain amount of understanding as to the ways of creatures of the wilds. But if many of these people were measured in their degree of accumulated knowledge of wildlife, they would be rated as only starting school, whereas Bill Douglas would have acquired his doctorate.

Much of the following has been gleaned from conversations with Douglas and reflect his many years of firsthand observations about wild animals in their natural habitat. Douglas noted that everybody with a viewpoint was, to some degree, influenced in his thinking by how it affected his way of life. In other words, one who makes his living by trapping or hunting predatory animals would, without realizing it, let his prejudices influence his thinking. But on the other hand, he had acquired facts from the many years' work that could not be duplicated in all the conservation courses in the world.

Many who make their living working in the outdoors feel as if there are more lions in Kern

This big cat stepped into one of J. C. Howe's traps on Greenhorn Mountain.

County in 1973 than during any period since the arrival of white men. Douglas himself believed there were more in 1973 than there were in 1949 when he first came to this country. He drew this conclusion from the number of lion tracks he found and the carcasses of deer killed by lions. Many people think that because they do not see lions running around in the daytime as they do squirrels, that the lions are becoming extinct. Lions will hardly move in the daytime; and when they do, they are very wary. Many times when a hunter thinks he saw a mountain lion during the day, it was only a bobcat or some other small animal.

The lion is a predatory animal, and the availability of buffer species such as snowshoe rabbits and porcupines will influence how many deer they kill. They will eat animals as small as a chipmunk, but it takes a great number of these little fellows to make even half a meal for a 150-pound lion. Therefore, the report previously cited that a lion's diet is principally deer probably is most accurate.

When lions kill more cattle than usual, this will take the pressure off the deer. One big tom followed the deer herd into the Loraine area every fall for three or four years, filling out a deer diet with beef, until Bilton ended his career. The last was a cow that weighed over 1,000 pounds; and after he made his kill, he dragged her for forty-five yards. This was quite a feat even for this big cat that weighed over 200 pounds. Lions kill more cattle than they are given credit, as they usually make only one or two meals of each victim before other animals come in and blot out the tracks. For example, a black bear might be blamed for killing a cow that he had been merely cleaning up after a lion had satisfied his hunger.

Lions are not migrators in the true sense, but they have to follow the food supply. Each fall when the deer leave the high country, you can find lion tracks coming out behind them.

One fall Douglas spent October and November camped on the east slope of Chimney Mountain, checking the number of deer by age and sex. These deer were migrating from the summer range in the Monache country to the winter range near Lamont Meadow. Knowing the route the largest number were taking, he counted and catalogued the tracks where they had to cross dirt roads. He did this every day, brushing out the tracks by dragging a tree limb behind his car to get ready for the next bunch that night. Although he did not know why, the mountain lions showed up about two weeks after the bulk of the deer got on their winter range.

According to Douglas, even with picking up an odd meal here and there, a full-grown lion will kill a deer about every three days. And regardless of the saying about a lion killing only to eat and eating everything it kills, many who have lived in the woods know better. Howard Bilton followed a tom one night who killed three deer, eating only one. The first was a buck that had papilloma (warts all over the head and neck) which possibly did not suit the cat's fancy. The next was another buck, which he killed and ate. Later in the night, on his way to where he was to bed down for the night, he killed another buck. It looked as if he had just stumbled on to him; and when he winded him, the killer instinct hit the lion. He jumped the buck, dragging him down, moving him 100 yards, and then went his way without eating a bite. This is not to say that it happens every night, but it happens fairly often. If you were not right on the lion's track, you might think the three deer had been killed by three separate lions. Douglas stated that they love to kill

and so would naturally kill some animals they do not eat. Have you ever seen a cat play with a mouse?

Conservationists have done an enormous amount of good; but as with any good movement, there are a few armchair experts who read one book and suddenly become an authority on a subject. Douglas, as well as Bilton and other men who worked with animals day in and day out, felt that the idea of predators killing only what they need to subsist on was ungrounded.

Favoring the deer is the slower reproduction rate of lions. A female lion will have cubs no more often than every two years, having 2.4 cubs per average litter, while deer multiply at least twice that fast.

The lion hunts almost totally at night, which accounts for the fact that very little is seen of them. Two cases have been noted when the female lion, who in both cases had young, was observed making a kill in daylight. One was recorded by a Forest Service employee on a lookout when he witnessed the mother bring her cubs back twice to feed on the carcass within eight hours, almost completely finishing it. The doe's fawn fled and was never seen again. The other case occurred in Grapevine Canyon when Ken Wortley, tracking a lion, came upon her making a kill. In both cases, the neck was broken almost instantly by a well-placed twist of the big, powerful paws. These females probably were hunting in the daylight only because of pressure from their young for more food.

The tom is pretty much a creature of habit, and he covers his circle, which might be 25 to 50 miles, with hardly any variation day after day. He hunts almost totally on the ridges where he is above his quarry and can wind their scent as it rises up the slope. At night there are usually air currents moving up the slope as the earth cools. More importantly, when he is above his prey, they cannot catch his scent.

Bill Douglas describes the female lion as being very erratic in her hunting pattern, but hunts and frequents the same type of country as the tom does. When she has young, though, she might stay in one small canyon until she has run out of deer and either is forced to move or becomes restless.

The mountain lion, like all the rest of the cat family, does not have the best smelling facilities. Almost everyone has watched a house cat being thrown a piece of meat. The cat runs around frantically trying to locate the source of that tantalizing smell. But if he is chasing a live mouse, let the mouse so much as flick its tail and the cat can spot it immediately. This is one of the secrets of the lion's reputation as a hunter.

While not actually watching any lions stalk their kill, Douglas had many times called up a bobcat with the use of a call that imitated a wounded fawn. As Douglas sat immobilized, he would catch the slightest glimpse of something move, first to one side, then to the other, using all available cover and depressions in the ground, coming ever nearer. If he had not been concentrating on watching the stalk, he would not have seen the cat at all. Then all of a sudden, from out of a depression that you would not think big enough to hide a small house cat, two ears would start to slip up. With his rifle ready, a bead was drawn right between the ears. As the eyes of the bobcat slipped up over the bank, Douglas squeezed a shot, nailing him dead center. He had to shoot the split second the cat's eyes came over the rim, or the cat would have disappeared as if the ground had swallowed him up.

Bill had checked out many sets of tracks that led up to lion kills and concluded that the same type of stalking was used by the lion as by the bobcat. He found belly hair on the snow or bare ground where the big cat had inched along, using all the patience in the world. If they missed, they might not eat that night.

Next to his exceptional eyesight, the lion's next best asset is his hearing — also without equal. These two attributes, coupled with his speed and phenomenal strength, make him the deadliest of killers.

Lions kill a lot of fawns but, of the adult deer, nearly two out of three are mature bucks. These isolated mountain ridges where the lions hunt is just the place where these bucks hide out. They lay up under some bluffs of rocks where they can watch the country below them. While does usually feed or bed down in groups of two or three, the big buck is alone most of the year and relies totally on his own alertness. When deer are in a group and feeding, there is at least one who acts as a sentinel. When a lion slips upwind of a lone buck, the buck's chances are slim. The only warning nature gives a lion's prey is the same warning that house cats and even African lions give—the nervous twitch of the end of their tails. This one bad habit has cost the mountain lion more than

Bobcats that are found on the Kern River rarely weigh over 30 pounds but are vicious fighters and many times will tackle another animal that is as much as four times its weight.

one good meal and caused more than one old buck to become a little wiser.

The average female lion weighs about 120 pounds and the average male 160, with very few of the biggest toms going over 200. When they jump a deer they almost always break the neck by catching it just right and giving a quick jerk and twist of their powerful paws or by biting into the occipital joint in the neck.

A lion always moves its kill, sometimes only 30 or 40 yards, but many times as much as 200 yards. And this might be uphill and in very rough country. In moving a deer, they usually drag it, but occasionally carry it bodily. They somehow get under the deer and carry it on their back and shoulders. Often the track of only one leg dragging the ground is observed. It is believed that the lion lies down beside the deer, grasps the throat at the base and rolls over, lifting most of the deer off the ground. In this manner they can carry an animal that equals or exceeds their own weight.

Some fourteen years after the Department of Fish and Game took off their predator control, a moratorium was held on taking the big cats as some preservationists felt they were disappearing. The following is a report on the findings during the first year:

LIONS DOUBLE IN CALIFORNIA IN TEN YEARS

Biologists estimate California's mountain lion population has at least doubled over the past ten years, according to the Wildlife Management Institute. This was among the findings of the California Department of Fish and Game in its first report to the State legislature on a mountain lion study conducted last year.

In 1971, a moratorium was established on lion taking and a study began to "ascertain the quantity

A young fawn is an easy target for predators such as lions, coyotes, and bobcats.

where few buffer species such as rabbits and squirrels are present, they hit the deer especially hard.

When the deer herd first enters the summer range, it is hit hard. Besides the lion and coyote, the bobcat, black bear, and bald eagle also take a few of the young fawns. But in all, coyotes kill more deer by far than all other predators combined.

Not many people have witnessed the coyote in action as he goes about the kill, but the following incidents were related to Bill Douglas:

Jerry Kenwood of the California Department of Fish and Game was out in the woods one day when he heard a terrible commotion and threshing around in the brush about a hundred yards away. He hurried ahead and found that two coyotes were trying to kill a fawn. Jerry did not have a gun, so he picked up a short piece of limb to use as a club and went closer. An old doe was charging full tilt around the clump of scrub oak, and staying just out of her reach was a coyote. Off to one side another coyote was standing with his eyes riveted to a little fawn who was lying with its head flat on the ground, as motionless as a statue. By this time Jerry was getting pretty close, but the participants of this deadly game were too engrossed in the business at hand to notice. Suddenly, while the one coyote and the doe were on the opposite side of the clump of oaks, the other coyote dashed in and killed the fawn; one grab, one short sound, and the fawn was dead.

Just as fast, the coyote started backing out, dragging the dead fawn with him. The coyote was so intent on what he was doing that he did not notice the man right at his heels. As Jerry swung his club, the coyote looked right up into his eyes and dodged to the side, causing the club to just graze him. All of a sudden the other coyote came back around, practically running between Jerry's legs, with the doe right behind. Jerry then had to fight her off with the club. She was so intent on protecting her fawn that she did not realize her target was now a human being.

This story was not told to make the coyote look like a bad guy, but only to point out that they are predators and live by their kill. To understand Mr. Coyote, it might be good to follow his life cycle through one year as Douglas told it.

The running season starts near Christmas and lasts about forty days. During this time as many as twelve male coyotes might follow one female in heat. Seeing so many coyotes together during this

of mountain lions in the state and to determine the best methods of providing sound management of this resource."

Department Director Ray Arnett said that in the 51,000 square miles of habitat studied, the estimated lion population is 2,242. The investigation included the capture, tagging and release of six lions which were fitted with radio telemetry collars.

Their movements were followed from the air at weekly intervals. Arnett said more intensive populations studies will follow the statewide survey.

THE MOUNTAIN COYOTE

Many locals in the Kern River Valley feel that the mountain lion is still a serious threat to California deer herds, but Douglas further stated that he felt that in 1973 the mountain coyote was the number one killer. Present in large numbers in the West and in no danger of becoming extinct, a female coyote averages six young yearly and sometimes has as many as eleven, so they multiply with amazing rapidity. Among other things significant in the coyote's well-being is that he feels at home fairly close to man. When he is allowed his freedom, he still often chooses relatively heavily populated areas.

The coyote can adjust his life style to almost any circumstance. Dry years, such as 1971 and 1972, are fairly hard on the desert coyote, for he must continually widen his range to find rabbits and other rodents. The coyotes become cannibalistic, eating carcasses of coyotes and other animals found dead. In an area like the Kern Plateau, time of year is responsible for many people believing that they generally travel in packs, when in reality the opposite is true. After a 63-day gestation period, the mother has her young.

The female coyote readies a number of dens several weeks before she has her litter of pups. She may have dug out old dens or located new ones, but she has at least six picked out. Every spring the trappers would pull their traps and, pairing up by twos for company, would search for these dens—being a good way to hold down the predators. Bill Douglas claims to have looked forward to this change of pace and noted that dens were found in every conceivable place.

In the San Joaquin Valley, the coyote would find a small mound and burrow a hole right down from the top. Being good diggers, they would dig out a comfortable home for their future family. The entrance was on top, which kept the den from being flooded. The female could also lay on top of this mound and, in flat country, a two or three foot rise in elevation enabled her to see a fair distance.

In the foothills, dens were located anywhere from a large 50-foot section of drainage pipe to a hollow log. However, most would be found in places similar to the edge of Hanning Flat, where the flat ends and the rocks start to climb the mountains. Here the coyote would choose a cave-like shelter—sometimes a natural passageway in the rocks and, at other times, she would just dig a hole.

Why does the coyote prepare so many dens? Because of fleas. When the fleas get too thick in one den and while the pups are still small, she picks them up by the nape of the neck and moves them, one by one, to a new den. Bill Douglas said that a person had only to lie down by a den to listen for the sound of pups and before long he would have fleas all over him.

Douglas found that the female keeps moving the pups nearer water, for by the time they are six to eight weeks old, they will have to have water available. That is why after the middle of May, when he was searching for coyote dens, he did not look more than several hundred yards from water.

By August the pups are big enough to follow the mother a short distance from home. Prior to this time she brought home a little meat, such as a squirrel, rabbit, or parts of a deer, to get them accustomed to the taste of meat. Helping the mother during this period was the old male coyote,

as he was a good family man. When his mate got "cabin fever" and needed to get out, the male "pup sat" while she brought home the bacon.

As the pups get old enough to follow a short distance, they begin to receive an education on taking care of themselves. They are shown how to catch grasshoppers, mice, and other small things and learn that these are not only a welcome change from mother's milk, but also are a lot of fun.

They stay together, not actually living in a den but staying within 300 or 400 yards of their last den for some time. The grass is knocked down where they play and the ground is littered with bones from small animals. You can tell by their droppings that they live in one spot.

By September the family is mobile and hunts together, with the older members training the younger ones according to their local habitat—whether valley or mountain country. Then near the end of the year, the running season starts again and the mother leaves the pups to fend for themselves. They are not full-grown experts, but are learning every day.

Douglas further stated that to run down a deer all they have to do is stay with it, as a coyote can run for an undetermined period of time while a deer starts off with a burst of speed and soon tires. After a short time, a lone coyote can kill a grown deer that is run to exhaustion by running up beside it and snapping the hamstrings, causing the deer to drop. Many times trappers and hunters have found where coyotes have pulled down a deer and proceeded to eat it alive, making no effort to kill it first.

One such case was noted by Earl Pascoe as he came down the Cherry Hill Road on his way back from taking men in on a snow survey. Coming over a ridge, he found a young buck struggling in the snow. He had been hamstrung, pulled down, and tracks indicated that three or four coyotes had systematically started to pull him apart without killing him. One quick bite in the jugular vein would have put him out of his misery. But the coyotes cannot be blamed, for nature is cruel in many ways and the coyotes were merely following their instincts.

To a trained observer, animal tracks can tell a story as clearly as if one had actually been on the scene. In the State Game Refuge at Hayfork, Trinity County, on September 28, 1921, State lion hunter, Jay Bruce, frightened two coyotes away from a deer they had just killed. The deer was a male fawn that had only recently lost its spots. The tracks showed that one coyote had lain in wait behind a log while the other one pursued the young deer down a steep hillside. The hidden coyote had rushed out and run the fawn fifty feet, dragging it down by apparently grabbing it by the rump. The coyotes had then eaten a large hole in the neck and belly of the deer and were still devouring the warm flesh when they were frightened away by the approach of the hunter.

In the 35 years Bill Douglas ran a trap line, he came to know coyotes as well as other wild animals—as only a trapper can. He also had the benefit of knowledge passed on to him from other veteran trappers.

His main job for the ten years prior to 1973 was to control predators that were doing agricultural damage. He worked for the U. S. Fish and Wildlife Service, with cooperating counties helping to finance the project.

If a sheepman had 1,000 sheep and one coyote started to kill five to ten sheep every night, you can well imagine how fast the owner would request action. On the other hand, deer herds are scattered over a large, unpopulated area, and no close count is taken. Coyotes could be killing every night without anyone being the wiser. The only way to be certain of coyote kills is to run stomach analyses on them to see what they have been eating.

In 1953 a report was published entitled, *The Food Habits of the California Coyote.* This report was based on the examination of 2,222 coyote stomachs and was exhaustive and comprehensive from the standpoint of the overall food habits of the California coyote. There was, however, a very limited sampling of stomachs of coyote from ranges of higher elevations, especially those inhabited by migratory deer. In other words, if you collected 2,222 coyote stomachs from an area where there were very few deer, you would naturally find a very small percentage of deer meat in the stomach. On the other hand, in areas where there were migratory deer herds such as on the Kern Plateau, many times rodents—particularly rabbits—are comparatively scarce. The higher deer ranges are also inhabited by a subspecies of coyote, known as the "mountain coyote," which is larger than its cousin, the "valley coyote." Many trappers, lion hunters, and other field men felt that this left a gap in our knowledge of the food habits

of the mountain coyote—leaving in question his effect on the biological dynamics of a deer herd. logical dynamics of a deer herd.

Bill Douglas was one State trapper who felt strongly enough about this matter to push additional research. At his suggestion, a study was initiated in June 1954 by the California Department of Fish and Game.

Douglas realized that this subject has always been controversial, with opinions ranging to both extremes. The collection of stomachs would have to be accompanied by an on-the-spot record of each stomach and a carefully thought out plan, rigidly adhered to, with complete professional honesty.

Before any stomachs were collected, Douglas selected three rules to be adhered to before a stomach could qualify for this study:

(1) It must be collected in the summer on a summer range or in the winter on a winter deer range.

(2) It must not be collected during deer season or for thirty days thereafter, unless the area had no open hunting season at all.

(3) A notation must be made at the time of collection as to the presence or absence of lions in the vicinity.

In June 1954, Bill Douglas trapped the first coyote for analysis. The following procedure was used at that time and throughout the entire study. Stomachs of trapped or shot coyotes were removed and placed in a ten percent formalin solution for shipment to the laboratory. A tag was attached listing pertinent data and assigning a number to the stomach. This number was then recorded on an information sheet to be kept on record.

Through May of 1957, Douglas had collected a total of 182 coyote stomachs. They were examined by Howard R. Leach, then Game Manager II, and Bruce M. Browning at the Fish and Game Laboratory in Sacramento. Of the 182 stomachs collected, 105 contained food.

This study was divided into the coyotes trapped or shot on the deer summer range and those taken on the winter range. Each of these was further divided as to location. The findings indicated that coyotes ate whatever was available. For instance, stomach contents of coyotes taken near Taylor Meadow showed the lowest incidences of deer meat, with 29 percent. Douglas explained that few deer were in the area. The principal portion of remaining stomach remnants were comprised of harvest mice, dusky-footed wood rats, meadow and deer mice, and chipmunks. One individual had eleven fence lizards in his stomach; another had an adult sparrow and five young sparrows; and remains of woodpeckers were also found. One caterpillar and seven cocoons were found in one stomach, as well as ladybugs, rain butterflies, spiders and other insects.

On the other side was the Greenhorn summer range, where the occurrence of deer meat in the stomachs was determined to be 79 percent. Deer meat comprised 99 percent of the volume of the food in these stomachs, verifying that deer meat made up the main part of their diet. Out of twelve stomachs examined, only one contained jackrabbit meat, one contained unidentified rodent hair, and and one contained bird feathers. Eight contained woody stem fragments; a great many contained fir needles, all varieties of pine needles, grass stems, and fern fronds.

In the years prior to the start of this survey, Douglas had opened possibly 1,500 coyote stomachs and many were empty. Unfortunately, no record was kept of these findings. But the stomach contents always reflected with great accuracy the food locally available to the coyotes and its proportions.

From the Fish and Game Department survey, there were 29 samples from the summer range collected between June 20 and September 20 when fawns are expected to be in the locality. Twelve of the stomachs contained fawn evidence and seventeen contained deer meat. This breaks down to 42 percent of fawn meat and 59 percent of deer meat, indicating a heavy toll of fawns taken during this period.

Of the 66 percent occurrence of deer meat in samples, Douglas deducted 20 percent that was due to natural deaths, other predators and poaching, and another 5 percent for lion kills that the coyotes had cleaned up. The remaining 41 percent was then attributed to healthy animals that the coyotes had killed themselves.

In making this study, data was also recorded by the laboratory as to the volume of deer meat in relation to other food found in the stomachs. This figure could not be judged too accurately, for in certain back country areas inaccessible by road, the stomachs had to be emptied of much of their contents in order to fit into the jar of formalin solution for shipment to the laboratory. Of the fifteen stomachs thus treated, one contained jackrabbit and juniper berries; one contained mouse and woodchuck meat; but the other thirteen contained large amounts of deer. The volume of deer meat came out to be 45 percent; but Douglas felt sure that if he had been able to ship out each stomach in its entirety, the volume of deer meat in relation to all else found in the stomachs would have been 50 to 55 percent.

Douglas seemed to lean over backwards in this study to present a true picture of the coyote's effect on the deer herds in the area he was working. He knew the country he was working as well as a person knows his back yard. With each stomach collected, he kept data on such miscellaneous information as the likelihood of a coyote finishing up a lion kill. Following is a list of coyote stomachs that all contained deer meat collected on the Greenhorn summer range an dthe possible relation to lion activity:

No. 91—Three lions using this area—likely lion kill.
    98—No lion in area.
    99—A lion in area.
    100—No lion present—coyote caught on return to previous coyote kill.
    102—Lion passed through going south two weeks ago—no return.
    103—Lion passed through three weeks previously—no return.
    159—No lion in vicinity—fawn hair in coyote.
    161—Fawn—lion passed through two days previously—possible lion kill, not likely.
    163—No lion in vicinity.
    164—No lion in vicinity.
    168—Fawn meat and hair—large lion passed two miles west four days previous—not likely lion kill.

The above notes show how closely Douglas checked each coyote he shot or trapped in the attempt to properly evaluate the eating habits of mountain coyotes in relation to the local deer herd. He even checked out the possibility of the collected stomachs containing deer meat obtained from road kills, but this only accounted for a small percentage. Even if a deer was injured and left the roadway, he could tell from the tracks whether it was a crippled deer or a healthy one.

In July of 1956, when 116 of the 182 stomachs had been collected, the study underway by Bill Douglas was mentioned in the *Quarterly Progress Report Surveys and Investigations* as required by Federal Aid in Wildlife Restoration Act, Project No. W-25-R. In a paper submitted by Howard R. Leach, project leader, it was reported that of the

116 stomachs, 59 were found to have contained sufficient food for stomach determination. The following is a quote from Mr. Leach's report:

The summary indicates that deer remains constituted the bulk of the coyote diet, having made up 50.5 percent of the food and occurred in 60.3 percent of the stomachs. Significantly, deer was the number one item of diet for every season of the year . . .

Mr. Leach went on to explain that the evaluation of the predator-prey relationship must be based on an analysis of the biological dynamics of the deer herd as a whole.

As 1957 drew to a close, Douglas sent in the last of the coyote stomachs. This ended three and a half years of running his trap lines, sending in stomachs for analysis, and his exhaustive study to determine if each coyote trapped or shot had the opportunity to feed on deer meat that he had not killed himself—such as by lion kills, road kills, or natural death.

This study has become a very important part in the life of Bill Douglas. In his twenty years of trapping coyotes in California, he had opened innumerable coyote stomachs and believed beyond a doubt that when coyotes became too plentiful they had a very adverse effect on deer herds in the area. Well, Douglas sat back to wait for these startling facts of this study to be made public, but it never came about. In 1973, some sixteen years after completing the study, he was still waiting and had nearly given up his claim to fame. As has been told before, the opinions stated in this book as to predator-prey relationship are the joint opinions of Bilton, Douglas, and a few other individuals who have spent their entire life working with wild animals. While ones such as Douglas were the first to admit that their close association with the trapping business might tend to make him somewhat biased in some of his opinions, these men with their many years in close contact with coyotes and lions undoubtedly would be able to contribute tremendous amounts of information on these animals not found in textbooks.

In 1959 the California Department of Fish and Game took off their predator control. So, in 1960, rather than be transferred to a game farm or similar job, Douglas took a position with the U. S. Fish and Wildlife Service in order to follow his lifelong vocation of trapping.

As stated before, the toll predators take on deer is just one factor to consider. The actual effect of predation must be based on an analysis of the biological dynamics of the deer herd as a whole. And as mentioned, the condition of the habitat has a definite effect on the deer herd.

In 1954, Bill Douglas worked on another study concerned with the over-use of winter deer range. The deer herd north of Bishop seemed to be getting progressively in poorer shape. The range was overgrazed, and the brush was eaten so close that each bush looked like a bunch of clumps. All vegetation has a certain tolerance point, and when pushed past this point, it starts to die.

There were just too many deer for the winter range, and the Department of Fish and Game wanted to begin special doe hunts the following year. They needed to convince sportsmen that the deer were literally eating themselves out of house and home. Does eat the same as bucks; and when too many have been bred, a certain number of each sex should be taken. The Department wanted to check at least 100 does. Because Douglas was an expert marksman, he was picked for the job. Each doe was to be shot in the neck. With his .222 Sako rifle equipped with a high-powered scope, Douglas made the neck shots from up to 200 yards.

A biologist accompanying Douglas would point out an old doe and, at the crack of the rifle, he would rush to the doe to get at least two vials of blood. The animal was then taken to Bishop, where the State had leased a building previously used for beef. The doe was dissected and every drop of blood retained. The large arteries and whole carcass was checked, with prime attention being given to the bone marrow. Marrow will tell the difference between a healthy deer and a sick or starving one. Close examination, therefore, proved that the deer range had been overgrazed, and the herd had become too numerous.

The most coyotes Bill Douglas trapped in a given period (eleven months) was 583 in Santa Barbara County, which set a state record for the California Department of Fish and Game. In 1971, he caught 381 coyotes and bobcats. And in 1972, he caught 365, or an average of one a day, from the 180 to 200 traps he ran daily.

Old style traps used to severely damage an animal's foot, but the type used for the past twenty years are made like handcuffs—hardly ever breaking bones. Systematic checks of a trap line means that an animal seldom stays in a trap more than

24 to 48 hours, and sometimes only 12 hours. Of the severity of the traps, Douglas said, "Oh, they smart; I've caught myself several times. One time I remember especially was when my dog, Red, was mixing it up with a fox caught accidently in one of the traps. I couldn't shoot, so was trying to get the other end of the chain that was fastened to the trap so I could get them separated. There was another trap set on the other end, and in my excitement, I glanced at it and thought it had been sprung. I reached down, with one eye still on Red and his opponent, and stuck my big hand right in the trap." The trap caught one finger; and while Douglas said it did not break the bone, it was sore for several days. You can well imagine that there was some fancy footwork going on, with a mad fox battling with a dog on one end of the chain while Douglas tried to get his finger out of the trap on the other end.

His dog, Red, was caught only once. Bill said that when he found the dog in the trap, Red was the most embarrassed dog he had ever seen. Red went with him to set the traps and could remember where each one was, to the exact inch. Many times he pulled up to the mouth of a canyon where he had a string of traps set, intending to run them on foot. He let Red out of the car, and the dog raced up the canyon. If he came back or did not bark within a few minutes, there was no need to go check as he knew the traps were all in order. If Red started barking, it meant there was an animal caught.

Many of the coyotes Douglas trapped during his thirty-five years required no special skills to be caught, but many were so smart that it was uncanny. The average trap was set in a saddle where coyotes came through, baited with a rabbit or other small animal, or doused with a special scent Douglas had manufactured. Coyotes are like dogs in most of their habits and establish scent posts much the same as a dog. This might be a clump of grass or bush, but it is not so much *what* it is but *where* it is. Each male coyote that comes along will urinate there and then back up and scratch dirt toward it, similar to a dog's actions. So places like this are selected for setting traps.

Douglas talked of one coyote who came out of the canyon every night and trotted down the road in one of the tire tracks. So Douglas set a trap in each of the tracks. The next morning he found where the coyote had traveled down the tire track to within four or five feet of the trap, trotted right out around it, and back into the road some six feet past the trap. The next night Douglas picked another spot and carefully set the traps. He then took a section of tire with tread matching that on the road and gently rolled it across the two fresh sets. That night he caught the coyote.

Douglas told about another area that had recently been heavily trapped. This left a bunch of surviving coyotes that had been partly educated by the sheep herders trapping for them around carcasses. Being a little smarter than the others, quite a few trappers had been after the remaining wary members, but with little success.

Then one of these animals started killing sheep for fun. The herders were jumping up and down, and the pressure was really on. Douglas found the track of the coyote where he came down off the same ridge every night. Until then he had been just another coyote to Bill, but by the next morning he knew quite a bit more about him. He set three or four scent sets on the ridge, and the coyote went straight to the traps as if attracted by a magnet. The traps were deep enough that the coyote could not possibly have smelled them and were set so that they blended with the ground. Nevertheless, the coyote somehow detected them, and starting on the edge, he dug up the trap— then dragged it off, still set. He then returned and dug the hole clear down to solid ground. Why? Nobody knows, unless he got some kind of personal satisfaction out of it.

The next day more traps were set along with others in back of them, called "backsets," so that the coyote would walk into them when he was circling around the first. That night the coyote dug out every one and dragged them out of the hole.

The next day Douglas dug an especially deep hole and set a trap on the bottom. He added protection to the bottom trap with a cedar stick under the pan so the extra weight would not set it off, then covered it with two inches of dirt. Another trap was set on top. He finished it off just like a normal set—even with the ground. The coyote came back, dug around the first trap, pulled it out, then went back over and put his big foot smack in the middle of the other trap.

The ones who dig are not the smartest ones, though, as they can be figured out. The coyotes that are tough to trap are the ones that will not come near a trap and are instinctively afraid of any bait they think may not be natural.

139

Douglas tried to trap a female coyote near Coalinga that was just such an individual. She would not come within fifty feet of any bait or attraction he put out. In the area where she was running, there was a little hill with lots of small trails running over it where sheep had crossed. At the base of this hill was a hole where someone had scooped out some dirt. This was just the spot Douglas was seeking. About fifty feet up the hill, four or five traps were set in these little trails. He punched holes in the bottom of a can and sprinkled water over the area of the traps so they would blend in completely, as it had just rained. He waited two days for all scent to leave, then dragged a recently killed sheep across the range and rolled it into the hole. The old female came by that night to look things over and wisely, she thought, climbed the little hill to look over the situation and "snap," that ended the adventures of one sly coyote.

There appears to be no pat answer to replenishing the deer herds on the Kern Plateau. There are hundreds of additional hunters in each fall, to say nothing of the many people scattered throughout the woods at all times of the year. With the nature of people, there will always be a few who are "sound shooters" — meaning that they shoot at every sound they hear in the brush, and every living creature is fair game. The sad part is that this type person rarely utilizes the meat he kills but, instead, leaves it to rot.

Many of the ranchers, packers, and some sportsmen who have spent much of their lives in the woods feel that control of predators should be continued when they get out of balance, as many feel the coyotes were in the 1970s. The proof of the pudding is in the eating; and the McNallys and others who are native to the area around the Kern Plateau saw the size and number of legal bucks jump sharply in the years following predator control. But, it is hard to convince these people that control is not necessary. Admittedly, there are many other aspects of game management these people would not be as knowledgeable about as a wildlife biologist; but there is no substitute for day by day field work such as a trapper would get to make him an expert on many things such as tracks. Since most predators hunt solely at night, there is not much chance to observe them during daylight, then only by reading sign left during these night hunting trips. As one coyote will make 25,000 individual tracks in one night, the sign left amounts

Bill Douglas gets out to check a "set" at the base of Nicolls Peak. Picture was taken in 1973 just before he retired after 36 years of trapping and working with wild animals.

to something like a jigsaw puzzle that no one but an expert could unscramble. Checking tracks coupled with stomach analysis and checking scats or dung are methods of studying animal behavior that is hard to substitute. There seems to be a fairly wide gap in our knowledge of the habits of predators. In the 1970s, the California Fish and Game continued to close this gap by stepping up the amount of research on wildlife by methods such as the use of small transmitters fastened to lion and coyotes.

Hunting is still a big business in California. In 1971 three-quarter million hunters bought licenses in that state, adding better than four million dollars to their treasury. The Department of Fish and Game has proven beyond a doubt that controlled hunting of game species is an effective and necessary management tool. They have also proven that none of the hunted species have ever been endangered, even though hard core preservationists would have people believe otherwise. Much of the money collected through the issuance of hunting licenses goes into activities directly related to environmental concerns, but not necessarily connected with the harvesting of fish and game. Some of these items are the studies related to rare or endangered species, reintroduction and reestablishment of certain species (Bighorn sheep for example), conservation education, water degradation, the protection of many marine animals and songbirds, as well as habitat improvement.

Douglas and Bilton, as well as many knowledgeable people who have lived in the Kern River Valley, felt that just as surely as the deer and other game species should be hunted under a controlled situation to insure lasting protection, the predators also should be controlled. This will only be possible by using the combined knowledge of experts in the field of predation such as Bill Douglas, who can tell by tracks and a limited amount of trapping what is actually going on, and the wildlife biologist, who can tie it to the biological dynamics of the deer herd as a whole.

The mountain men have been the unsung heroes of the West. True, they did what they loved to do and would have been like fish out of water in any other line of business. It is true that some fur trappers in the past were partly responsible for placing some mammals on the rare and endangered list; but in most cases of those who hunted and trapped on the Kern River, they were dedicated to keeping the west what it was—a sportsman's paradise. Few of them gained recognition, as they were a group that stayed to themselves. There was one of these mountain men, though, that gained a measure of local fame posthumously. In front of the Kernville park there is a monument erected by the Sportsmen's Council of Central California which reads: "Memorial Award to Howard Bilton, A Modern John Muir of the Sierra Nevada Mountains. In recognition of his work and contributions in conservation of California wildlife and natural resources, 1904-1961."

Our hats are off to not only Howard Bilton, but also to Bill Douglas and all the rest of that hardy breed of mountain men who have, in their own way, dedicated their lives to helping keep California's natural resources what they are today.

Roads End and Points North

THE LITTLE SETTLEMENT which was later to be called Roads End came into existence in 1910 when the Southern California Edison Company set up one of their camps on this little flat beside the River. It was their uppermost camp, known then as Camp No. 8.

In those days it literally was the end of the road, although a rough wagon track had been pushed one and a half miles upriver to where the Edison Company was constructing the intake for their K.R. No. 3 power plant.

In 1922, Earl and Lucille Pascoe started a pack station with summer headquarters in this location; and until 1937, it was known as "Pascoes." For the first five years of the pack station, the Pascoes moved to Old Kernville each winter. Then, after 1927, they made it their year-round home. They slowly started building up their packing business, as well as their overall operation, and by 1934 they had built a lodge, store, as well as a number of cottages, and also served meals to guests and tourists. Over the years the Pascoes instigated many "firsts." In 1937 they obtained the first post office for that area; and when the post office had to be named, Roads End was picked. That same year, they became the first voting precinct for that part of Tulare County, with sixteen registered voters. Earl Pascoe not only became the first deputy, but the first road maintenance manager for this section of Tulare County as well.

When it came time for the Pascoe children to start school, the county paid a teacher $20 a month, and the Pascoes gave her room and board. Carolyn and Raymond, the two Pascoe children, were the only pupils when the school first opened. When the logging community of Johnsondale was built, they also needed a school; so for the first six months Earl Pascoe drove up and hauled the Johnsondale children down to school. Then the Roads End School, of thirty-five students, was moved to Johnsondale.

Building up his packing business, Earl used as many as 150 head of horses and mules and twelve or thirteen packers or guides in the peak season. Packers long remembered are Cisco Acosta, Sandy Severns, Tom Downs, Dutch Williams, and Al Bernard. In talking about these former packers, Earl said, "We were mighty lucky in those days

The Road's End Store, built by Earl and Lucille Pascoe in the early 1930s.

Earl Pascoe's pack train heads into the back country.

to have these boys who worked for us. They were conscientious; they took good care of their parties and stock and were just an A-number-one bunch of boys."

One of the favorite camping spots of the early parties was Round Meadow, and many customers wanted to return there year after year.

Frank Knapp was a friend who packed into the high country with the Pascoes for over thirty years. Frank built some fine rock cabins at Horse Meadow, and he and the Pascoes used these cabins for many years. They finally had to be removed at the Forest Service's request, having been constructed on public domain.

In 1952, after twenty-five years at Roads End, the Pascoes retired from actively managing their business there and bought the Pala Ranches Motel in "new" Kernville. Having increased the motel's capacity and made many improvements, they retired to the Pascoe homestead west of Wofford Heights, where they still lived in 1973.

"RANGER" MOORE

Almost counted as a permanent fixture at Roads End was Ranger Jack Moore. Jack will long be remembered by the countless thousands who visited the upper Kern River from the 1940s through the 1970s, as well as the many natives living in that area. During the twenty-eight years Jack was stationed at his little guard station at Roads End, he watched the Cannell Meadow District change and grow from an area visited by only a few thousand people each year to the skyrocketing use in 1972 of over one million visitor days.

Christened John T. Moore, but known to most as "Jack," he was born and raised in Lemon Cove, California. In 1941 he was offered a six-week job on the Needles Lookout on the Tule River District, and that "temporary" job stretched over a period of thirty-one years. In 1942 he moved to the Mountain Home Guard Station on the Tule River.

Then in 1944 he came to the Cannell Meadow District to work as fire patrolman. From 1944 to 1947 Jack was the only man patrolling the upper Kern Canyon, and in those days patrolling also included taking care of the campgrounds. Each campground had a garbage pit fitted with a cover and lid. When full, Jack had to pull the lid to one side, set the pit afire, and watch to see that flying sparks did not cause any wild fire. When it cooled, he would shovel the charred and unburned material into a trailer to haul to the dump. He also had to take care of the toilets, which included cleaning them and digging a new hole when a pit filled.

As more people began to use the area, more money was appropriated and more help obtained, but Jack's job continued to be one that lasted twenty-four hours a day, for his living room at the small Roads End guard station was also the only Forest Service office within twenty miles. Recognition should be paid to Jack, whose home resembled a railway station. It should also be given

Jack Moore, the "Silver Fox," *second from right*, had a great sense of humor. *Above*, he tells a joke for the benefit of three of his co-workers. They are, *from left to right*, Burt Hutchison, Cannell Meadow Fire Control Officer for 15 years; Jim James, long-time Forest Supervisor; and, *far right*, Bob Powers, District Recreation and Range Officer.

to his wife, Loreen, who made her home available day and night for twenty-nine years, though she received no government pay. What made this situation even more of a problem was that the living room that doubled for an office was also their bedroom!

Night and day, calls came in of highway accidents, lost children, and campfires that had burned out of control. Disputes among campers were brought to Jack in the middle of the night, and Jack never failed to pull on his trousers, start up his pickup, and do what he could to help. Most of these after-duty chores were performed without pay, and Jack did it because he loved the Forest and liked to help people. During the summer he was obliged to warn thousands of campers of the dangers of swimming in the Kern River, and for some who did not heed his warnings, he spent

hours searching for their bodies after the drownings.

Summer also meant other problems, such as people pulling off the road to find a camping spot and becoming stuck fast in the sand. Jack could be seen along the road, helping shovel out the sand and putting rocks under the wheels so the campers could be on their way. During some summers the fire danger was critical, but no laws were then in force to prevent people from building campfires. Jack would ask campers to move to another area with less fire danger, and if they refused, he would more or less move in with them. He would make such a pest of himself, making sure their fire did not get away, that people would finally give up and follow his advice to find a safer camping spot.

Although use of the forest dropped way off dur-

143

The first mill in Johnsondale—taken in 1939. This mill burned in the winter of 1943.

ing the winter, Jack had his midnight calls then too. Finding that someone had slid off the road on the ice or their car had broken down, off he would go to put chains on the car or whatever was needed.

Jack retired in 1972, and when his many friends honored him with a retirement dinner on December 16 of that year, more than 150 people attended the dinner held at McNally's Steak House. Among those who attended were U. S. Magistrate John Halsey, several highway patrol officers and Kern County deputies. Also attending were many of Jack's former co-workers, a good number of local residents, and people from the Southland who made the long trip to show their appreciation to "Ranger Moore" who had made their trips to the mountains safer over the years.

After the Pascoes left Roads End, Mildred and Skeets Byers operated the store and lodge there, In 1973 Al and Fran Keegan had taken over the lease. Although there have been changes down through the years, this spot is still enjoyed by countless thousands each year.

JOHNSONDALE

Nestled in the mountains some five miles north of Roads End is the logging town of Johnsondale. It was in 1935 when negotiations were opened between the Dwyer-Rucker Timber Company of Detroit and the U. S. Forest Service to work out a timber and land exchange. Many years before Dwyer-Rucker had acquired a considerable acreage of timbered land, in several parcels, extending from Double Bunk on the south to Camp Nelson and Lloyd Meadow on the north. Included in these parcels were several groves of "big trees," or

giant sequoias. Because these timber lands were so widely scattered and intermingled with public lands, sustained operation of a sawmill would have been most difficult.

Under an act of Congress, it was made possible for a private owner to consolidate his holdings by offering them to the Forest Service in exchange for government timber, and thereby create a more economical logging unit. This area had, at that time, just come through a very serious depression and the Forest Service was interested in this exchange as it would help create an industry where people could earn a living. They were also interested in returning to government ownership several large "big tree" groves owned by the Dwyer-Rucker interests.

After the land exchange was made, it became necessary to find a company who would be willing to put up a sawmill and build a town. A group of men, which included Walter S. Johnson, W. E. Arblaster, Horace Webster, George Arblaster and C. T. Gruenhagen, became interested in establishing a logging operation here. But the only access into this wild, undeveloped area was by trail except for a partially constructed Forest Service fire road between Hot Springs and Double Bunk. This group of men were shown over the area on foot and horseback as they looked for a mill site. They felt the mill should be located along the lower edge of the timber belt where a large piece of level ground for a lumber yard was available. Also needed was a stream for the sawmill pond. The site was tentatively selected at the confluence

Dedication of the Johnsondale Bridge in 1937. *Left to right, front row*, Joan Berry, Donald Jones, Emmett Berry, Joe Elliott—Supervisor of the Sequoia National Forest, and Betty Jones. Others not identified.

of South Creek and Parker Meadow Creek. The next problem was that of a road out to the south. The potential of constructing a road down South Creek and along the main Kern River to the intake for the Edison Company power plant had to be determined.

The surveys were made and it was decided to build the road cooperatively with the U. S. Forest Service. The newly organized lumber company was named the Mt. Whitney Lumber Company. They immediately contributed their pro-rated share of the road's cost.

A mill was purchased in Florida, and shipped by rail to Ducor, then trucked through California Hot Springs and up over the Forest Service fire road to Double Bunk. To complete the haul, a trail was constructed by bulldozers to the present mill site. This first mill was carried on new 1936 Ford trucks and, even after filling up with gas at California Hot Springs, another gas stop had to be arranged at Cold Springs Saddle for the remaining 19 miles from there to Johnsondale.

The Mt. Whitney Lumber Company entered into an agreement with the Dwyer-Rucker interests on June 30, 1936, to cut the timber. The logging operation was to be under complete control of the U. S. Forest Service. By the fall of 1936, the Forest Service had completed its survey of the road to be constructed between Johnsondale and Roads End. Later that fall the Forest Service established a 25-man C.C.C. camp on South Creek— located where the rodeo grounds were later built, and a 100-man C.C.C. camp at Roads End so that work could be started from both ends.

The following winter proved to be one of the most severe ever experienced in this area. The thermometer dropped to —24 degrees and the snow depth was far greater than expected. The

Wilbur Kelin, Mill Superintendent, running log deck due to absence of operator. Note snow on the log.

Cars stream across the Johnsondale Bridge on the dedication day.

C.C.C. boys were living in tents, and suffered severely from this extreme cold. The road to California Hot Springs was closed by snow, thereby requiring food, powder and other supplies to be brought in by pack trains. That winter thousands of deer died from being caught in snow drifts or breaking through the ice on Kern River, accounting for one of the greatest losses of wildlife ever recorded for this area.

The road construction was done under Forest Service supervision, with a brilliant young engineer named Hamilton (Ham) Files designing the bridge and selecting its location. The road and Kern River bridge was completed fourteen months after work started. The time of year that this project was started and the unusually severe winter caused the men to work under most difficult and demanding conditions.

On October 10, 1937, the new scenic highway from Kernville to Johnsondale was formally opened with a dedication program sponsored by the Kern River Chamber of Commerce. Supervisors Roy Woollomes of Kern County and Jay G. Brown of Tulare County officially opened the highway. Emmett Berry, who had taught school in Old Kernville some 20 years earlier, was asked by Joe Elliott, Sequoia National Forest Supervisor, to give the dedication speech. His daughter, Joan Berry, and Betty Jones, daughter of Mr. and Mrs. Donald Jones of Porterville, cut the ribbon of pine cones, thus officially opening the new road and bridge.

In 1973, the only employee who had been with the Mt. Whitney Lumber Company since the mill opened was Wilbur Kelin. Wilbur had started his sawmill career at Dinkey Creek where he had worked for a year at the Pine Logging Company. He then departed for Johnsondale with his wife,

Hurshella, and have ever since made this little logging town their home.

Coming to the mill from Dinkey Creek at the same time was H. J. Reasonover, Wilbur's father-in-law. Mr. Reasonover had acquired the nickname of "Steamer" early in his logging career, and it stuck with him through his life. A big part of his mail even came addressed to this name. As a young man he worked as a "pond monkey," a man who walks the logs in the pond that keeps the mill supplied. One day he slipped off and went in the water over his head. When he came up, he spurted water so high they started calling him Steamer. Steamer was a sawyer, as was his brother, and their father before them. The family had worked many years for the Madera Sugar Pine Company. The sawyer is generally considered to be the most important person in the sawmill operation, as he can easily make-or-break the operation. He must have a quick eye, an alert mind, a good memory and a head for figures to know the exact cut of each log to maximize lumber and minimize waste.

Wilbur first started as oiler in the mill at 50 cents per hour. Their first home was a 20-by-20 foot tent on a wooden platform. That winter there was 61 inches of snow on the level and only the main roads had been cleared by bulldozers. Each family added to the network of paths which ran from one dwelling to another. The Kelins tell about one night that winter when it was snowing and the wind was blowing. Wilbur was, at that time, working as night watchman, or "carrying the clock," at $54.00 per month. It was almost midnight, Wilbur had finished dinner and was preparing to go out into the blizzard to his job, when they heard something hit the porch in front of their tent. It was the watchman from the previous shift, covered with snow, bringing the clock and the keys. He said it was too miserable for anyone to be out, and suggested that Wilbur work his job from his tent until the weather let up.

By the next winter the Kelins had moved into a house, or at least the resemblance of a house. It had been a 20-by-20 foot tent platform to start with, belonging to a carpenter who had been hired for the initial building of the logging camp. When he left camp he sold the Kelins his house for $20.00. It was a two room affair, built primarily of two-by-fours and building paper. At first their dwelling had no inside plumbing, but by the end of the first winter Wilbur had piped in water.

In the winter of 1943 the mill burned. As the country was at war and the demand for building materials was at its peak, this was an enormous loss. But with little wasted time, they started to clean up the mess and rebuild. In the spring of 1944 they had set up a small mill on the flat across from the commissary and began cutting timbers for the new mill. Wilbur Kelin and a helper cut timbers up to 40 feet long on a 60-inch top and bottom saw. In the summer of 1944 the sawmill was completed. In 1973 the same mill was still in operation. Wilbur started in 1944 as mill superintendent, a job he still held some 29 years later until his retirement in 1973.

The first mill had been completed in the fall of 1935 and, when in full production, maintained a crew of 28 men, with an annual cut of 25 million feet of lumber. In 1972, by automation and efficient management, a mill crew of 11 were able to put out 38 million board feet. Of approximately 165 employees, some 60 work in the woods.

The job of timber fallers has always been one of the hardest in the woods, and those remembered as being among the best of the early fallers were names such as Pappy Hall, Joe Birtch, and Joe Settie. In the early days the fallers worked in pairs, and after the timber was felled it was skidded to where it was to be loaded. When the Johnsondale mill started, this skidding was done mainly with Allis-Chalmers tractors. As the years passed, the method of skidding was gradually improved, causing less damage to the ground cover and reducing erosion. By 1972 much of the equipment used for skidding, and for loading the trucks as well, was rubber tired, which was even easier on the forest soil. In some cases a "high lead" operation is employed where a system of cables are set up to transport logs out of country too steep and rough to economically build roads. With this type of logging only a portion of the log drags the ground. Even more advanced is aerial logging, where large helicopters are used to pick up the giant logs from where they are felled and transport them to where there is easy road access.

Logging trucks also have come a long way since the days when early drivers such as Johnny McNally nosed the first trucks over those steep mountain roads. The Jacob brakes, or "Jake brakes," have been a time and money saving invention. With this brake system, compression from the truck engine is used to help hold back the load. Drivers in the early days, as those in the 1970s, had to be experts in their field or they did not last long. A twenty ton load pushing you down the mountain calls for quick judgment as well as stamina.

Once at the mill, the logs were unloaded into the mill pond. Then, with the guidance of the pond men, the logs were floated to where they entered the mill. To one of these "pond monkeys," a misstep meant a plunge into the icy cold water.

A local employee named Bob Greenwood once had aspirations of being a pond man, but found it was not as easy as it looked. Bob watched other pond men jump from a big log to a small one, then onto a big log, and it looked as easy as stepping on stepping stones across a creek. When Greenwood tried it he hesitated for a brief second on the small log, which caused it to start sinking. Once the log started down, there was nothing he could do to keep from getting dunked. Along with being a cold fall morning, this experience helped to interest Bob in other occupations at the mill. However, the men did not let him forget his early morning bath.

In 1970 the mill pond was discontinued, with the logs being "drydecked," or stacked and kept wet with sprinklers to keep the bugs out. When they went into the mill, they were cleaned with air. One man operating a jammer unloaded the trucks, piled the logs, and also kept feeding logs to the mill. With these changes, one man could do the work of five.

Formerly, when the pond was in use, the logs would be directed by long poles to where an endless chain hooked the log and took it up into the mill. A giant crosscut saw first cut the logs into 16-foot lengths. Then the log entered the relentless teeth of the nine-foot bandsaw—the log being cut remains on a wheeled carriage on rails called a "block setter." The logs are flipped from side to side and run through the bandsaw at what appears to be express train speeds. The blade on the saw must be changed twice a day as millions of board feet are run through this saw annually. The sawyer must constantly alter, or tell the block-setter to alter, the cut to get the most lumber from the log. Odd slices from the log, cut when the log is being squared up, are diverted mechanically to where they are saved for posts or narrow boards of various dimensions.

The short pieces, too short to make marketable lumber, are sent to the box factory. After the knots are cut out, the good sections are sawed into

Hilt lumber stacker — taken in 1938. Commonly known as the "Iron Swede."

various sized boards needed for making fruit and vegetable crates. Some of these pre-cut pieces are sent to the Harbor Box Company of Los Angeles.

The lumber that came out of the mill went through what was called the "green chain." This again was one of the many jobs associated with the logging industry that could be filled only by men in top physical condition. The pace was killing, and each board was so "green," or full of water, that they seemed to be made of lead. In later years an automatic green chain was installed which took care of a lot of the back breaking work.

The same type men were required to work on the "Iron Swede." This contraption looked like a ferris wheel, with a log or arms to hold a board every three or four feet. As one man fed the lumber into one side, it went up and over to where another man took the boards off and stacked them.

One of Hurshella Kelin's extra services on the route was delivering fresh bread to patrons that could not make it to the store. It is interesting to note price on the bread wrapper. Picture was taken in 1961.

In this manner, a pile 30 or 40 feet high would be achieved. In later years this, too, was mechanized.

Not only did the mill change through the years, but the logging town itself also changed from the days of "tent city" to where over 100 houses were maintained in Johnsondale. The first store was a little one Pappy Hall had in his own house. Pappy, who was one of the early timber fallers in camp, had built his own home and had one small room set aside for a grocery store until the commissary was built. Mr. Bates, from California Hot Springs, brought over fresh vegetables and milk several times a week during these early times. The rest of the grocery shopping was done either with Bert James in Old Kernville or Gus Suhre in Old Isabella. Trips down the river were not planned very often because a few trips down that rugged dirt road would wear out a good set of tires.

Besides homes for employees, it also became necessary to provide dormitories, a commissary and cook house, as well as install water systems and the many other necessities for some 650 residents that were eventually to live there.

As the family population increased in the new town, one of the first essentials was a school. The first school was a little two room affair that was later remodeled and used for a dwelling. The company deeded land to the school district from time to time to accommodate the growing needs of the elementary school, and in 1972 some 112 students were enrolled. Later a high school was built, complete with all facilities including athletic fields, and, in the above year, 31 high school students were enrolled. This high school was one of

the few branch schools in California, being part of the Porterville Union High School District centered some 65 curving road miles to the west.

In 1951 a community center was completed and dedicated to Joe Elliot, who was instrumental in the planning and erection of the building. Joe, after retirement from the Forest Service, was later active in Management and Forestry phases, and from 1946 to 1952 was resident manager at Johnsondale. This new hall, finished inside with knotty cedar, had a main floor of 36 by 72 feet and a stage 14 by 36 feet. The dedication of this hall was a major event in these mountains. Because of the remote location of the community, it had become almost a self-contained town—with grocery store, pool hall, post office, and small hospital with a doctor and nurse in attendance. Except for hunting, fishing, the annual rodeo, and roping club, there was little entertainment until the company built the new recreation hall. Dances were held regularly, but room in any of the older buildings was insufficient to take care of this activity in the best style. The hall came to be used for these dances, church services, Boy Scout activities, card parties, as well as serving as a movie theatre.

Hurshella, wife of the long-time mill superintendent, Wilbur Kelin, has made somewhat of a record herself. In 1973 she was still on the job after 26 years as mail carrier, along with being a housewife and mother of two girls. Each year she has logged an average of 16,800 miles, or approximately 420,000 miles in all. Besides carrying mail, she also delivers groceries and telephone messages to isolated people, takes shoes to the repairman, pulls cars out of sand and mud, has prescriptions filled, and has also used her mail vehicle as an ambulance. In 1959 the Johnsondale bridge burned down and, for ten days, Mrs. Kelin had to travel 179 miles a day. She had to leave at 9 in the morning, drive west over Parker Pass, down through Pine Flat, and back over Greenhorn Summit. She would take mail from Kernville up as far as Lila Lofberg's at the Edison intake, then return down the river, over Greenhorn, and back to Johnsondale. She would then deliver mail as far as Lower Durrwood Meadows. After making this grueling trip for ten days, the loggers built a foot bridge for her, and she kept a truck on each side of the river, carrying the mail across the foot bridge by herself. She did this for four months until the new bridge was completed. Hurshella received an award from the Safety Council of Tulare County, a commendation from the Post Office Department in San Francisco, and a commendation from her Congressman, who at that time was Harlan Hagen.

In the early days of her mail run she many times carried more bread than she did mail. Perhaps the thing for which Hurshella will be remembered best was her willingness to take the old pensioners from Johnsondale and Roads End into Kernville to get their monthly checks. This, in itself, was no small undertaking. Take the case of Dick Weed, for instance. Dick was an old miner who had a cabin below Roads End and wore the same clothes so long that he smelled like an old billy goat. Once a year Dick caught a ride down to Bath House Canyon. He took with him a complete change of clothes, usually purchased in Kernville for the occasion. He would bathe in the little bath house where the tub was filled by gravity flow from a hot mineral water spring. After Dick had taken his yearly bath and washed his hair and beard, he would throw away his old clothes he had bought the previous spring. He then would be all set for another year. Many times toward the end of winter Dick got so odorous that Hurshella insisted he ride in the back of her truck with the mail bags. This made him angry, and he would complain that she let other people ride in front with her. But she stuck by her decision, telling him that she had too many things up front with her and did not have room for him too. Dick sup-

This picture, taken in 1961, shows Hurshella Kelin making a call from the Kern Lodge Motel. This was before the installation of phones between Kernville and Johnsondale. She ordered many items for the lumber company as well as made a lot of calls for friends.

plied a lot of color around Roads End with his gum rubber boots and his hat with no top, which he called his "new hat."

Of course, there were many other people too numerous to mention whom Hurshella took the time to haul around and do their shopping. One has only to drive the twenty-odd miles from Kernville to Johnsondale to appreciate the job she has taken on for the last quarter century. Even now the Johnsondale Road is a super highway compared to what it was in years past. This little lady mail carrier has had to have the ingenuity and stamina of a burly logger to stick with her job.

As with any lumber operation, there is always a steady stream of employees coming and going. Those who had, in 1973, worked continuously for the Mount Whitney Lumber Company at Johnsondale for over 20 years were Jack Montgomery,

Aerial view of Johnsondale. South Creek that was used to feed the mill pond runs through the left of the picture. Note all the stacks of lumber in the foreground. Grove of trees to the right shades the cookhouse, commissary, dormitories, post office, school, and comunity hall. Most of the homes for the employees are farther to the right of the picture.

The Sherman Peak Tungsten Mine discovered and developed by Gil Embree and his family.

Kenny Gritton, Clinton Young, Clifford Piephoff, Cliff Bailey, Clyde Dobbs, Billy Cole, Leo Williams and his wife, Rosie, who in 1973 had retired after 21 years as postmaster at Johnsndale, and, of course, Wilbur Kelin who retired in that year with 37 years service.

At times there have been as many as 100 employees working for contractors in the woods operation. These contractors play a large part in the production of the mill, and one of the best known was Jim Heath.

The direction of the work at Johnsondale has been under the direct supervision of resident managers, who include Hyalmar Holmberg, Warren Wood, Joe Elliott, Bill Arblester, Simon Alsaker, Walt LaCasse, and William Lantsberger.

Logging camps have always had a reputation for huge amounts of food they put forth, and the mess hall at Johnsondale is no exception. In 1973, as for many years, a person could eat with the loggers by first calling and making a reservation. Eating at the big tables, where everything is served family style and nobody goes away hungry, is an experience. There is also a complete store

and commissary operated for many years by Oscar and Caroline Greene.

The residents of this little logging community have had their share of hardships, most of them connected with the elements. There have been three floods since the mill opened, and one time it rained for five days and nights. Each time the flood came the mill pond broke, once taking the burner, machinery, and several buildings with it. A lot of cold weather, mud, and snow could be expected every winter. But all in all, the pay was good, they had their own roping club, rodeos, box socials, dances and shows, and most of the residents admitted it was a pretty good place to live.

SHERMAN PEAK

The story of the discovery and development of the Sherman Peak Mine by Gil Embree and his family reminds one in many ways of the pioneer mining families from some 100 years before. This mine was located on Sherman Peak, some six miles as the crow flies northeast of Roads End. The original discovery was made by Gil Embree in 1940 while on a hunting trip out of Pascoe's Lodge at Roads End.

Gil had come into the Valley in 1938 to work on the building of the original mill at Johnsondale. He later worked as a logger and, still later, operated the steam donkey on the mill pond. Embree was an experienced miner and was amazed at the outcropping of tungsten ore there on the side of Sherman Peak. He made his way to northern California to work in the gold mines, but all he could think or talk about was the strike on Sherman Peak.

Finally, in 1948, he had the capital to start developing his mine. Earl Pascoe packed Gil and his wife, Beulah (known to everyone as "Babe") up to the mine site. It was nine miles from the road and rose 4,000 feet from the road to an altitude of 8,000 feet. The packers must have been completely bewildered as they unloaded the portable compressor, jackhammer, blasting powder, and other mining supplies on the side of that mountain.

Gil had also brought a tent, a supply of food, and believe it or not, their two boys, Wayne, age 6½, and Lee, who was not quite 4. The Embrees had arrived in May and accomplished the nearly impossible during the next six months. The compressor had been dismantled for loading on the mules, so it was reassembled, drilling was begun, and a tunnel blasted under the main outcropping.

The whole family worked. Even the boys helped load powder in the holes and do many of the chores connected with camp life.

When enough ore had been stockpiled to start moving it to the roadhead, Gil walked out the nine miles to the road and brought back two of Earl Pascoe's packers, Al Bernard and Foster Webb, and 20 mules. A total of 3,000 pounds of ore were packed out, with 150 pounds loaded on each mule. The ore was then taken by truck to a mill in Havilah, where it was milled the same day.

By the time this first shipment was milled out the Embrees had been awake for three days and three nights, but still they started to Fresno with their payload. They got as far as Miracle Hot Springs and decided they were too worn out to drive down the canyon road. They stopped to get a room for the night. The rooms were all sold out, but a kindly soul, whose name has been forgotten, moved in with a friend and gave them his room.

Early the next day they started out again, reached Fresno without further delay, and sold the shelite, which was the product of the tungsten ore. They hurried to the bank with the check, but

The cabin built of native stone on top of Sherman Peak by Gil and Babe Embree.

The Forest Service lookout on Sherman Peak, where the Embree family met their special friends, the Lofbergs. The lookout has long since been dismantled.

it bounced. They did finally get their badly needed money, and were soon back digging in the side of their mountain.

The Embrees lived in a tent on Sherman Peak for several years, coming out only when they were forced out by heavy snows. Those first few years were lean ones, and many times they survived on deer meat and sourdough bread, spending their small supply of cash on the more important items such as blasting powder and drill steel. They later had a house built of native rock by Henry and Ruddy Leibel who were working for them. By this time the Embrees also had a daughter, Linda.

Gil then obtained a permit to put a road up to the mine. Strictly a road for four wheel drive vehicles, he pioneered it with a Caterpillar tractor with a cable dozer, which was quite a feat in itself.

The Embrees then set up a roller mill with a nine-foot flywheel. John Dilts was the foreman

Suspension bridge that crossed the Kern River to Camp Durrwood established by Bill and Lou Calkins in 1921.

of the mill; Red Smith and Kenny Keillor were among those who worked there; also two local teenagers, Bruce and Larry Wagner.

In reminiscing about their first year on Sherman Peak, Babe Embree's fondest memories were of meeting her good friends, Ted and Lila Lofberg. Ted had retired from the Edison Electric Company after 25 years of service, and the Forest Service had offered them a summer position on Sherman Peak lookout. The Embrees' mine was about two miles down from the lookout, and Gil would pick up the Lofberg's mail when he was in town. The two young Embree boys started delivering the mail and came to love this exceptional couple. Babe met Lila in the town of Old Kernville when Lila was picking up groceries at Bert James' store. She felt a little shadow following her and turned to find Wayne Embree. Lila had a special way with children, as well as animals, and the boys soon brought their mother to be introduced to Mrs. Lofberg. This started a lasting friendship and for the last 18 years of her life, Lila counted Babe Embree as her closest friend.

After Wayne and Lee Embree grew up they gave up mining and used the skills they had acquired with heavy equipment to hold responsible, well paying construction jobs. Gil, however, continued to play the mining game. When the mining bug hits you it's almost impossible to give it up.

When one drives up the Cherry Hill Road toward Sherman Pass and looks across the canyon at the Embree claim that seems to hang on the side of that 9,000 foot peak, it is cause for wonder at the persistence and patience it took for a family to tackle a seemingly impossible feat. For that's what this was—developing and operating a paying tungsten mine in what was then a roadless and almost inaccessible wilderness.

CAMP DURRWOOD

About a half-mile above the settlement of Roads End and on a sharp bend of the river, domestic grapevines could be found growing in 1973. During the 1920s and 1930s this was the base of operations for Bill Calkins' resort, Camp Durrwood, located 15 miles upriver.

Bill Calkins and his wife, Lou, had been running the Mountain Inn in Kernville, but this country was getting too civilized for Bill. So in the spring of 1921 he took his future son-in-law, Earl Pascoe, with him and started out to find a spot for a back country resort. The two men got caught by a late snowstorm and when they left the Rincon Trail and started to work their way down through the two miles of rough terrain to the Kern River, it became quite a chore. They wrapped their feet in barley sacks and pushed on down-slope. When they got to where Durrwood Creek empties into the Kern, Bill knew it was what he had been looking for. Both went back to Roads End and started packing in supplies for Camp Durrwood. Before the camp could be started, they had to build two miles of trail from the Rincon down to the river. Then all the lumber and other bulky materials were packed in the 15 miles. It took all of Earl Pascoe's packing knowledge to get some of the loads down those rough trails.

All the buildings at Camp Durrwood were of frame construction except for the recreation room made of rock. Shakes for the roofs were split out of native pine. That first year Bill built a ditch around the rock bluff from Durrwood Creek to the lodge. Part of the ditch had to be blasted from solid rock. It was given just the right amount of gravity fall by using a level fastened onto a long board.

After water was brought to the camp, fruit trees and flowers were planted, and a vegetable garden reworked each year. A sprinkling system was put in later, utilizing the same fall of the water line from Durrwood Creek to produce the necessary

Everything and everybody was rugged on the Upper Kern. Here, Tim, the lion cub, gets his milk from a whiskey bottle served by Bill Calkins.

pressure to run the system. The fishing was fabulous in those early days on that portion of the Kern River, and each fall the deer hunters brought many large bucks down to the lodge. Bill also built a swinging bridge so his guests could cross the river to fish and hunt on the west bank.

After the road was pushed on to Johnsondale, Calkins moved his lower camp up across the river and past South Creek Falls to what later became known as Lower Durrwood. He then built a trail up the west side of the river through Bean Camp to Peppermint Creek. From there, the trail led down the creek to the river and across the swinging bridge to the river bench and camp. Two of the men who helped Calkins build this new trail were Joe Hall and Alphy Neill. Neill worked for Calkins for most of the 22 years he ran Camp Durrwood.

Bill once went lion hunting with a State trapper and came home with an unusual pet. They had

Tim takes his leisure in the sun. This friendly mountain lion had learned to come in and out of the Calkins' home in the summertime by either pushing the screen door open or pulling it with his paw. He then would jump through before the door closed, but not quite fast enough to keep the door from banging on the end of his tail. Because of this, he would give a loud yowl each time he came in, before the door hit his tail.

Bill and Lou Calkins pose outside their marvelous Upper Durrwood Resort.

treed a female lion, killed her, and then found that she was nursing young. By backtracking from where the dogs first jumped her trail, they located her litter. There they found two lion cubs, so small they had not yet opened their eyes. They carried them out in a feed bag, and Bill decided to keep one for a pet. He was dubbed "Timothy Tickle Britches," "Tim" for short, and raised on a baby bottle.

After a few weeks, Tim started playing with the Calkins' mother house cat and her litter of kittens. The mother cat kept Tim in line the same way she did her own—by slapping him with her paw. He took the chastisement meekly, and it looked pretty silly for a mother house cat to slap around a mountain lion four times bigger than she was. Then one day when the mother cat slapped Tim, he slapped back. It probably surprised both of them, but at any rate, she did not try to push Tim around again.

153

Bill Calkins romps with Tim, his pet mountain lion.

Tim kept growing and growing until he measured eight feet from the tip of his tail to the end of his nose. He loved to play, and Bill had to keep his dangerous claws trimmed back to the quick. When Bill went to Kernville, he took Tim along on a long leash. You can imagine a stranger's amazement when they walked by Bill's parked car and a grown mountain lion jumped up to look them over.

Tim made several trips out of the Valley with Bill Calkins, but one memorable trip occurred when Bill was invited to a Lion's Club dinner in the Southland. This was one of the rare occasions when Bill wore a suit, and Tim did not like it at all. By the time they got to Kernville, Bill decided he did not want to wear the suit anyway, so he stopped off at the A. Brown Store and bought a new wool plaid shirt and a pair of Levis—leaving his suit there. As soon as Bill changed clothes, Tim was his old self again, and they were on their way.

Tim created quite a sensation at the dinner when he sat at the table and ate chicken with seemingly no interest in his surroundings. When Bill went to check in at the hotel, it was another matter altogether, as the clerks had not heard about Calkins' tame lion and wanted no part of him. Bill was finally able to get a room on the ground floor and left Tim in the car. After dark he went out to the car, untied the lion, and told him to "stay." Back in the room, he raised his window and gave a whistle. Out of the car jumped Tim, up through the window, and into Bill's room where he spent a peaceful night. The next morning Bill knew it would be harder to get Tim out without being detected. He left Tim in the room with the window open and paid the bill. Then he drove the car close to the building, whistled, and into the car sprang Tim. At that moment a city policeman walked around the corner, his mouth dropping open with amazement. Bill asked, "Anything you want to do about it son?" With the big cat staring him in the eye, the policeman merely stated, "Oh no, just go on." So Bill drove out of the parking lot and back to the hills.

In 1944 the Calkins sold Camp Durrwood. Bill, who was then 72 and in good health after working so hard all his life, should have lived at least another 20 years. But the rugged old mountain man was stricken with an attack of acute appendicitis and passed away in 1945. His wife, Lou, known as Grandma Calkins, followed him in death in 1965.

There have been many other lodges in the high Sierras, but none ever furnished more enjoyment to its guests than Camp Durrwood did in its picturesque setting, nestled securely by the Kern in the heart of the deep canyon. Just another of the picturesque spots along the River that made "North Fork Country" so unique.

Index

Weed, Dick, 120, 123-125, 149
Welch, Beverly, 22
Welch, Bob, 118-121
Wells, John, 50
Werth, Ben, 97
Wheldon, Charlie, 65
Whistman, Allie, 36
Whitesides, Joan, 99
Whitesides, Stan, 77, 99
Willett, Rev. Arthur D., 29, 30
Willett, Donald, 30
Willett, Mrs., 30
Williams, 80
Williams, Dutch, 141
Williams, Leo, 150
Williams, Richard, 26
Williams, Rosie, 150

Williams, Spencer, 65
Winslow, Slim, 45
Wirth, Milta Ross, 20
Wirth, Willy, 47
Witt, Hy, 44
Witt, Tim, 44
Witt's, 63
Wofford, Gail, 58, 67
Wofford, Irven, 17, 47, 59, 61-66, 120
Wofford, John, 58, 60, 62, 67
Wofford, Lucille, 60
Wofford, Naomi, 60, 66
Wood, Dr. C. H., 115
Wood, Warren, 110, 150
Woodard, Charlie, 62
Woollomes, Roy, 72, 74, 145

Worrell, Colene, 22
Worthington, Bill, 123
Wortley, Chet, 114, 115
Wortley, Ken, 114, 124, 132
Worton, Will, 6, 7
Wren, Ruth, 22
Wright, Walter S., 84
Wyatt, Gwenevere, 70
Wyatt, Mark, 4, 70
Wyatt, Mrs. Mark, 4

Yarbrough, Dave, 27, 68
Yarbrough, Nettie, 27, 28, 68
Yates, Lizzie, 19
Yeargen, LaVida, 48
Young, Clinton, 150

Zook, Clyde, 41

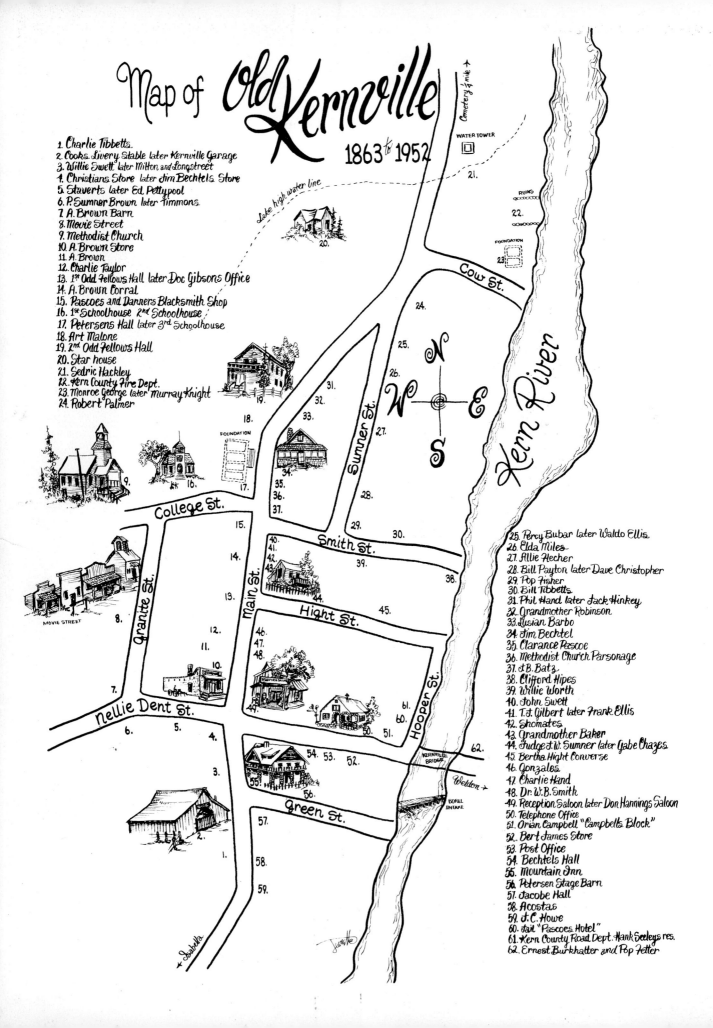

Map of Old Kernville
1863 to 1952

1. Charlie Tibbetts
2. Cooks Livery Stable later Kernville Garage
3. Willie Swett later Milton and Longstreet
4. Christians Store later Jim Bechtels Store
5. Stauerts later Ed. Pettypool
6. P. Sumner Brown later Timmons
7. A. Brown Barn
8. Movie Street
9. Methodist Church
10. A. Brown Store
11. A. Brown
12. Charlie Taylor
13. 1st Odd Fellows Hall later Doc Gibsons Office
14. A. Brown Corral
15. Pascoes and Danners Blacksmith Shop
16. 1st Schoolhouse 2nd Schoolhouse
17. Petersens Hall later 3rd Schoolhouse
18. Art Malone
19. 2nd Odd Fellows Hall
20. Star house
21. Sedric Hackley
22. Kern County Fire Dept.
23. Monroe George later Murray Knight
24. Robert Palmer

25. Percy Bubar later Waldo Ellis
26. Elda Miles
27. Allie Hecher
28. Bill Payton later Dave Christopher
29. Pop Fisher
30. Bill Tibbetts
31. Phil Hand later Jack Hinkey
32. Grandmother Robinson
33. Lusian Barbo
34. Jim Bechtel
35. Clarance Pascoe
36. Methodist Church Parsonage
37. J.B. Batz
38. Clifford Hipes
39. Willie Worth
40. John Swett
41. T.J. Gilbert later Frank Ellis
42. Shomates
43. Grandmother Baker
44. Judge J.W. Sumner later Gabe Chazes
45. Bertha Hight Converse
46. Gonzales
47. Charlie Hand
48. Dr. W.B. Smith
49. Reception Saloon later Don Hannings Saloon
50. Telephone Office
51. Orian Campbell "Campbells Block"
52. Bert James Store
53. Post Office
54. Bechtels Hall
55. Mountain Inn
56. Petersen Stage Barn
57. Jacobe Hall
58. Acostas
59. J.C. Howe
60. Jail "Pascoes Hotel"
61. Kern County Road Dept. Hank Seeleys res.
62. Ernest Burkhalter and Pop Fetter

Cemetery ½ mile

WATER TOWER

Lake high water line

RUINS

FOUNDATION

Cow St.

Kern River

College St.

Movie Street

Smith St.

Hight St.

Granite St.

Main St.

Sumner St.

Hooper St.

Nellie Dent St.

Green St.

Kernville Bridge

Weldon →

Borel Intake

← Isabella